The Korn Shell

The Korn Shell

Unix and Linux Programming Manual

Third Edition

Anatole Olczak

Addison-Wesley

An imprint of **Pearson Education**

Harlow, England · London · New York · Reading, Massachusetts · San Francisco
Toronto · Don Mills, Ontario · Sydney · Tokyo · Singapore · Hong Kong · Seoul
Taipei · Cape Town · Madrid · Mexico City · Amsterdam · Munich · Paris · Milan

PEARSON EDUCATION LIMITED

Head Office:
Edinburgh Gate
Harlow CM20 2JE
Tel: +44 (0)1279 623623
Fax: +44 (0)1279 431059

London Office:
128 Long Acre
London WC2E 9AN
Tel: +44 (0)20 7447 2000
Fax: +44 (0)20 7240 5771

Website: www.aw.com/cseng/

First published in Great Britain in 1991

This edition published 2001

© Anatole Olczak 2001

The right of Anatole Olczak to be identified as the author of this work has been asserted by him in accordance with the Copyright, Designs and Patents Act 1988.

ISBN 0-201-67523-4

British Library Cataloguing in Publication Data
A CIP catalogue record for this book can be obtained from the British Library

Library of Congress Cataloging in Publication Data
Applied for.

The programs in this book have been included for their instructional value. The publisher does not offer any warranties or representations in respect of their fitness for a particular purpose, nor does the publisher accept any liability for any loss or damage arising from their use.

Many of the designations used by manufacturers and sellers to distinguish their products are claimed as trademarks. Pearson Education Limited has made every attempt to supply trademark information about manufacturers and their products mentioned in this book. Where those designations appear in this book and Addison-Wesley were aware of a trademark claim, the designations have been printed in initial or capital letters.

10 9 8 7 6 5 4 3 2

Printed and bound in Great Britain by Biddles Ltd, Guildford and King's Lynn.

The Publishers' policy is to use paper manufactured from sustainable forests.

Table of Contents

Korn Shell User and Programming Manual

Table of Contents

Table of Contents

Table of Contents

Table of Contents

List of Tables:

Table of Contents

Preface

The **Korn Shell User and Programming Manual** is designed to be a reference and learning tool for a range of users - from the novice with some experience to the pro who is familiar with both the Bourne and C shells. It contains complete technical information, as well as hands-on examples and complete programs to help guide you and illustrate all the features of the Korn shell. This edition of the book has been updated to cover Korn Shell 93, the latest version of the Korn shell. This book also assumes that you are familiar with the basic Unix commands, and understand file system concepts. You should also be able to login to a system, and enter basic commands.

If you are an experienced user, you may want to skip Chapter 1 and the first half of Chapter 2. The first seven chapters deal primarily with interactive use, while Chapter 8 and 9 cover the programming concepts.

The goal of this book to teach you the Korn shell, and this is done by walking you through examples. So by the time you are finished reading the book, you'll be comfortable with it, and writing your own Korn shell scripts.

But don't just read the book. The best way for you to learn about the Korn shell is to type in the examples yourself. Then do some experimentation on your own by either modifying the examples or coming up with your own commands.

Chapter 1 contains an overview of the major features in the Korn shell. It covers where to get it, how your login shell is configured, and setting up the Korn shell to co-exist with other shells while you are on the learning curve. It also includes brief descriptions of other related shells, including the Born Again shell (**bash**), Mortice Kern shell (**ksh**) for PC/Windows, and the public domain Korn shell (**pdksh**) for Linux.

Chapter 2 covers the Korn shell basics: how commands can work together to do other things, and some basic shortcuts to improve productivity, and Korn shell I/O. You'll also be introduced to file name, command, and tilde substitution: important concepts that are the basis of much of the Korn shell.

Chapter 3 teaches you about Korn shell variables, variable attributes, and parameters. You'll learn about all the different types of variable expansion, including the substring features. Array variables and quoting are also discussed in detail.

Chapter 4 discusses the Korn shell command history mechanism and vi and emacs in-line editors. Here you will learn how to call up previous commands and manipulate them.

Chapter 5 shows you how to manage and manipulate multiple processes using the job control mechanism, a feature almost directly copied from the C shell.

In Chapter 6, you will learn how to perform arithmetic with the Korn shell. It contains sections on multi-base arithmetic, declaring integer-type variables, and random numbers, along with examples for each type of arithmetic operator.

XVIII

Chapter 7 will show you how to set up your own customized environment: from setting up the prompt how you like it, to configuring your personal email. Korn shell options, environment variables, aliases, the **.profile** file, and subshells are also covered.

In Chapter 8, you are taught how to write programs using the many Korn shell commands and features. Executing and debugging scripts, input/output commands, positional parameters, flow control commands such as **case**, **for**, **if**, **select**, **while**, and **until** are also discussed. Step-by-step examples are included, and complete usable scripts are built from the bottom up. For those experienced Unix programmers, important differences between the Korn and Bourne shells are discussed, and something else new to Unix shell programming - performance. You'll learn a few tricks that can speed up execution of your Korn shell scripts.

Chapter 9 covers miscellaneous commands, such as **readonly**, **ulimit**, **whence**, and Korn shell functions.

Appendix A and B include a sample ready-to-use profile and environment file.

Appendix C contains the Korn shell versions of a number of C shell commands and functions.

Appendix D contains the source code listing for a number of handy ready-to-run Korn shell scripts, including an interactive calendar program.

Appendix E contains the Korn shell man pages.

Appendix F contains information about pdksh, the public domain version of the Korn shell for Linux.

Appendix G contains the Pdksh quick reference guide, and Appendix H contains the Pdksh man page.

Korn Shell 93: The Latest Version

This edition is based on the latest edition of the Korn shell. There have been a number of new features and enhancements added to Korn Shell 93 including:

Datatypes: New data types: floats and structures.

Variables: New variable typer: compound and nameref variables.

Arrays: Associative arrays and additional commands for array manipulation.

Functions: Discipline functions to support further manipulation of variables.

String Manipulation:

        Search, replace, and substring operators.

Acknowledgements

Thanks to David Korn for developing the Korn shell, Steven Bourne for the Bourne shell, and Bill Joy for the C shell. Other thanks to Mike Veach and Pat Sullivan for contributing to the development of the Korn shell, and Mark Horton, Bill Joy (again), and Richard Stallman for developing the vi and emacs editors which were used in the development of the Korn shell.

Special thanks to Peter Collinson, Cynthia Duquette, Ian Jones, Peter Kettle, Heather Prenatt, the ASP staff, Aspen Technologies, O'Reilly & Associates (who reviewed the initial draft of this book before publishing their own Korn shell book!), James Lamm, Darian Edwards and others for reviewing drafts of this book.

Miscellaneous

The information and material has been tested and verified to the best of our ability. This does not mean that it is always 100% correct! Subtle differences and variations may exist between implementations and features may have changed. And of course there may even be bugs or mistakes! Please send us any comments or suggestions for future editions, along with information about your environment. Please visit our Web site for more information **www.aw.com/cseng.**

Conventions

For readability sake, the default **$** prompt is used in the examples in this publication. Control characters are given as **Ctl** followed by the character in boldface. For example, **Ctl-d** specifies **Control-d** and is entered by pressing the **d** key while holding down the **Control** key. Special keys, like carriage-return and backspace, are enclosed in <>'s. Long command lines are continued onto the next line using the \ character.

Source Code Listing

If you would like the source code listing to the Korn shell scripts listed in the appendices, please visit our web site at **www.aw.com/cseng**.

Licensing Agreement

This book comes with a CD software package. By opening this package you are agreeing to be bound by the license terms contained on the CD-ROM.

Chapter 1:
Introduction

The Korn shell is an interactive command and programming language that provides an interface to the Unix and other systems. As an interactive command language, it is responsible for reading and executing the commands that you enter. For example, when you type in the **date** command to check the system date, your login shell is responsible for interpreting the command before it is executed. It also provides the ability to customize your working environment. You can set up your own commands, specify environment variables for other programs, change your command prompt, and a lot more. As a programming language, its special commands allow you to write sophisticated programs. These programs are called scripts in Unix shell speak and are just text files that contain programs written in the Korn shell programming language. You can use any Unix editor, such as **vi** or **emacs** to create scripts.

Major Features

The Korn shell offers compatibility with the Bourne shell, while providing a more robust programming language and command interpreter. It also contains some features of the C shell. The major features of the Korn shell are:

- **Improved performance.** Programs written in the Korn shell can run faster than similar programs written in the Bourne or C shells.

- **Bourne shell compatibility.** Programs written for the Bourne shell can run under the Korn shell without modification.

- **Command-line editing.** Instead of backspacing or retyping, commands can be edited in **vi**, **emacs**, or **gmacs** mode.

- **Command history.** Commands are stored in a history file, which can then be modified and re-executed or just re-executed as is. The commands are saved, up to a user-specified limit, across multiple login sessions.

- **Enhanced I/O facilities.** File descriptors and streams can be specified. Multiple files can be opened at the same time and read. Menus can be formatted and processed more easily.

- **Added data types and attributes.** Variables can now have a type, as well as size and justification attributes.

- **Integer arithmetic support.** Integer arithmetic can be performed in any base from two to thirty-six using variables and constants. A wide range of arithmetic operators is supported, including bitwise operators.

• **Arrays.** One-dimensional and associative arrays can be used.

• **Improved string manipulation facilities.** Substrings can be generated from the value of strings. Strings can be converted to upper or lower case.

• **Regular expressions.** Better support of regular expressions in variable expansion and filename wildcards has been added.

• **Job control.** The Korn shell job control feature is virtually the same as that of the C shell. Programs can be stopped, restarted, or moved to and from the background. Programs can be identified for **kill** with their job numbers.

• **Aliases.** Programs, and Korn shell scripts, along with their options can be aliased to a single name.

• **New options and variables.** These have been added to provide more control over environment customization.

• **Functions.** Increases programmability by allowing code to be organized in smaller, more manageable units, similar to procedures in other languages. Functions also allow Korn shell programs to be stored in memory.

• **Enhanced directory navigation facilities.** The previous directory, and home directory of any user can be referred to without using pathnames. Components of previous pathnames can be manipulated to generate new pathnames.

• **Enhanced debugging features.** More robust diagnostic facilities have been provided, and functions can be traced separately.

- **Other miscellaneous features.** New test operators, special variables, special commands, control commands, command-line options, and security features have also been added.

Where To Get the Korn Shell

The Korn shell is included as an optional shell, along with the Bourne and C shells by most vendors, including Sun for Solaris, SCO for UnixWare, Hewlett-Packard for HP-UX, and others. It is also available as an unbundled product from many vendors.

The Desktop Korn shell (**dtksh**) is another version of the Korn shell that is available by many vendors as an upgrade to Kornshell88-based versions. It is usually located in **/usr/dt/bin/dtksh**.

The Public Domain Korn shell, or **pdksh**, as the name suggests, is a public domain version of the Korn shell. It's compatible with most any version of Unix, but is mostly used on Linux-based systems. At the time of this writing, the current version (5.2.14) has most of the Kornshell88, as well as some of the Kornshell93 and additional features that are not in either. For more detailed information, refer to Appendices F-H.

David Korn and AT&T offer U/WIN, a non-commercial version of the Korn shell for Windows-based systems (NT and 98). It is based on KornShell98 and contains almost 200 of the popular Unix commands. We've included a version in the accompanying CD, but it is also available from **http://www.research.att.com/sw/tools/uwin**.

More information including links for the source distribution for the Korn Shell and U/Win is available at this URL:
http://www.kornshell.com.

Mortice Kern Systems sells a version of the Korn shell for MS-DOS and Windows. There are also a number of shareware shells that have Korn shell-like functionality.

Which Version Do You Have?

To determine which version of the Korn shell you are using, run the following command:

```
$ print ${.sh.version}
Version 1993-12-28 i
```

If you don't get a version back from this command, then you are probably using an older version of the Korn shell. Try running the **what** command on the Korn shell binary (usually located in **/bin/ksh**):

```
$ what /bin/ksh
Version   12/28/93
```

Logging In

A number of things happen before you see the **login:** prompt on your terminal. After you enter the login name, the **login** program is started. It finishes the process of logging you in by prompting for a password, checking the **/etc/passwd** file, and finally starting up your login shell. Your login shell is specified in the **/etc/passwd** file like this:

```
larissa:*:101:12::/home/larissa:/bin/sh
renata:*:102:101::/home/renata:/bin/ksh
```

For **larissa**, the login shell is **/bin/sh**, while for **renata** it is **/bin/ksh**.

Changing the Login Shell

To make the Korn shell your default login shell, have your system administrator change it to **/bin/ksh** or the pathname of wherever the Korn shell binary is located, or run the **chsh** command (if available on your system). Until that is done, you can still run the Korn shell by simply invoking:

```
$ ksh
```

This will give you a Korn subshell. To get back to your login shell, type **Ctl-d** (**Control-d**). If you get an error message complaining about ksh not being found, you can try to find it by executing:

```
$ find / -name ksh -print
/usr/local/bin/ksh
```

Once you've found it, add the directory in which it was found to your **PATH** variable. If you're using the Bourne shell, it would be done like this:

```
$ PATH=$PATH:/usr/local/bin
$ export PATH
$ ksh
```

while for the C shell:

```
% set path=($path /usr/local/bin)
% ksh
```

You could also invoke the Korn shell with the full pathname:

```
$ /usr/local/bin/ksh
```

More about the **PATH** variable is explained later in **Chapter 7**.

Invoking The Korn Shell Separately

If you would like to use the Korn shell, but keep your login shell the same, you can avoid conflicts between the two shells by putting all of your Korn shell environment and startup commands in the environment file. This is specified by the **ENV** variable, which could be set in your Bourne shell **.profile** file like this:

```
$ grep ENV $HOME/.profile
ENV=$HOME/.kshrc
```

or in the C shell **.login** file:

```
$ grep ENV $HOME/.login
setenv ENV $HOME/.kshrc
```

This way, when you invoke the Korn shell, it will know where to look and find the environment settings. Here are some basic commands that should be in the environment file:

```
$ cat $HOME/.kshrc
SHELL=/usr/local/bin/ksh
EDITOR=vi
export SHELL EDITOR
```

The **EDITOR** variable specifies the editor to use for command-line editing. Here it is set to **vi**, but it can also be set to **emacs** or **gmacs**. This will be covered in detail later in **Chapter 7**.

Using The Korn Shell in Scripts

For those experienced users that are ready to dive into writing some
Korn shell scripts, but do not have their login shells configured for the
Korn shell, make sure to add this to the top of your Korn shell script to
make sure that it is executed by the Korn shell:

```
#!/bin/ksh
```

Use the full pathname of **ksh** if it is not located in **/bin**.

Chapter 2:
Korn Shell Basics

Simple Script
Process Execution
Input/Output Redirection
File Name Substitution
Command Substitution
Tilde Substitution

This chapter covers some of the basic features of the Korn shell. If you've worked with the Bourne and/or C shells, then most of the **Process Execution** section will be a review of what you are already familiar with. The **Input/Output Redirection** section shows how you can use the special Korn shell I/O operators with regular commands to perform more sophisticated programming tasks. The last three sections in this chapter, **File Name Substitution**, **Command Substitution**, and **Tilde Substitution** show you how these powerful features can be used as shortcuts to help simplify your work.

Simple Script

Most of this chapter deals with how the Korn shell interacts with Unix , but to briefly explain the scripting concept a very simple example is provided. First of all, **ls** is a Unix command that lists the name of the files in the current directory, and **print** is a Korn shell command that displays its argument. Using your favorite Unix editor, enter the following text into a file called **simple_script.ksh**:

```
print "Here are the current files:"
ls
```

Assuming that you are using the Korn shell, have execute permission in your default umask and that you have the current path included in your environment (this will also be covered later!), run the script like this:

```
$ simple_script.ksh
Here are the current files:
simple_script.ksh   /tmp          report.txt
```

If this does not work, you cna also try running the script like this:

```
$  ksh simple_script.ksh
Here are the current files:
simple_script.ksh   tmp    report.txt
```

As you can see, a script is just a 'batch' file of commands that is passed to the Korn shell to be executed. More about writing Korn shell scripts is covered in Chapter 8.

Process Execution

This section provides a quick overview of how the Korn shell interacts with Unix . For the following sections, it is assumed that you are logged as a regular user, therefore you have the default command prompt - $.

Multiple Commands

Multiple commands can be given on the same line if separated with the ; character. Notice that the command prompt is not displayed until the output from all three commands is displayed:

```
$ pwd ; ls dialins ; echo Hello
/home/anatole
dialins
Hello
$
```

This is also useful when you want to run something more complex from the command line, like rename all the files in the current directory using flow control commands:

```
$ for i in $(ls); do mv $i $i.bak; done
```

The **for** loop command is covered in more detail in **Chapter 8**.

Continuing Commands

If a command is terminated with a \ character, it is continued on the next line. Here, the **echo** arguments are continued onto the next line:

```
$ echo a b \
> c
a b c
```

This is often used to make Korn shell scripts mode readable. Refer to **Appendix D** for some good examples. The **echo** command itself can be continued onto the next line by using the \ character:

```
$ ec\
> ho a b c
a b c
```

Background Jobs

Commands terminated with a **&** character are run in the background. The Korn shell does not wait for completion, so another command can be given, while the current command is running in the background. In this example, the **ls** command is run in the background while **pwd** is run in the foreground:

```
$ ls —1R /usr > ls.out &
[1] 221
$ pwd
/home/anatole/bin
```

This feature is discussed in detail in **Chapter 5**.

Pipes

The output of a command can be directed as the input to another command by using the | symbol. Here, a pipe is used to see if **root** is logged on by connecting the output of **who** to **grep**:

```
$ who | grep root
root   console  Sep 12 22:16
```

It can also be used to count the number of files in a directory by connecting the **ls** and **wc** commands. This shows that there are eleven files in the current directory:

```
$ ls | wc -l
11
```

You can also have multiple pipes to connect a series of commands together. The name of each unique user that is logged on is displayed using this command:

```
$ who | cut -f1 -d' ' | sort -u
anatole
root
```

You could even add another pipe to give you just the count of unique users:

```
$ who | cut -f1 -d' ' | sort -u | wc -l
3
```

Conditional Execution

The Korn shell provides the **&&** and **||** operators for simple conditional execution. First you need to know that when programs finish executing, they return an exit status that indicates if they ran successfully or not. A zero exit status usually indicates that a program executed successfully, while a non-zero exit status usually indicates that an error occurred.

If two commands are separated with **&&**, the second command is only executed if the first command returns a zero exit status. Here, the **echo** command is executed, because **ls** ran successfully:

```
$ ls temp && echo "File temp exists"
temp
File temp exists
```

Now, file **temp** is removed and the same command is run again:

```
$ rm temp
$ ls temp && echo "File temp exists"
ls: temp: No such file or directory
```

If two commands are separated with ||, the second command is only executed if the first command returns a non-zero exit status. In this case, the **echo** command is executed, because **ls** returned an error:

```
$ ls temp || echo "File temp does NOT exist"
ls: temp: No such file or directory
File temp does NOT exist
```

Remember that basic conditional execution using these operators only works with two commands. Appending more commands to the same command-line using **;** does not cause these to also be conditionally executed. Here, the **touch temp** command is executed, regardless if **ls temp** failed or not. Only the **echo** command is conditionally executed:

```
$ ls temp || echo "File temp does NOT exist"; \
touch temp
ls: temp: No such file or directory
File temp does NOT exist
```

The next section talks about how you can conditionally execute more than one command by using {}'s or ()'s. As you can see, the **&&** and || operators can come in handy. There are certainly many situations where they can be more efficient to use than the **if** command.

There is one more type of logic you can perform using these operators. You can implement a simple **if** command by using the **&&** and || operators together like this:

command1 **&&** *command2* || *command3*

If *command1* returns true, then *command2* is executed, which causes *command3* to not be executed. If *command1* does not return true, then *command2* is not executed, which causes *command3* to be executed.

Confusing, right? Let's look at a real example to make sense out of this. Here, if the file **temp** exists, then one message is displayed, and if it doesn't exist, the another message is displayed:

```
$ touch temp
$ ls temp && echo "File temp exists" || echo \
File temp does NOT exist
temp
File temp exists
```

Now we remove file **temp** and run the same command:

```
$ rm temp
$ ls temp && echo "File temp exists" || echo \
"File temp does NOT exist"
ls: temp: No such file or directory
File temp does NOT exist
```

Although compact, this format may not be considered as readable as the **if** command. We look at comparing the **&&** and || operators to the **if** command later in **Chapter 8**.

Grouping Commands

Multiple commands can be grouped together using {} or (). Commands enclosed in {} are executed in the current shell. This is useful for when you want to combine the output from multiple commands. Here is file **temp**:

```
$ cat temp
The rain in Spain
falls mainly on the plain
```

Let's say we want to add a header to the output, then line-number the whole thing with the **nl** command (or **pr −n** if you don't have **nl**). We could try it like this:

```
$ echo "This is file temp:" ; cat temp | nl
This is file temp:
1  The rain in Spain
2  falls mainly on the plain
```

Only the output from **cat temp** was line numbered. By using {}'s, the output from both commands is line numbered:

```
$ { echo "This is file temp:"; cat temp ; } | nl
1  This is file temp:
2  The rain in Spain
3  falls mainly on the plain
```

There must be whitespace after the opening {, or else you get a syntax error. One more restriction: commands within the {}'s must be terminated with a semi-colon when given on one line. This keeps commands separated so that the Korn shell knows where one command ends, and another one begins.

This means that commands can be grouped within {}'s even when separated with newlines like this:

```
$ { pwd ; echo "First line"
> echo "Last line"
> }
/usr/spool/smail
First line
Last line
```

Another use for this feature is in conjunction with the **&&** and **||** operators to allow multiple commands to be conditionally executed. This is similar to the example from the previous section. What we want this command to do is check if file **temp** exists, and if it does, display a message, then remove it. Unfortunately, the way it is written, **rm temp** is executed regardless of whether it exists or not.

```
$ rm temp
$ ls temp && echo "temp exists.removing";rm temp
ls: temp: No such file or directory
rm: temp: No such file or directory
```

16

Table 2.1: Command Execution Format

command1 **;** *command2*

        execute *command1* followed by *command2*

command **&**   execute *command* asynchronously in the background; do not wait for completion

command1 | *command2*

        pass the standard output of *command1* to standard input of *command2*

command1 **&&** *command2*

        execute *command2* if *command1* returns zero (successful) exit status

command1 **||** *command2*

        execute *command2* if *command1* returns non-zero (unsuccessful) exit status

command **|&**   execute *command* asynchronously with its standard input and standard output attached to the parent shell; use **read –p**/**print –p** to manipulate the standard input/output (see **Chapter 8**)

command ****   continue *command* onto the next line

{ *command* **; }**

        execute *command* in the current shell

(*command* **)** execute *command* in a subshell

By using {}'s, both the **echo** and **rm** commands are only executed if **temp** exists:

```
$ touch temp
$ ls temp && { echo "temp exists..removing" ;
> rm temp ; }
temp
temp exists..removing
```

Commands enclosed in ( ) are executed in a subshell. This is discussed in detail in **Chapter 7**.

Input/Output Redirection

The Korn shell provides a number of operators than can be used to manipulate command input/output and files. For example, you can save command output to a file. Or instead of typing in the input to a command, it can be taken from a file. The following sections describe some of the features of Korn shell I/O redirection.

Redirecting Standard Output

The standard output of a command is by default directed to your terminal. By using the > symbol, the standard output of a command can be redirected to a file, instead of your terminal. In this example, the standard output of the **echo** command is put into the file **p.out**:

```
$ echo "Hello" > p.out
$ cat p.out
Hello
```

If the file doesn't exist, then it is created. Otherwise, the contents are usually overwritten, usually, but not always. If you have the

noclobber option set (discussed in the next section), or the file attributes (permissions and/or ownership) do not permit writing, the file will not be overwritten. If we change permission on **p.out** and try to direct output to it again, we get an error message:

```
$ chmod 444 p.out
$ echo "Hello again" > pwd.out
/bin/ksh: p.out: cannot create
```

We'll see in the next section how to force overwriting of existing files using a variation of the > redirect operator.

You can also use the > command to create an empty file:

```
$ > tmp
$ ls -s tmp
0 tmp
```

This is equivalent to **touch tmp**.

Standard output can be appended to a file by using the >> redirect operator. Here, the output of **find** is appended to **deadfiles.out**:

```
$ echo "Dead File List" > junk.out
$ find . -name dead.letter -print >>junk.out
$ find . -name core -print >>junk.out
$ cat junk.out
Dead File List
./mail/dead.letter
./bin/core
```

Standard output is closed with the >&- redirect operator:

```
$ echo "This is going nowhere" >&-
$
```

This feature can be used in a Korn shell script to close the output of a group of commands instead of redirecting the output of each command individually.

The noclobber Option

To prevent redirecting output to an existing file, set the **noclobber** option. By default, this feature is usually disabled, but can be enabled with the **set −o noclobber** command:

```
$ ls > file.out
$ set —o noclobber
```

Now when we try to redirect output to **file.out**, an error message is returned:

```
$ ls > file.out
/bin/ksh: file.out: file already exists
```

The >| operator is used to force overwriting of a file, even if the **noclobber** option is enabled. Here, **file.out** can now be overwritten, even though the **noclobber** option is set:

```
$ ls >| file.out
```

Redirecting Standard Input

Standard input to a command is redirected from a file using the < operator. This feature can be used to read in a mail message from a file, instead of typing it in:

```
$ mail dick jane spot < mlist
```

This could also be implemented using a pipe:

```
$ cat mlist | mail dick jane spot
```

In both cases, file **mlist** becomes the standard input to **mail**.

Table 2.2: Some I/O Redirection Operators

<*file*	redirect standard input from *file*.
>*file*	redirect standard output to *file*. Create *file* if non-existent, else overwrite.
>>*file*	append standard output to *file*. Create *file* if non-existent.
>|*file*	redirect standard output to *file*. Create *file* if non-existent, else overwrite even if **noclobber** is enabled.
<>*file*	open *file* for reading and writing as standard input.
<&−	close standard input.
>&−	close standard output.

Standard input can be closed with the **<&−** redirect operator. Here, the standard input to the **wc** command is closed:

```
$ cat mlist | wc −l <&−
0
```

Not really exciting. This is useful when manipulating file descriptors with the **exec** command, which is discussed later in **Chapter 8**.

File Descriptors

File descriptors are used by processes to identify their open files. The Korn shell automatically assigns file descriptor 0 to standard input for reading, file descriptor 1 to standard output for writing, and file descriptor 2 to standard error for reading and writing. The file descriptors 3 through 9 can be used with I/O redirection operators and are opened, closed, and/or copied with the **exec** command, which is discussed later in **Chapter 8**.

Redirecting Standard Error

Most Unix commands write their error messages to standard error. As with standard output, standard error is by default directed to your terminal, but it can be redirected using the standard error file descriptor (2) and the > operator. For example, the **ls** command displays a message on standard error when you attempt to display information about a non-existent file:

```
$ ls tmp
tmp not found
```

Now, if you do an **ls** on an existent and non-existent file on the same command-line, a message about the non-existent file goes to standard error, while the output for the existent file goes to standard output:

```
$ ls tmp t.out
tmp not found
t.out
```

By using the **2>** operator, the standard error of the same command is redirected to **ls.out**. The standard output is still displayed directly to your terminal:

```
$ ls tmp t.out 2>ls.out
t.out
$ cat ls.out
tmp not found
```

There can be no space between the **2** and > symbol, otherwise the **2** is interpreted as an argument to the command.

Table 2.3: File Descriptors

0	standard input
1	standard output
2	standard error
3–9	unassigned file descriptors

More with File Descriptors

The **>&***n* operator causes output to be redirected to file descriptor *n*. This is used when you want to direct output to a specific file descriptor. To send the output of the **echo** command to standard error, just add **>&2** to the command-line:

```
$ echo This is going to standard error >&2
This is going to standard error
```

In the next command, the standard error and output are sent to **ls.out** by specifying multiple redirections on the same command line. First, **>&2** causes standard output to be redirected to standard error. Then, **2>ls.out** causes standard error (which is now standard output and standard error) to be sent to **ls.out**:

```
$ ls tmp t.out 2>ls.out 1>&2
$ cat ls.out
tmp not found
t.out
```

This command causes output to be redirected to both standard output and standard error:

```
$ { echo "This is going to stdout" >&1 ; \
echo "This is going to stderr" >&2 ; }
This is going to stdout
This is going to stderr
```

If the output of the last command was redirected to a file using the `>` operator, then only the standard output would be redirected. The standard error would still be displayed on your terminal.

```
$ { echo "This is going to stdout" >&1 ; \
echo "This is going to stderr" >&2 ; } >out
This is going to stderr
$ cat out
This is going to stdout
```

The *n>&m* operator causes the output from file descriptors *n* and *m* to be merged. This operator could be used in the previous command to direct both the standard output and standard error to the same file.

```
$ { echo "This is going to stdout" >&1 ; \
echo "This is going to stderr" >&2 ; } >out 2>&1
$ cat out
This is going to stdout
This is going to stderr
```

If you wanted the standard output and standard error appended to the output file, the `>>` operator could be used:

```
$ { echo "This is going to stdout again" >&1 ; \
echo "This is going to stderr again" >&2 ; } \
>>out 2>&1
$ cat out
This is going to stdout
This is going to stderr
This is going to stdout again
This is going to stderr again
```

As seen in the previous example, multiple file descriptor redirections can also be specified. To close the standard output and standard error of this **ls** command:

```
$ ls tmp t.out >&- 2>&-
$
```

The **print** and **read** commands have special options that allow you to redirect standard output and input with file descriptors. This is discussed in **Chapter 8**.

Here Documents

Here documents is a term used for redirecting multiple lines of standard input to a command. In looser terms, they allow batch input to be given to programs and are frequently used to execute interactive commands from within Korn shell scripts. The format for a here document is:

> *command* << *word*
> or
> *command* <<–*word*

where lines that follow are used as standard input to *command* until *word* is read. In the following example, standard input for the **cat** command is read until the word **END** is encountered:

```
$ cat >> .profile <<END
> export TERM=sun-cmd
> export ORACLE_HOME=/apps/oracle
> END
```

The other variation, *command* <<– *word*, deletes leading tab characters from the here document. It is often used over the first variation to produce more readable code when used within larger scripts. A good use for here documents is to automate **ftp** file transfers. This snippet of code could be used within a larger script to automatically **ftp** code to or from another server.

```
$ ftp <<- END
open aspsun
user anonymous
cd /usr/pub
binary
get ksh.tar.Z
quit
END
```

Here Documents and File Descriptors

Here documents can also be used with file descriptors. Instead of reading multiple lines from standard input, multiple lines are read from file descriptor *n* until *word* is read.

> *command n<<word*
> or
> *command n<<–word*

Discarding Standard Output

The **/dev/null** file is like the system trash bin. Anything redirected to it is discarded by the system.

```
$ ls >/dev/null
```

This is not the same as:

```
$ ls >&—
```

which closes standard output.

Table 2.4: Redirect Operators and File Descriptors

<&n	redirect standard input from file descriptor *n*.
>&n	redirect standard output to file descriptor *n*.
n<file	redirect file descriptor *n* from *file*.
n>file	redirect file descriptor *n* to *file*.
n>>file	redirect file descriptor *n* to *file*. Create *file* if non-existent, else overwrite.
n>|file	redirect file descriptor *n* to *file*. Create *file* even if **noclobber** is enabled.
n<&m	redirect file descriptor *n* input from file descriptor *m*.
n>&m	redirect file descriptor *n* output to file descriptor *m*.
n<>file	open *file* for reading and writing as file descriptor *n*.
n<<word	redirect to file descriptor *n* until *word* is read.
n<<−word	redirect to file descriptor *n* until *word* is read; ignore leading tabs.
n<&−	close file descriptor *n* for standard input.
n>&−	close file descriptor *n* for standard output.
print −u*n args*	redirect arguments to file descriptor *n*. If *n* is greater than **2**, it must first be opened with **exec**. If *n* is not specified, the default file descriptor argument is **1** (standard output).
read −u*n args*	read input line from file descriptor *n*. If *n* is greater than **2**, it must first be opened with **exec**. If *n* is not specified, the default file descriptor argument is **0** (standard input).

File Name Substitution

File name substitution is a feature which allows strings to be substituted for patterns and special characters. This provides greater flexibility and saves a lot of typing time. Most frequently this feature is used to match file names in the current directory, but can also be used to match arguments in **case** and **[[...]]** commands.

The syntax for file name substitution is not the same as regular expression syntax used in some Unix commands like **ed**, **grep**, and **sed**. The examples in the following sections assume that the following files exist in the current directory:

```
$ ls —a
.         .molog   abc       dabkup3   mobkup1
..        a        dabkup1   dabkup4   mobkup2
.dalog    ab       dabkup2   dabkup5
```

The * Character

The * character matches any zero or more characters. This is probably the most frequently used pattern matching character. If used alone, * substitutes the names of all the files in the current directory, except those that begin with the "**.**" character. These must be explicitly matched. Now, instead of typing in each individual file name to the **cat** command:

```
$ cat dabkup1 dabkup2 dabkup3 dabkup4 ...
. . .
```

You can do this:

```
$ cat *
. . .
```

The * character can also be used with other characters to match only certain file names. Let's say we only wanted to list the monthly backup files. We could do it like this:

```
$ ls m*
mobkup1          mobkup2
```

The **m*** matches any file name in the current directory that begins with **m**, which here would be **mobkup1** and **mobkup2**. This command lists file names that end in **2**:

```
$ ls *2
dabkup2          mobkup2
```

This command lists file names that contain **ab**. Notice that **ab** and **abc** are also listed:

```
$ ls *ab*
ab       dabkup1    dabkup3         dabkup5
abc      dabkup2    dabkup4
```

Remember that file name substitution only works with files in the current directory. To match file names in subdirectories, the / character must be explicitly matched. This pattern would match file names ending in **.Z** from any directories one-level under the current directory:

```
$ ls */*.Z
bin/smail.Z         bin/calc.Z         bin/testsh.Z
```

To search the next level of directories, another /* would need to be added.

```
$ ls */*/*.Z
bin/fdir/foo.Z
```

Be careful, because on some systems, matching files names in extremely large directories and subdirectories will generate an argument list error.

Don't forget that the "**.**" character must be explicitly matched. Here, the **.** files in the current directory are listed:

```
$ echo .*
. .. .dalog .malog
```

The ? Character

The **?** character matches exactly one character. It is useful when the file name matching criteria is the length of the file name. For example, to list two-character file names in the current directory, **??** could be used.

```
$ echo ??
ab
```

What if you wanted to list the file names in the current directory that had at least three or more characters in the name. The **???** pattern would match file names that had exactly three characters, but not more. You could try this:

```
$ echo ??? ???? ????? . . .
```

but that is not correct either. As you probably already guessed, the pattern to use would be **???***, which matches files names with three characters, followed by any zero or more characters. Let's try it:

```
$ echo ???*
abc dabkup1 dabkup2 dabkup3 dabkup4 dabkup5
mobkup1 mobkup2
```

If you only wanted to list the **dabkup***, you could you the following pattern:

```
$ echo dabkup?
dabkup1 dabkup2 dabkup3 dabkup4 dabkup5
```

The [] Characters

The [] characters match a single, multiple, or range of characters. It is useful for when you want to match certain characters in a specific character position in the file name. For example, if you wanted to list the file names in the current directory that began with **a** or **m**, you could do it like this:

```
$ ls a* m*
a          ab          abc          mobkup1  mobkup2
```

or do it more easily using []:

```
$ ls [am]*
a          ab          abc          mobkup1  mobkup2
```

This command lists file names beginning with **d** or **m**, and ending with any number **1** through **5**:

```
$ echo [dm]*[12345]
dabkup1          dabkup3          dabkup5                    mobkup2
dabkup2          dabkup4          mobkup1
```

You could do the same thing using a range argument instead of listing out each number:

```
$ echo [dm]*[1-5]
dabkup1          dabkup3          dabkup5                    mobkup2
dabkup2          dabkup4          mobkup1
```

In the range argument, the first character must be alphabetically less than the last character. This means that [**c–a**] is an invalid range. This also means that pattern [**0–z**] matches any alphabetic or

alphanumeric character, [**A**–**z**] matches any alphabetic character
(upper and lower case), [**0**–**Z**] matches any alphanumeric or upper
case alphabetic character, and [**0**–**9**] matches any alphanumeric
character.

Multiple ranges can also be given. The pattern [**a**–**jlmr3**–**7**] would
match files names beginning with the letters **a** through **j**, **l**, **m**, **r**, and **3**
through **7**.

The ! Character

The **!** character can be used with [] to reverse the match. In other
words, [**!a**] matches any character, except **a**. This is another very
useful pattern matching character, since frequently you want to match
everything except something. For example, if the current directory
contained these files:

```
$ ls
a         abc        dabkup2      dabkup4        mobkup1
ab        dabkup1    dabkup3      dabkup5   mobkup2
```

and we wanted to list all of the file names, except those that started
with **d**, we could do this:

```
$ ls [0-ce-z]*
a         abc       mobkup2
ab        mobkup1
```

or it could be done more easily using [**!d**]:

```
$ ls [!d]*
a         abc       mobkup2
ab        mobkup1
```

Multiple and range arguments can also be negated. The pattern

Table 2.5: Basic Pattern-Matching Characters

?	match any single character
*****	match zero or more characters, including null
[abc]	match any character or characters between the brackets
[x–z]	match any character or characters in the range *x* to *z*
[a–ce–g]	match any character or characters in the range *a* to *c*, *e* to *g*
[!abc]	match any character or characters not between the brackets
[!x–z]	match any character or characters not in the range *x* to *z*
.	strings starting with **.** must be explicitly matched

[!lro]* would match strings not beginning with **l**, **r**, or **o**, ***[!2–5]** would match strings not ending with **2** through **5**, and ***.[!Z]** would match strings not ending in **.Z**.

Matching . Files

Certain characters like "**.**" (period) must be explicitly matched. This command matches the file names **.a**, **.b**, and **.c**:

```
$ ls .[a-c]
.a   .b   .c
```

To remove all the files in the current directory that contain a ".", except those that end in **.c** or **.h**:

```
$ rm *.[!ch]
```

Complex Patterns

The latest version of the Korn shell also provides other matching capabilities. Instead of matching only characters, entire patterns can be given. For demonstration purposes, let's assume that we have a command called **match** that finds words in the on-line dictionary, **/usr/dict/words**. It's like the **grep** command, except that Korn shell patterns are used, instead of regular expression syntax that **grep** recognizes. The source code for **match** is listed in **Appendix D**.

*(pattern)

This format matches any zero or more occurrences of *pattern*. You could find words that contained any number of consecutive **A**'s:

```
$ match *(A)
A
AAA
AAAAAAAA
```

Multiple patterns can also be given, but they must be separated with a | character. Let's try it with **match**:

```
$ match *(A|i)
A
AAA
AAAAAA
i
ii
```

```
iii
iiiiii
```

This pattern matches **anti**, **antic**, **antigen**, and **antique**:

```
$ match anti*(c|gen|que)
anti
antic
antigen
antique
```

This format is also good for matching numbers. The **[1–9]*([0–9])** pattern matches any number **1–9999999*** (any number except **0**).

?(*pattern*)

This format matches any zero or one occurrences of *pattern*. Here we look for one, two, and three letter words beginning with **s**:

```
$ match s?(?|??)
s
sa
sac
sad
...
```

Here are some more patterns using this format:

```
1?([0-9])
```
matches
```
1, 10, 11, 12, ..., 19
```

```
the?(y|m|[rs]e)
```
matches
```
the, they, them, there, these
```

+(*pattern*)

This format matches one or more occurrences of *pattern*. To find any words beginning with **m** followed by any number of **iss** patterns:

```
$ match m+(iss)*
miss
mississippi
```

Here is another pattern using this format. It matches any number.

```
+([0-9])
matches
0-9999999*
```

@(*pattern*)

This format matches exactly one occurrence of *pattern*. Let's look for words beginning with **Ala** or **Cla**:

```
$ match @([AC]la)*
Alabama
Alameda
Alamo
Alaska
Claire
Clara
Clare
...
```

Now for another number-matching pattern. This one matches any number **0–9**:

```
@([0-9]
matches
0, 1, 2, 3, ..., 9
```

Table 2.6: Other File Name Patterns

?(*pattern-list*)	match zero or one occurrence of any *pattern*
*(*pattern-list*)	match zero or more occurrences of any *pattern*
+(*pattern-list*)	match one or more occurrence of any *pattern*
@(*pattern-list*)	match exactly one occurrence of any *pattern*
!(*pattern-list*)	match anything except any *pattern*
pattern-list	multiple patterns must be separated with a | character

!(*pattern*)

This format matches anything except *pattern*. To match any string that does not end in **.c**, **.Z**, or **.o**:

```
!(*.c|*.Z|*.o)
```

or any string that does not contain digits:

```
!(*[0-9]*)
```

More Complex Patterns

The complex file patterns can be used together or even nested to generate even more sophisticated patterns. Here are a few examples:

```
@([1-9])+([0-9])
matches
1-9999999*

@([2468]|+([1-9])+([02468]))
matches any even numbers
2, 4, 6, 8, ...

@([13579]|+([0-9])+([13579]))
matches any odd numbers
1, 3, 5, 7, ...
```

Disabling File Name Substitution

File name substitution can be disabled by setting the **noglob** option using the **set** command:

```
$ set —o noglob
or
$ set —f
```

The **—o noglob** and **—f** options for the **set** command are the same. Once file name substitution is disabled, pattern-matching characters like *, ?, and] lose their special meaning:

```
$ ls a*
a* not found
$ ls b?
b? not found
```

Now we can create some files that contain special characters in their names.

```
$ touch *a b?b c-c d[]d
$ ls
*a      b?b     c-c     d[]d
```

Within [...] patterns, a \ character is used to remove the meaning of the special pattern-matching characters. This means that the [*\?]* pattern would match file names beginning with * or ?.

Command Substitution

Command substitution is a feature that allows output to be expanded from a command. It can be used to assign the output of a command to a variable, or to imbed the output of a command within another command. The format for command substitution is:

$(*command*)

where *command* is executed and the output is substituted for the entire $(*command*) construct. For example, to print the current date in a friendly format:

```
$ echo The date is $(date)
The date is Fri Jul 27 10:41:21 PST 1996
```

or see who is logged on:

```
$ echo $(who -q) are logged on now
root anatole are logged on now
```

Any commands can be used inside $(...), including pipes, I/O operators, metacharacters (wildcards), and more. We can find out how many users are logged on by using the **who** and **wc -l** commands:

```
$ echo $(who | wc -1) users are logged on
There are 3 users logged on
```

Bourne Shell Compatibility

For compatibility with the Bourne shell, the following format for command substitution can also be used:

> `command`

Using `...` command substitution, we could get the names of the files in the current directory like this:

```
$ echo `ls` are in this directory
NEWS asp bin pc are this directory
```

If you wanted a count of the files, a pipe to **wc** could be added:

```
$ echo There are `ls | wc -1` files here
There are 4 files here
```

Directing File Input

There is also a special form of the **$(...)** command that is used to substitute the contents of a file. The format for file input substitution is:

> **$(<** *file*)

This is equivalent to **$(cat** *file*) or `cat *file*`, except that it is faster, because an extra process does not have to be created to execute the **cat** command. A good use for this is assigning file contents to variables:

```
$ cat foo
a b c
$ X=$(<foo)
$ echo $X
a b c
```

We will talk about this later in **Chapter 3**.

Arithmetic Operations

Another form of the **$(...)** command is used to substitute the output of arithmetic expressions. The value of an arithmetic expression is returned when enclosed in double parentheses and preceded with a dollar sign.

> **$((***arithmetic-expression***))**

Here are a few examples.

```
$ echo $((3+5))
8
$ echo $((8192*16384%23))
9
```

Performing arithmetic is discussed in detail in **Chapter 6**.

Tilde Substitution

Tilde substitution is used to substitute the pathname of a user's home directory for *~user*. Words in the command line that start with the tilde character cause the Korn shell to check the rest of the word up to a slash. If the tilde character is found alone or is only followed by a slash, it is replaced with the value of the **HOME** variable. This is a handy shortcut borrowed from the C shell. For example, to print the pathname of your home directory:

```
$ echo ~
/home/anatole
```

or to list its contents:

```
$ ls ~/
NEWS          bin          pc
asp           mail         src
```

If the tilde character is followed by a login name file, it is replaced with the home directory of that user. Here we change directory to the **tools** directory in **smith**'s home directory:

```
$ cd ~smith/tools
$ pwd
/home/users/admin/smith/tools
```

If the tilde character is followed by a + or −, it is replaced with the value of **PWD** (current directory) and **OLDPWD** (previous directory), respectively. This is not very useful for directory navigation, since **cd** ~+ leaves you in the current directory. The **cd** ~− command puts you in the previous directory, but the Korn shell provides an even shorter shortcut: **cd** − does the same thing, except that it also displays the current directory.

```
$ pwd
/home/users/admin/smith/tools
$ cd /usr/bin
$ cd ~-
$ pwd
/home/users/admin/smith/tools
$ cd -
/usr/bin
```

Table 2.7: Tilde Substitution

~	replaced with **$HOME**
~*user*	replaced with the home directory of *user*
~—	replaced with **$OLDPWD** (previous directory)
~+	replaced with **$PWD** (current directory)

Chapter 3:
Variables and Parameters

Variables
Special Parameters
Variable Expansion
Array Variables
Compound Variables
Quoting

Variables and parameters are used by the Korn shell to store values. Like other high-level programming languages, the Korn shell supports data types and arrays. This is a major difference with the Bourne, C shell, and other scripting languages, which have no concept of data types.

The Korn shell supports four data types: *string*, *integer*, *float*, and *array*. If a data type is not explicitly defined, the Korn shell will assume that the variable is a *string*.

By default, all variables are global in scope. However, it is possible to declare a local variable within a function. This is discussed in more detail later in this chapter.

Variables

Korn shell variable names can begin with an alphabetic (**a–Z**) or underscore character, followed by one or more alphanumeric (**a–Z, 0–9**) or underscore characters. Other variable names that contain only digits (**0–9**) or special characters (**!, @, #, %, *, ?, $**) are reserved for special parameters set directly by the Korn shell.

To assign a value to a variable, you can simply name the variable and set it to a value. For example, to assign **abc** to variable **X**:

```
$ X=abc
```

The **typeset** command can also be used to assign values, but unless you are setting attributes, it's a lot more work for nothing. If a value is not given, the variable is set to null. Here, **X** is reassigned the null value:

```
$ X=
```

This is not the same as being undefined. As we'll see later, accessing the value of an undefined variable may return an error, while accessing the value of a null variable returns the null value.

Accessing Variable Values

To access the value of a variable, precede the name with the **$** character. There can be no space between **$** and the variable name. In this example, **CBIN** is set to **/usr/ccs/bin**.

```
$ CBIN=/usr/ccs/bin
```

Table 3.1: Assigning Values to Variables

variable=	declare *variable* and set it to null
typeset *variable=*	declare *variable* and set it to null
variable=value	assign *value* to *variable*
typeset *variable=value*	assign *value* to *variable*

Now you can just type **$CBIN** instead of the long pathname:

```
$ cd $CBIN
$ pwd
/usr/ccs/bin
```

Here is a new command to go along with this concept: **print**. It displays its arguments on your terminal, just like **echo**.

```
$ print Hello world!
Hello world!
```

Here we use **print** to display the value of **CBIN** :

```
$ print $CBIN
/usr/ccs/bin
```

Variable Attributes

Korn shell variables can have one or more attributes that specify their internal representation, access or scope, or the way they are displayed. This concept is similar to a data type in other high-level programming languages, except that in the Korn shell it is not as restrictive. Variables can be set to integer type for faster arithmetic operations, read-only so that the value cannot be changed, left/right justified for formatting purposes, and more. To assign a value and/or attribute to a Korn shell variable, use the following format with the **typeset** command:

> **typeset** *—attribute variable=value*
> or
> **typeset** *—attribute variable*

Except for **readonly**, variable attributes can be set before, during, or after assignment. Functionally it makes no difference. Just remember that the attribute has precedence over the value. This means that if you change the attribute after a value has been assigned, the value may be affected.

Lowercase (–l) and Uppercase (–u) Attributes

These attributes cause the variable values to be changed to lower or uppercase. For example, the lowercase attribute and uppercase value **ASPD** are assigned to variable **MYSYS**:

```
$ typeset —l MYSYS=ASPD
```

Despite the fact that **MYSYS** was assigned uppercase **ASPD**, when accessed, the value is displayed in lowercase:

```
$ print $MYSYS
aspd
```

This is because the attribute affects the variable value, regardless of the assignment. Variable attributes can also be changed after assignment. If we wanted to display variable **MYSYS** in uppercase, we could just reset the attribute:

```
$ typeset -u MYSYS
$ print $MYSYS
ASPD
```

Table 3.2: Assigning Values/Attributes to Variables

typeset *−attribute variable=value*
>   assign *attribute* and *value* to *variable*
typeset *−attribute variable*
>   assign *attribute* to *variable*
typeset *+attribute variable*
>   remove *attribute* from *variable*

Readonly (−r) Attribute

Once the readonly attribute is set, a variable cannot be assigned another value. Here, we use it to set up a restricted **PATH**:

```
$ typeset -r PATH=/usr/rbin
```

If there is an attempt to reset **PATH**, an error message is generated:

```
$ PATH=$PATH:/usr/bin:
/bin/ksh: PATH: is read only
```

We'll come back to this in a few pages. Unlike other variable attributes, once the readonly attribute is set, it cannot be removed.

The **readonly** command can also be used to specify a readonly variable.

Integer (–i) Attribute

The integer attribute (**–i**) is used to explicitly declare integer variables. Although it is not necessary to set this attribute when assigning integer values, there are some benefits to it. We'll cover this later in **Chapter 6**. In the meantime, **NUM** is set to an integer-type variable and assigned a value:

```
$ typeset -i NUM=1
$ print $NUM
1
```

We could also assign **NUM** the number of users on the system using command substitution like this:

```
$ typeset -i NUM=$(who | wc -1)
$ print $NUM
3
```

There is one restriction on integer variables. Once a variable is set to integer type, it can't be assigned a non-integer value:

```
$ typeset -i NUM=abc
/bin/ksh: NUM: bad number
```

Float (–E, –F) Attribute

The float attributes (**–E, –F**) are used to declare float variables. The **–E** is used to specify the number of significant digits, while **–F** is used to specify the precision. We'll cover this later in **Chapter 6**. In the following example, **X** is set to a float variable and assigned a value using both formats:

```
$ typeset —E5 X=123.456
$ print $X
123.46
$ typeset —F5 X=123.456
$ print $X
123.45600
```

The **float** command can also be used to declare a float variable, but does not allow for specifying the precision.

Right (–R) and Left (–L) Justify Attributes

The right and left justify attributes cause variable values to be justified within their width and are be used to format data. Here, variables **A** and **B** are set to right-justify with a field width of 7 characters. Notice that integer values are used, even though the integer attribute is not set.

```
$ typeset —R7 A=10 B=10000
$ print :$A:
:     10:
$ print :$B:
:  10000:
```

If the field width is not large enough for the variable assignment, the value gets truncated. Variable **X** is assigned a seven-character wide value, but the field width is set to **3**, so the first four characters are lost:

```
$ typeset -R3 X=ABCDEFG
$ print $X
EFG
```

If a field width is not given, then it is set with the first variable assignment. Variable **Y** is assigned a three-character wide value, so the field width is set to **3**.

```
$ typeset -L Y=ABC
$ print $Y
ABC
```

Without explicitly resetting the field width, a subsequent assignment would be restricted to a three-character wide value:

```
$ Y=ZYXWVUT
$ print $Y
ZYX
```

Autoexport (-x) Attribute

This is another useful attribute. It allows you to set and export a variable in one command. Instead of

```
$ typeset X=abc
$ export X
```

you can do this:

```
$ typeset -x X=abc
```

We could use this attribute to add the **/lbin** directory to the **PATH** variable and export it all in one command:

```
$ typeset -x PATH=$PATH:/lbin
```

Table 3.3: Some Variable Attributes

typeset **–i** *var*	Set the type of *var* to be integer
typeset **–l** *var*	Set *var* to lower case
typeset **–L** *var*	Left justify *var*; the field width is specified by the first assignment
typeset **–L***n* *var*	Left justify *var*; set field width to *n*
typeset **–LZ***n* *var*	Left justify *var*; set field width to *n* and strip leading zeros
typeset **–r** *var*	Set *var* to be readonly (same as the **readonly** command)
typeset **–R** *var*	Right justify *var*; the field width is specified by the first assignment
typeset **–R***n* *var*	Right justify *var*; set field width to *n*
typeset **–RZ***n* *var*	Right justify *var*; set field width to *n* and fill with leading zeros
typeset **–t** *var*	Set the user-defined attribute for *var*. This has no meaning to the Korn shell.
typeset **–u** *var*	Set *var* to upper case
typeset **–x** *var*	Automatically export *var* to the environment (same as the **export** command)
typeset **–Z** *var*	Same as **typeset –RZ**

Removing Variable Attributes

Except for readonly, variable attributes are removed with the **typeset** +*attribute* command. Assuming that the integer attribute was set on the **NUM** variable, we could remove it like this:

```
$ typeset +i NUM
```

and then reassign it a non-integer value:

```
$ NUM=abc
```

Once the readonly attribute is set, it cannot be removed. When we try to do this with the **PATH** variable that was previously set, we get an error message:

```
$ typeset +r PATH
/bin/ksh: PATH:  is read only
```

The only way to reassign a readonly variable is to unset it first, then assign a value from scratch.

Multiple Attributes

Multiple attributes can also be assigned to variables. This command sets the integer and autoexport attributes for **TMOUT**:

```
$ typeset -ix TMOUT=3000
```

To set and automatically export **ORACLE_SID** to uppercase **prod**:

```
$ typeset -ux ORACLE_SID=prod
$ print $ORACLE_SID
PROD
```

Obviously, some attributes like left and right justify are mutually exclusive, so they shouldn't be set together.

Checking Variable Attributes

Attributes of Korn shell variables are listed using the **typeset** – *attribute* command. For example, to list all the integer type variables and their values:

```
$ typeset -i
ERRNO=0
MAILCHECK=600
PPID=177
RANDOM=22272
SECONDS=4558
TMOUT=0
```

To list only the names of variables with a specific attribute, use the **typeset** +*attribute* command.

More with Variables

You can do other things with variables, such as assign them the value of another variable, the output of a command, or even the contents of a file. Here **Y** is assigned the value of variable **X**:

```
$ X=$HOME
$ Y=$X
$ print $Y
/home/anatole
```

Variables can be assigned command output using this format:

> *variable=$(command)*
> or
> *variable=`command`*

The second format is provided for compatibility with the Bourne shell. Here, **UCSC** is set to its internet ID by assigning the output of the **grep** and **cut** commands:

```
$ UCSC=$(grep UCSC /etc/hosts | cut -f1 -d" ")
$ print $UCSC
128.114.129.1
```

Variables can also be assigned the contents of files like this:

> *variable=$(<file)*
> or
> *variable=`cat file`*

The first format is equivalent to *variable=$(cat file)*. The second format is much slower, but is provided for compatibility with the Bourne shell. Here, the **FSYS** variable is set to the contents of the **/etc/fstab** file:

```
$ FSYS=$(</etc/fstab)
$ print $FSYS
/dev/roota / /dev/rootg /usr
```

Notice that the entries were displayed all on one line, instead of each on separate lines as in the file. We'll talk about this in the **Quoting** section later in this chapter.

A **nameref** variable is a synonym for another variable and will always have the same value as its associated variable They are created using the following formats:

nameref *nameref_variable=variable*
or
typeset −n *nameref_variable=variable*

For example:

```
$ X=abc
$ nameref Y=X
$ print $X
abc
$ print $Y
abc
```

Unsetting Variables

Variable definitions are removed using the **unset** command. The **TMOUT** variable is not being used, so let's unset it:

```
$ unset TMOUT
```

Now to check and see:

```
$ print $TMOUT

$
```

This is not the same as being set to null. As we'll see later in this chapter, variable expansion may be performed differently, depending on whether the variable value is set to null.

Unsetting either the base or **nameref** variable will unset both variables.

```
$ unset Y
$ print $X

$ print $Y

$
```

Special Parameters

Some special parameters are automatically set by the Korn shell and usually cannot be directly set or modified.

The ? Parameter

The **?** parameter contains the exit status of the last executed command. In this example, the **date** command is executed. It ran successfully, so the exit status is **0**:

```
$ date +%D
05/24/96
$ print $?
0
```

Notice that there was no output displayed from the **date** command. This is because the **>&−** I/O operator causes standard output to be closed. The next command, **cp ch222.out /tmp**, did not run successfully, so **1** is returned:

```
$ cp ch222.out /tmp
ch222.out: No such file or directory
$ print $?
1
```

When used with a pipe, **$?** contains the exit status of the last command in the pipeline.

Table 3.4: Some Preset Special Parameters

?	exit status of the last command
$	process id of the current Korn shell
–	current options in effect
!	process id of the last background command or co-process
ERRNO	error number returned by most recently failed system call (system dependent)
PPID	process id of the parent shell

The $ Parameter

The **$** parameter contains the process id of the current shell.

```
$ print $$
178
```

It is useful in creating unique file names within Korn shell scripts.

```
$ touch $0.$$
$ ls *.*
ksh.218
```

Other Special Parameters

The – parameter contains the current options in effect. The output of the next command shows that the **interactive** and **monitor** options are enabled:

```
$ print $-
im
```

To display the error number of the last failed system call, use the **ERRNO** variable. Here, an attempt to display a non-existent file returns an error, so **ERRNO** is checked for the error number:

```
$ cat tmp.out
tmp.out: No such file or directory
$ print $ERRNO
2
```

This is system dependent, so it may not be available on your system. Check your documentation or **/usr/include/sys/errno.h** for more information.

Special Reserved Variables

The Korn shell has two types of reserved variables - those that are set and updated automatically by the Korn shell, and those that are set by each user or the system administrator. These are listed in detail in **Chapter 7**.

Variable Expansion

Variable expansion is the term used for the ability to access and manipulate values of variables and parameters. Basic expansion is done by preceding the variable or parameter name with the **$** character. This provides access to the value.

```
$ UULIB=/usr/lib/uucp
$ print $UULIB
/usr/lib/uucp
```

Other types of expansion can be used to return portions or the length of variables, use default or alternate values, check for mandatory setting, and more.

For the sake of convenience, the term *variable* will refer to both variables and parameters in the following sections that discuss variable expansion.

$variable, ${variable}

This is expanded to the value of *variable*. The braces are used to protect or delimit the variable name from any characters that follow. The next example illustrates why braces are used in variable expansion. The variable **CA** is set to **ca**:

```
$ CA=ca
```

What if we wanted to reset **CA** to **california**? It could be reset to the entire value, but to make a point, let's try using the current value like this:

```
$ CA=$CAlifornia
$ print $CA

$
```

Nothing is printed, because without the braces around the variable **CA**, the Korn shell looks for a variable named **$CAlifornia**. None is found, so nothing is substituted. With the braces around variable **CA**, we get the correct value:

```
$ CA=${CA}lifornia
$ print $CA
california
```

Braces are also needed when attempting to expand positional parameters greater than 9. This ensures that both digits are interpreted as the positional parameter name.

${#variable}

This is expanded to the length of *variable*. In this example, **X** is set to a three-character string, so a length of **3** is returned:

```
$ X=abc
$ print ${#X}
3
```

Whitespace in variable values is also counted as characters. Here the whitespace from the output of the **date** command is also counted:

```
$ TODAY=$(date)
$ print ${#TODAY}
28
```

${*variable:–word*}, ${*variable–word*}

This is expanded to the value of *variable* if it is set and not null, otherwise *word* is expanded. This is used to provide a default value if a variable is not set. In the following example, the variable **X** is set to **abc**. When expanded using this format, the default value **abc** is used:

```
$ X=abc
$ print ${X:-cde}
abc
```

After **X** is unset, the alternate value **cde** is used:

```
$ unset X
$ print ${X:-cde}
cde
```

Notice that the value of **X** remains unchanged:

```
$ print $X

$
```

Let's say we needed a command to get the user name. The problem is that some people have it set to **USER**, while others have it set to

LOGNAME. We could use an **if** command to check one value first, then the other. This would be quite a few lines of code. Or we could use this form of variable expansion to have both values checked with one command. Here, if **USER** is set, then its value is displayed, otherwise the value of **LOGNAME** is displayed.

```
$ print USER=$USER, LOGNAME=$LOGNAME
USER=anatole, LOGNAME=AO
$ print ${USER:-${LOGNAME}}
anatole
```

Now we unset **USER** to check and make sure that **LOGNAME** is used:

```
$ unset USER
$ print ${USER:-${LOGNAME}}
AO
```

But what if both **USER** and **LOGNAME** are not set? Another variable could be checked like this:

```
$ print ${USER:-${LOGNAME:-${OTHERVAR}}}
```

But to demonstrate other ways that the alternate value can be expanded, let's just use some text.

```
$ unset USER LOGNAME
$ print ${USER:-${LOGNAME:-USER and LOGNAME \
not set!}}
USER and LOGNAME not set!
```

In this version, the output of the **whoami** command is used:

```
$ print ${USER-${LOGNAME:-$(whoami)}}
anatole
```

For compatibility with the Bourne shell, it could also be given as:

```
$ echo ${USER:-${LOGNAME:-`whoami`}}
anatole
```

Remember that the alternate value is only used and not assigned to anything. The next section shows how you can assign an alternate value if a default value is not set. The other format, $*{variable-word}*, causes the variable value to be used, even if it is set to null:

```
$ typeset X=
$ print ${X-cde}

$
```

${*variable*:=*word*}, ${*variable*=*word*}

This is expanded to the value of *variable* if set and not null, otherwise it is set to *word*, then expanded. In contrast to the variable expansion format from the previous section, this format is used to assign a default value if one is not already set. In the next example, the variable **LBIN** is set to **/usr/lbin**. When expanded using this format, the default value **/usr/lbin** is used:

```
$ LBIN=/usr/lbin
$ print ${LBIN:=/usr/local/bin}
/usr/lbin
```

After **LBIN** is unset, this form of variable expansion causes **LBIN** to be assigned the alternate value, **/usr/local/bin**:

```
$ unset LBIN
$ print ${LBIN:=/usr/local/bin}
/usr/local/bin
```

Notice that **LBIN** is now set to **/usr/local/bin**.

```
$ print $LBIN
/usr/local/bin
```

Command substitution can also be used in place of *word*. This command sets the **SYS** variable using only one command:

```
$ unset SYS
$ print ${SYS:=$(hostname)}
aspd
```

The other format, **${*variable=word*}**, causes the variable value to be used, even if it is set to null. Here **LBIN** is not assigned an alternate value. If **:=** was used instead of **=**, then **LBIN** would be set to **/usr/local/bin**:

```
$ LBIN=
$ print ${LBIN=/usr/local/bin}

$
```

${*variable:?word*}, ${*variable:?*}, ${*variable?word*}, ${*variable?*}

This is expanded to the value of *variable* if it is set and not null, otherwise *word* is printed and the Korn shell exits. If *word* is omitted, **'parameter null or not set'** is printed. This feature is often used in Korn shell scripts to check if mandatory variables are set. In this example, variable **XBIN** is first unset. When expanded, the default error is printed:

```
$ unset XBIN
$ : ${XBIN:?}
/bin/ksh: XBIN: parameter null or not set
```

The **?** as the *word* argument causes the default error message to be used. You could also provide your own error message:

```
$ print ${XBIN:?Oh my God, XBIN is not set!}
/bin/ksh: XBIN: Oh my God, XBIN is not set!
```

The other formats, **${*variable*?*word*}** and **${*variable*?}**, cause the variable value to be used, even if it is set to null.

${*variable*:+word}, ${*variable*+word}

This is expanded to the value of *word* if *variable* is set and not null, otherwise nothing is substituted. This is basically the opposite of the **${*variable*:−word}** format. Instead of using *word* if *variable* is not set, *word* is used if *variable* is set. In the first example **Y** is set to **abc**. When expanded, the alternate value **def** is displayed because **Y** is set:

```
$ Y=abc
$ print ${Y:+def}
def
```

Here, **Y** is unset. Now when expanded, nothing is displayed:

```
$ unset Y
$ print ${Y:+def}

$
```

Like the ${*variable*:–*word*} format, the alternate value is only used and not assigned to the variable. **Y** is still set to null:

```
$ print $Y

$
```

The other format, ${*variable*+*word*}, causes the variable value to be used, even if it is set to null:

```
$ Y=
$ print ${Y+def}
def
```

${*variable#pattern*}, ${*variable##pattern*}

This is expanded to the value of variable with the smallest (#) or largest (##) part of the left matched by *pattern* deleted. What these expansion formats allow you to do is manipulate substrings. To demonstrate the basic functionality, **X** is set to a string that contains a recurring pattern: **abcabcabc**.

```
$ X=abcabcabc
```

When expanded to return the substring that deletes the smallest left pattern **abc**, we get **abcabc**:

```
$ print ${X#abc*}
abcabc
```

Table 3.5: Variable Expansion Formats

${#*variable*}   length of *variable*

${*variable*:−*word*}

> value of *variable* if set and not null, else print *word*

${*variable*:=*word*}

> value of *variable* if set and not null, else *variable* is set to *word*, then expanded

${*variable*:+*word*}

> value of *word* if *variable* is set and not null, else nothing is substituted

${*variable*:?}   value of *variable* if set and not null, else print '*variable*: **parameter null or not set**'

${*variable*:?*word*}

> value of *variable* if set and not null, else print value of *word* and exit

${*variable*#*pattern*}

> value of *variable* without the smallest beginning portion that matches *pattern*

${*variable*##*pattern*}

> value of *variable* without the largest beginning portion that matches *pattern*

${*variable*%*pattern*}

> value of *variable* without the smallest ending portion that matches *pattern*

${*variable*%%*pattern*}

> value of *variable* without the largest ending portion that matches *pattern*

${*variable*//*pattern1*/*pattern2*}

> replace all occurrences of *pattern1* with *pattern2* in variable

while the substring that deletes the largest left pattern **abc** is **abcabcabc**, or the entire string:

```
$ print ${X##abc*}

$
```

We could use this concept to implement the Korn shell version of the Unix **basename** command. The pattern in this command causes the last directory to be returned if variable **X** is set to a full pathname:

```
$ X=/usr/spool/cron
$ print ${X##*/}
cron
```

${*variable%pattern*},
${*variable%%pattern*}

This is expanded to the value of *variable* with the smallest (**%**) or largest (**%%**) part of the right matched by *pattern* deleted. This is the same as the parameter expansion format from the previous section, except that patterns are matched from the right instead of left side. It could also be used to display file names without their *.suffixes*:

```
$ X=file.Z
$ print ${X%.*}
file
```

Here, any trailing digits are stripped:

```
$ X=chap1
$ print ${X%%[0-9]*}
chap
$ X=chap999
$ print ${X%%[0-9]*}
chap
```

70

The pattern in this command causes it to act like the Unix **dirname** command. Everything except the last directory is returned if variable **X** is set to a full pathname.

```
$ X=/usr/spool/cron
$ print ${X%/*}
/usr/spool
```

${*variable//pattern1/pattern2*},
${*variable/pattern1/pattern2*},
${*variable#pattern1/pattern2*},
${*variable/%pattern1/pattern2*}

The Korn shell supports four search and replace operations on variables. This example changes all occurrences of **abc** in **X** to **xyz**:

```
$ X=abcabcabc
$ print ${X//abc/xyz}
xyzxyzxyz
```

while this one only changes the first occurrence of **abc** in **X** to **xyz**:

```
$ X=abcabcabc
$ print ${X/abc/xyz}
xyzabcabc
```

See Table 3.6 for detailed explanation of the other formats.

${*variable:start*}, ${*variable:start:length*}

This format returns a substring. The first returns *variable* from position *start* to end, while the second returns *length* characters from *variable* from character position *start* to end. For example, this returns the first 3 characters of **X**:

```
$ X=abcdefghij
$ print {$X:0:3}
abc
```

while this example returns the value of **X** starting at character position 5:

```
$ X=abcdefghij
$ print {$X:5}
fghij
```

Array Variables

One-dimensional arrays are supported by the Korn shell. Arrays can have a maximum of 4096 elements. Array subscripts start at 0 and go up to 4096 (or the maximum element minus one). Any variable can become a one-dimensional array by simply referring to it with a subscript. Here, variable **X** is set to **A**:

```
$ X=A
```

By explicitly assigning **X[1]** a value, variable **X** is transformed into an array variable:

```
$ X[1]=B
```

The original assignment to variable **X** is not lost. The first array element (**X[0]**) is still assigned **A**.

Table 3.6: More Variable Expansion Formats

${*variable*//*pattern1*/*pattern2*}
> replace all occurrences of *pattern1* with *pattern2* in *variable*

${*variable*/*pattern1*/*pattern2*}
> replace first occurrence of *pattern1* with *pattern2* in *variable*

${*variable*/#*pattern1*/*pattern2*}
> replace first occurrence of *pattern1* with *pattern2* in *variable* if *variable* begins with *pattern1*

${*variable*/%*pattern1*/*pattern2*}
> replace last occurrence of *pattern1* with *pattern2* in *variable* if *variable* ends with *pattern1*

${*variable*:**start**}
> return *variable* from character position *start* to end

${*variable*:**start**:**length**}
> return *length* characters from *variable* from character position *start* to end

Array Variable Assignments and Declarations

Arrays can be assigned values by using normal variable assignment statements, the **set −A** command, or the **typeset** command:

> *variable*[**0**]=*value variable*[**1**]=*value . . . variable*[*n*]=*value*
> or
> **set −A** *variable value0 value1 . . . valuen*
> or
> **typeset** *variable*[**0**]=*value variable*[**1**]=*value . . .* \
> *variable*[*n*]=*value*

The only difference between the formats is that with the **set** command format, the values are assigned to the array variable sequentially starting from element zero. In the other formats, the array elements can be assigned values in any order. This example assigns the weekday names to the array variable **DAY** using normal variable assignment format:

```
$ DAY[0]=Mon DAY[1]=Tue DAY[2]=Wed  \
DAY[3]=Thu DAY[4]=Fri DAY[5]=Sat DAY[6]=Sun
```

The same variable can be assigned values using the **set** command:

```
$ set −A DAY Mon Tue Wed Thu Fri Sat Sun
```

or the **typeset** command:

```
$ typeset DAY[0]=Mon DAY[1]=Tue DAY[2]=Wed \
DAY[3]=Thu DAY[4]=Fri DAY[5]=Sat DAY[6]=Sun
```

Not all the elements of an array need to exist. You can assign values to non-successive elements of an array. Here, the first and fourth elements of the **TEST** array are assigned values.

```
$ typeset TEST[0]=a TEST[3]=b
```

Table 3.7: Array Variables

${*array*}, $*array* array element zero
${*array*[*n*]} array element *n*
${*array*[*n+2*]} array element *n+2*
${*array*[**$i**]} array element **$i**
${*array*[*]}, ${*array*[@]}
    all elements of an array
${#*array*[*]}, ${#*array*[@]}
    number of array elements
${#*array*[*n*] length of array element *n*
${!*array*[*]}, ${!*array*[@]}
    all initialized subscript values
${!*array*[*]:*n*:*x*} x array elements starting with element n
${!*array*[@]:*n*} all array elements starting with element n

Array Variable Expansion

Array variables are expanded in the same manner as normal variables and parameters: using the $ character. Without a subscript value, an array variable refers to the first element, or element **0**.

```
$ print $DAYS is the same as $DAY[0]
Mon is the same as Mon
```

To access the value of a specific array variable element use a subscript. Array variable names and subscripts must be enclosed in braces for proper expansion:

```
$ print ${DAY[3]} ${DAY[5]}
Thu Sat
```

If an element does not exist, nothing is substituted:

```
$ print ${DAY[25]}

$
```

All the elements of an array can be accessed by using the * or @ as the subscript value. They both return the same value. These examples print the values of all the elements of the **DAY** array variable:

```
$ print ${DAY[*]}
Mon Tue Wed Thu Fri Sat Sun
$ print ${DAY[@]}
Mon Tue Wed Thu Fri Sat Sun
```

The number of elements of an array variable is returned by using the# in front of the array variable name and using * or @ as the subscript value. Let's try it with **DAY**:

```
$ print ${#DAY[*]}
7
$ print ${#DAY[@]}
7
```

To get values for a subset of an array, use this format:

${*variable*[*]:*start_subscript*:*num_elements*}
or
${*variable*[@]:*start_subscript*}

Arithmetic expressions can be used to return a subscript value. This example prints the fifth element of the **DAY** array variable. Remember that array subscripts start with **0**, so the third array element has a subscript of **2**, and the fifth element has a subscript of **4**:

```
$ print ${DAY[4/2]}
Wed
$ print ${DAY[7-6+5-4+3-2+1]
Fri
```

Variable expansion can also be used to generate a subscript value.

```
$ X=6
$ print ${DAY[$X]}
Sun
```

Array Variable Attributes

As with ordinary variables, attributes can be assigned to array-type variables. Arrays can also be declared, and assigned values and attributes with the **typeset** command:

typeset −*attribute variable*[**0**]=*value variable*[**1**]=*value* . . .

Once set, attributes apply to all elements of an array. This example sets the uppercase attribute for the **DAY** array variable using the **typeset −u** command:

```
$ typeset −u DAY
```

Now all the element values are displayed in upper case:

```
$ print ${DAY[*]}
MON TUE WED THU FRI SAT SUN
```

Array element attributes can be set before or after assignment. Here, **XVAR** is initially assigned lowercase **aaa**, **bbb**, and **ccc**:

```
$ set —A XVAR aaa bbb ccc
$ print ${XVAR[*]}
aaa bbb ccc
```

Now, the uppercase, left-justify, two-character-wide attributes are set and the new element values are displayed. Notice that the third character from each element has been dropped, and the value is now in uppercase:

```
$ typeset —uL2 XVAR
$ print ${XVAR[*]}
AA BB CC
```

Array Variable Reassignments

Besides using regular *array-element*[*n*]*=value* or **typeset** *array-element*[*n*]*=value* syntax to reassign values, array variables can also have their values reassigned with the **set +A** command:

> **set +A** *variable value0 value1 . . .*

This is helpful when you don't want to reassign values to all the elements of an array. In this example, the array variable **X** is assigned six values:

```
$ set -A X one two three d e f
$ print ${X[*]}
one two three d e f
```

Using the **set +A** command, the first three elements are reassigned **a**, **b**, and **c**:

```
$ set +A X a b c
$ print ${X[*]}
a b c d e f
```

Notice that values of the fourth, fifth, and sixth elements have not been affected.

Associative Arrays

This version of the Korn shell also supports associative arrays, that is arrays that use string subscripts rather than integer subscripts. Associative arrays are declared using this format:

typeset -A *variable*

where *variable* is the name of the associative array. Additional arguments can be given to the typeset command to specify a data type. For example, we can create an associative array to store some exchange rates:

```
$ typeset -AE exchange_rate
$    exchange_rate["DM"]=1.7
$    exchange_rate["FF"]=.15
$    exchange_rate["AS"]=.04
```

To display a list of associative array subscripts:

${!*variable*[*]}* or ${!*variable*[@]}*

To display the values for all or parts of an associative array:

${!*variable*[*subscript*]}*

For example, all and a specific exchange rate is displayed here:

```
$ print ${!exchange_rate[*]}
0.15 1.7
$ print "The DM exchange rate is:${exchange_rate[DM]}"
1.7
```

Compound Variables

The Korn shell also supports compound variables, which are similar to structures or records in other languages, that is a meta-datatype which is a group of related values, each of which can have a different data type. The syntax for declaring compund variables is:

compound_variable=(
    [*datatype*] *field1*[=*value*]
    . . .
    [*datatype*] *fieldn*[=*value*]
)

For example, we can use a compound variable to manage employee information:

```
$ employee=(
typeset name=Allenby
integer id=1243
float salary=9000.50
)
```

The syntax to display the value of a compound variable field is:

${*compound_variable.field*}

Here we access the employee compound variable:

```
$ print $employee
    ( typeset -E salary=9000.5 name=Allenby typeset -i
id=1243 )
    $ print ${employee.name}
    Allenby
```

Quoting

Quotes are used when assigning values containing whitespace or special characters, to delimit parameters and variables, and to assign command output.

There are three types of quotes: single quotes, double quotes, and back quotes. Single and double quotes are similar, except for the way they handle some special characters. Back quotes are used for command output assignment.

Look what happens when you try to perform a variable assignment using a value that contains whitespace without enclosing it in quotes:

```
$ GREETING=Hello world
/bin/ksh: world:  not found
$ print $GREETING

$
```

No assignment is made. To assign **Hello world** to **GREETING**, you would need to enclose the entire string in quotes, like this:

```
$ GREETING='Hello world'
$ print $GREETING
Hello world
```

Single Quotes

Single quotes are also used to hide the meaning of special characters like $, *, \, !, ", ` and /. Any characters between single quotes, except another single quote, are displayed without interpretation as special characters:

```
$ print '* $ \ ! ` / "'
* $ \ ! ` / "
```

This also means that variable and command substitution does not take place within single quotes (because $ and `` lose their special meaning). If you want to access the value of a variable, use double quotes instead of single quotes (discussed in the next section). So, instead of displaying **/home/anatole**, we get **$HOME**:

```
$ print '$HOME'
$HOME
```

and instead of the date, we get `**date**`:

```
$ print 'Today is `date`'
Today is `date`
```

Korn shell command substitution **$(...)** also doesn't work in single quotes, because of the $ character. You may be thinking what good are single quotes anyway? Well, there are still some good uses for them. You could print a menu border like this:

```
$ print '*****************MENU*****************'
*****************MENU*****************
```

or use the $ character as the dollar symbol:

```
$ print 'Pass GO — Collect $200'
Pass GO — Collect $200
```

You couldn't do that with double quotes! Actually there are quite a
few good uses for single quotes. They can be used to print a double-
quoted string:

```
$ print '"This is in double quotes"'
"This is in double quotes"
```

or just to surround plain old text that has embedded whitespace. This
improves readability by separating the command from the argument.
Variables can be set to null with single quotes:

```
$ X=''
```

Single quotes are also used to assign values to aliases and **trap**
commands, and prevent alias substitution, but we'll get to that later.

Double Quotes

Double quotes are like single quotes, except that they do not remove
the meaning of the special characters $, `, and \. This means that
variable and command substitution is performed.

```
$ DB="$HOME:`pwd`"
$ print $DB
/home/anatole:/tmp
```

Double quotes also preserve embedded whitespace and newlines. Here are some examples:

```
$ print "Line 1
> Line 2"
Line 1
Line 2
$ print "A                           B"
A                   B
```

The > is the secondary prompt, and is displayed whenever the Korn shell needs more input. In this case, it waits for the closing double quote:

```
$ ADDR="ASP,Inc
> PO Box 23837
> San Jose CA 95153 USA
> (800)777-UNIX * (510)531-5615"
```

Without double quotes around **ADDR**, we get this:

```
$ print $ADDR
ASP,Inc PO Box 23837 San Jose CA 95153 USA (800) 777-
UNIX * (510)531-5615
```

Not quite what we wanted. Let's try it again:

```
$ print "$ADDR"
ASP,Inc
PO Box 23837
San Jose CA 95153 USA
(800)777-UNIX * (510)531-5615
```

There are also other uses for double quotes. You can set a variable to null:

```
$ NULL=""
$ print $NULL

$
```

or display single quotes.

```
$ print "'This is in single quotes'"
'This is in single quotes'
```

If you really wanted to display the $, `, \, or " characters using double quotes, escape them with a backslash like this:

```
$ print "\$HOME is set to $HOME"
$HOME is set to /home/anatole
$ print "\`=back-quote \\=slash \"=double-quote"
`=back-quote \=slash "=double-quote
```

Back Quotes

Back quotes are used to assign the output of a command to a variable. This format, from the Bourne shell, is accepted by the Korn shell but considered obsolescent. This command sets the variable **SYS** to the system name:

```
$ SYS=`uuname -l`
$ print $SYS
aspd
```

Chapter 4:
Editing
Commands

Terminal Requirements
Command History File
*The **fc** Command*
In-Line Editor

One of the major features of the Korn shell is the ability to manipulate current and previous commands using the built-in editors and the **fc** command.

If you make a mistake on the current command line, instead of having to backspace to fix it, or killing the entire line and starting over, you can use the in-line editor to make the correction much more quickly and efficiently.

If you want to re-execute a command, instead of having to type it in all over again, you can use the command re-entry feature to call it back up. You can even make changes to it before re-executing!

Terminal Requirements

The in-line editor and command re-entry features require that the terminal accepts <Return> as carriage return without line-feed, and the space character to overwrite the current character on the screen and move right. Some terminals may require special settings. For more information, see **Appendix E**.

Command History File

The Korn shell stores the commands that you enter at your terminal in a file, called the command history file. This file is specified by the **HISTFILE** variable. If not set, the default is **$HOME/.sh_history**.

The number of commands accessible via the command history file is specified by the **HISTSIZE** variable. If not set, the last 128 commands are saved, starting from your most recent command. The command history file operates on a first-in, last-out basis, so that as new commands are entered, the oldest commands are not accessible.

There are two ways to access the command history file: using the **fc** command, or the in-line editor. These are discussed in the following sections.

The fc Command

The **fc** command allows you to list, or edit and re-execute history file commands. It is the simplest interface to the command history file provided with the Korn shell. The **fc** command also allows you to manipulate the history file using your own choice of editors.

Displaying the Command History File

The command history file can be displayed using the **fc** command in a number of ways: with or without command numbers, using a range of line numbers, in reverse order, and more. The format for displaying the command history file with the **fc −l** command is:

fc —l[nr] [*range*]

where the **−n** option causes the command numbers to not be displayed, and the **−r** option specifies reverse order (latest commands first). The range of commands to list is given as:

n1 [*n2*]	display list from command *n1* to command *n2*. If *n2* is not specified, display all the commands from current command back to command *n1*.
−count	display the last *count* commands
string	display all the previous commands back to the command that matches *string*

If no *range* argument is given, the last sixteen commands are listed. Let's look at the last five commands:

```
$ fc —l —5
250         set
251         vi /etc/env
252         . /etc/env
253         set
254         alias
255         functions
```

The **history** command is equivalent to **fc −l**. It is much easier to remember than **fc −l**, especially for C shell users. The last command could also be given like this. Notice that the order is reversed.

```
$ history -r -5
255          functions
254          alias
253          set
252          . /etc/env
251          vi /etc/env
250          set
```

By using a string instead of a count argument, we could search backward for a specific command.

```
$ history -r set
258          fc -lr set
257          fc -ln -10
256          fc -l 250 265
255          functions
254          alias
253          set
```

The argument **set** could also be given as **s**, or **se**, since partial strings are also matched. This means that the string **f** would match **functions** and **fc**, while **fu** would only match **functions**.

Editing the Command History File

Besides displaying the command history file, it can also be edited using the **fc** command with the following format:

> **fc** [−e *editor*] [−r] [*range*]
> or
> **fc** −e − [*old=new*] [*command*]

where the −e *editor* option is used to specify an editor. If not given, the value of the **FCEDIT** variable is used, and if not set, the default /**bin/ed** is used. The −r option reverses the order of the commands, so that the latest commands are displayed first. The first format allows you to edit a list of commands before re-executing. The range of commands to edit is given as:

n1 n2	edit list from command *n1* to command *n2*
n	edit command *n*
−n	edit the last *nth* command
string	edit the previous command that matches *string*

If no range argument is given, the last command is edited. The second format listed allows you to edit and re-execute a single command, where *old=new* specifies to replace the string *old* with *new* before re-executing, and *command* specifies which command to match. The *command* can be given as:

n	edit and re-execute command number *n*
−n	edit and re-execute the last *nth* command
string	edit and re-execute the most previous command that matches *string*

If no *command* argument is given, the last command is edited. Command **173** could be edited and re-executed like this:

```
$ fc −e − 173
```

Another way to do this is with the **r** command. It is the same as the **fc −e −** command. Using **r**, the last command could also be given as:

```
$ r 173
```

As you can see, the **r** command is easier to use (and remember) than the **fc −e −** command. What else can be done with this command? The substitution feature is used to make minor changes to a previous command. Let's start with **print Hello**:

```
$ print Hello
Hello
```

We could change **Hello** to something else like this.

```
$ r Hello=Goodbye print
print Goodbye
Goodbye
```

The next section covers an easier way to edit and re-execute commands using the in-line editor.

In-Line Editor

In-line editing provides the ability to edit the current or previous commands before executing them. There are three in-line editing modes available: **emacs**, **gmacs**, and **vi**. The in-line editing mode is specified by setting the **EDITOR** or **VISUAL** variables, but if neither variable is set, the default is **/bin/ed**. The in-line editing mode can also be specified with the **set −o** command like this:

```
$ set −o option
```

where *option* can be **emacs**, **gmacs**, or **vi**. This is usually specified in your **$HOME/.profile** file.

The size of the editing window is specified by the **COLUMNS** variable. The default is **80**, unless **COLUMNS** is set. Some systems use the window size as the default. The size of your command prompt also affects the width of the editing window.

In the examples in the following sections, the **Before** column shows what was displayed at the prompt, the **Command** column lists the edit mode command, and the **After** column displays the result. The underbar character (_) represents the cursor. Control characters are given as **Ctl** followed by the character in bold face. For example,

Ctl-h specifies **Control-h** and is entered by pressing the **h** key while holding down the **Control** key.

Vi Edit Mode

If you know the Unix **vi** text editor, then learning how to use the vi in-line editor is relatively easy. The vi in-line editor is a subset of the **vi** editor program, so most of the commands are the same.

In vi edit mode, there are two operating modes: input and command. Operating in and out of input mode is virtually the same. Commands are entered and executed just as if you were not using the in-line editor. As soon as you press the <Escape> key, you are put in command mode. This is where you can enter your vi commands to access and edit commands from the history file, or current command line.

Input Mode

Once the vi edit mode is set, you are placed in input mode. If the vi mode is set in your **.profile** file, then you are automatically in input mode whenever the Korn shell starts up. As stated in the previous section, operating in and out of vi input mode is virtually the same.

The next example shows some of the basic vi input mode commands. We start with **'print Hi again world'**. The **Ctl-w** commands delete the strings **world**, and **again**, then the **Ctl-h** command deletes **i**. The @ command kills the entire line, and we get a new command prompt.

Table 4.1: Vi Input Mode Commands

Ctl-h, #, <Backspace>
        delete the previous character (system dependent)

Ctl-d   terminate the shell

Ctl-x, @   kill the entire line (system dependent)

<Return>   execute the current line

\\   escape the next *Erase* or *Kill* character

Ctl-v   escape the next character

Ctl-w   delete the previous word

Before	Command	After
$ print Hi again world_	Ctl-w	$ print Hi again _
$ print Hi again _	Ctl-w	$ print Hi _
$ print Hi _	Ctl-h	$ print Hi_
$ print Hi_	Ctl-h	$ print H_
$ print H_	Ctl-h	$ print _
$ print _	@	$ _

The *Erase* and *Kill* characters can be set with the **stty** command.

Command Mode

When you press the <Escape> key in vi input mode, you are put in command mode. This is where the **vi** commands can be given to edit a single command from the history file. Editing commands can be given until the <Return> key is pressed, then the result is executed. To cancel current editing, press the <Escape> key again. If you enter an invalid command, or a search command fails, the Korn shell will cause your terminal to beep or flash.

Table 4.2 lists the basic commands available in command mode. A complete listing of the commands can be found in Appendix E.

Moving Around the History File

In this example, we navigate through the command history file using some basic vi edit mode commands. Assume that these are the last two commands that were executed:

```
$ history −2
339          pwd
340          date
341          history −2
```

At the command prompt, the <Escape> key is pressed to enter command mode, then a series of **k** commands are given to successively retrieve the previous command. The **j** command is given to retrieve the next commands, until we get to the **date** command. After the <Return> key is pressed, **date** is executed.

Before	**Command**	**After**
$ _	<Escape>k	$ history -2
$ history -2 k	$ date	
$ date	k	$ pwd
$ pwd	j	$ date
$ date	<Return>	

Of course, a more efficient way to retrieve the **date** command would be with a single backward search command, <Escape>/**da**<Return>. Notice that **da** is used to match **date**.

Before	Command	After
$ _	<Escape>/da<Return>	$ date
$ date	<Return>	

Editing Previous Commands

In the next example, we want to change the word **Hello** to **Goodbye** in the **print** command. The <Escape> key is pressed to enter command mode. Then the **k** command retrieves the last command, and the **h** command moves the cursor left one character. The **b** command is given to move the cursor back one word, to the beginning of **world**. Another **b** command is given, and the cursor is at the beginning of **Hello**. Now the **cw** command is used to change the word **Hello**, and we can type over the new word **Goodbye**. When we are finished typing, the <Return> is pressed, and the result is executed.

Before	Command	After
$ print Hello world_	<Escape>	$ print Hello world
$ print Hello world	h	$ print Hello world
$ print Hello world	b	$ print Hello world
$ print Hello world	b	$ print Hello world
$ print Hello world	cwGoodbye	$ print Goodbye world
$ print Goodbye world	<Return>	

There are a number of ways that the same results could have been achieved. The cursor could have been moved back to **Hello** using **FH** (move left to character H), and then deleted using **dw** (delete word).

Table 4.2: Some Vi Command Mode Commands

h, <Backspace>

	move left one character
l, <Space>	move right one character
b	move left one word
B	move left one word; ignore punctuation
w	move right one word
W	move right one word; ignore punctuation
e	move to the end of the next word
E	move to end of next word; ignore punctuation
^	move to beginning of the line
$	move to end of line
f*c*	move right to character *c*
F*c*	move left to character *c*
a	add text after the current character
A	append text to end of the current line
i	insert text left of the current character
r*c*	replace current character with *c*
x	delete the current character
u	undo the last text modification command
k	get previous command from history file
j	get next command from history file
/string	search backward in the history file for command that matches *string*
?*string*	search forward in the history file for command that matches *string*
.	repeat the last text modification command
~	toggle the case of the current character

Goodbye could have then been inserted using the **i** (insert) command.

Let's say we want to just add an exclamation point to the **print Hello world** command. Instead of typing it all over again, we enter <Escape> for command mode and **k** to get the last command. Then the **$** command moves the cursor to the end of the line, and the **a!** command appends the **!** character. After the <Return> key is pressed, **print Hello world!** is displayed.

Before	Command	After
$ _	<Escape>k	$ print Goodbye world
$ print Hello world	$	$ print Hello world
$ print Hello world	a !	$ print Hello world!_
$ print Hello world!_	<Return>	

Here, a typo is spotted in the **chmod** command. Instead of backspacing fourteen times to make the correction, or killing the entire line and typing over, we enter command mode by pressing <Escape>. The **^** command moves the cursor to the beginning of the line, and **e** (end of word) moves it to the **s** character, where we want to make the correction. The **rd** command (replace current character with **d**) is given, followed by <Return> to execute.

Before	Command	After
$ chmos 777 /tmp/foo_	<Escape>	$ chmos 777 /tmp/foo
$ chmos 777 /tmp/foo	^	$ chmos 777 /tmp/foo
$ chmos 777 /tmp/foo	e	$ chmos 777 /tmp/foo
$ chmos 777 /tmp/foo	rd	$ chmod 777 /tmp/foo
$ chmod 777 /tmp/foo	<Return>	

Displaying Long Command Lines

For lines longer than the window width, a mark is displayed at the end of the line to indicate the position. Only part of the command is displayed. The text position markers can be:

>   line extends to the right of the edit window
<   line extends to the left of the edit window
*   line extends on both sides of the edit window

Moving around the command line makes different parts of the command line visible. If the cursor is moved past the last character, the line is redisplayed with the cursor in the middle of the screen. The **COLUMNS** variable setting, and the size of your command prompt also affect the width of the editing window.

Emacs/Gmacs Edit Modes

Like the vi in-line editor, the emacs/gmacs in-line editor is also basically a subset of the same text editors. However, there are a few commands in the emacs/gmacs in-line editors that are not in the regular program.

This only difference between the emacs and gmacs editors is the way **Ctl-t** is handled. In emacs mode, **Ctl-t** transposes the current and next character. In gmacs mode, **Ctl-t** transposes the previous two characters.

Table 4.3 lists the basic commands available in emacs/gmacs edit mode. **Appendix E** contains a complete listing of the commands.

Editing Commands in Emacs/Gmacs Mode

Before we look at some emacs/gmacs in-line editor command examples, here are the last three commands from the history file:

```
$ history −r −n −3
history −r −n −3
grep ksh /etc/passwd
print $PATH
cd /usr/etc/yp
```

In the following example, the **Ctl-n** and **Ctl-p** commands are used to get the next and previous commands from the history file. Assuming that **history −r −n −3** just completed execution, the **Ctl-p** command brings it back, and another **Ctl-p** goes back to **grep**. To get back to the **cd** command, the **Ctl-r** command is given. The <Return> key is pressed, and the current directory is changed to **/usr/etc/yp**.

<u>Before</u>	<u>Command</u>	<u>After</u>
$ _	Ctl-p	$ history -n -3_
$ history -n -3_	Ctl-p	$ grep x /etc/passwd_
$ grep x /etc/passwd_	Ctl-rcd	$ cd /usr/etc/yp_
$ cd /usr/etc/yp_	<Return>	

In the next example, we want to make a correction to the current command line. The **Ctl-b** commands moves the cursor one character left, then **Esc-b** moves the cursor one word left. The **Ctl-d** command deletes character **C**, and **Ctl-]E** moves forward to the next **E** character. The <Return> key is pressed, and the result is executed.

Table 4.3: Some Emacs/Gmacs In-Line Edit Commands

Ctl-b	move left one character
Ctl-f	move right one character
Esc-b	move left one word
Esc-f	move right one word
Ctl-a	move to beginning of line
Ctl-e	move to end of line
Ctl-]*c*	move right to character *c*
Ctl-h	delete preceding character
Ctl-x, @	kill the entire line
Ctl-k	delete from cursor to end of line
Ctl-d	delete current character
Esc-d	delete current word
Ctl-w	delete from cursor to mark
Ctl-y	undo last delete (w/**Esc-p**)
Ctl-p	get previous command from history file
Ctl-n	get next command from history file
Ctl-r*string*	search backward in history file for command that contains *string*
Ctl-c	change current character to upper case
Esc-l	change current character to lower case
Esc-p	save to buffer from cursor to mark
Esc-\<Space\>	mark current location
Ctl-l	redisplay current line

Before	Command	After
`$ print AB CD EF_`	Ctl-b	`$ print AB CD EF`
`$ print AB CD EF`	Esc-b	`$ print AB CD EF`
`$ print AB CD EF`	Ctl-d	`$ print AB D EF`
`$ print AB D EF`	^E	`$ print AB D EF`
`$ print AB D EF`	<Return>	

What about inserting text? To add characters to the command line, in emacs/gmacs mode, you just type them in. Characters are inserted before the cursor. Here we get the last command using **Ctl-p**. Then we move to the beginning of the line using **Ctl-a**, and to the next word with **Esc-f**. **Ctl-k** deletes to the end of the line, and we insert **hello** by typing it in. To display **hello**, we just press <Return>.

Before	Command	After
`$ _`	Ctl-p	`$ print AB D EF_`
`$ print AB D EF_`	Ctl-a	`$ print AB D EF`
`$ print AB D EF`	Esc-f	`$ print_AB D EF`
`$ print AB D EF`	Ctl-k	`$ print_`
`$ print_`	hello	`$ print hello_`
`$ print hello_`	<Return>	

This example shows another way in which a command can be edited using emacs/gmacs mode. The **Ctl-a** command moves the cursor to the beginning of the line, and ^]s moves to the **s** character. The **Ctl-d** command deletes **s**, then **d** is typed in. The <Return> key is pressed, and the command is run.

Before	Command	After
$ chmos 777 /tm/foo_	Ctl-a	$ <u>c</u>hmos 777 /tmp/foo
$ <u>c</u>hmos 777 /tm/foo	^]s	$ chmo<u>s</u> 777 /tmp/foo
$ chmo<u>s</u> 777 /tm/foo	Ctl-d	$ chmo_777 /tmp/foo
$ chmo_777 /tm/foo	d	$ chmo<u>d</u> 777 /tmp/foo
$ chmo<u>d</u> 777 /tmp/foo	<Return>	

Chapter 5:
Job Control

Manipulating Jobs
Checking Job Status
Background Jobs and I/O
Job Names
Leaving Stopped Jobs

The Korn shell provides a job control mechanism that is virtually identical to the C shell version of BSD Unix. Job control allows programs to be stopped and restarted, moved between the foreground and background, their processing status to be displayed, and more. To enable the job control feature, the **monitor** option must be enabled with the **set** command:

```
$ set —o monitor
or
$ set —m
```

This can be put into the **.profile** file so that job control is automatically enabled at login. On most systems that provide the job control mechanism, this option is automatically enabled for interactive shells.

It can be checked by executing the **set –o** command. Let's see if it is set:

```
$ set —o | grep monitor
monitor                on
```

If a command is run in the background, the Korn shell returns a job number and process id. Here, the **find** command is assigned job number **1** and process id **1435**:

```
$ find / —name core —exec rm —rf {} \; &
[1] 1435
```

The next command is assigned job number **2** and process id **1437**:

```
$ cpio —iBcdu < /dev/rmt0 &
[2] 1437
```

When background jobs are completed, a message is given before the next prompt is displayed. This is done so that other work is not interfered with. In this example, the **ls** command is put in the background. Although it finished before the **sleep** command, the completion message is not displayed until **sleep** is finished:

```
$ ls —x > ls.out &
[3] 1438
$ sleep 30
[3] + Done           ls —x > ls.out &
$
```

Manipulating Jobs

Jobs running in the foreground are suspended by typing **Ctl-z** (**Control-z**). So instead of waiting for the long-running **split** command to complete, it is interrupted using **Ctl-z**:

```
$ split —5000 hugefile
Ctl-z
[3]  + Stoppedsplit —5000 hugefile
$
```

Stopped and backgrounded jobs are brought back into the foreground with the **fg** command. If no argument is given, the current (most recently stopped or backgrounded) job is used. The stopped **split** job is brought back into the foreground with **fg**:

```
$ fg
split —5000 hugefile
```

Stopped jobs are put into the background with the **bg** command. If no argument is given, the most recently stopped job is used. In the next example, we want to put the **split** job back in the background. It is currently running in the foreground, so it must first be suspended with **Ctl-z** again:

```
$ fg
split —5000 hugefile
Ctl-z
```

Now, it can be put into the background using **bg**:

```
$ bg
[3]    split —5000 hugefile &
```

The **split** job is brought into the foreground with **fg**, and we are back to where we started. This time we use the job number as the argument to **fg**:

```
$ fg %3
split -5000 hugefile
```

Checking Job Status

The status and other information about all jobs is displayed using the **jobs** command. The following **jobs** output shows that there is one stopped job, and two running jobs. The + indicates the current job, and – indicates the previous job:

```
$ jobs
[3]   + Stopped          split -5000 hugefile
[2]   - Running          find / -name core -print &
[1]     Running          sleep 25 &
```

The **jobs –l** command shows the same information, along with the process ids, while **jobs –p** only gives you the process ids.

```
$ jobs -l
[3]   + 466 Stopped  split -5000 hugefile
[2]   - 465 Running  find / -name core -print &
[1]     463 Running  sleep 25 &
```

Killing Jobs

Stopped or background jobs are terminated with the **kill** command.
Unlike **bg** or **fg**, a job argument must be given. Here, a **sleep**
command is put in the background, then killed:

```
$ sleep 100 &
[1]   254
$ kill %1
```

It could also be given as **kill 254**.

Waiting for Jobs

You can make the Korn shell wait for some or all background jobs to
complete with the **wait** command. If no argument is given, the Korn
shell waits for all background jobs to complete.

Background Jobs and I/O

Jobs being executed in the background will stop if they attempt to
read input from your terminal. If you tried to interactively remove
$PUBDIR/junk in the background, this is what would happen:

```
$ rm -i $PUBDIR/junk &
[2]   +Stopped (tty input) rm -i $PUBDIR/junk &
```

The job is stopped because it needs to prompt you for input. The **rm
−i** job is brought back into the foreground with the **fg** command and its
prompt is displayed:

```
$ fg %2
rm −i $PUBDIR/junk
rm: remove /usr/spool/uucppublic/junk? y
```

By default, jobs send their output to your terminal, even while running
in the background. Here, the **find** command sends its output to the
terminal, even though it is running in the background:

```
$ find / −name core −print &
[2]   1453
$ /usr/lbin/core
/home/anatole/bin/core
```

That can be annoying, especially if you are in the middle of something
else. To avoid this problem, redirect the output of background jobs to
a file. Make sure to be careful with the redirection. If you don't
redirect standard error, error messages will go to your terminal and
not to the output file. Let's kill the **find** job, then restart it and send the
output to **c.out**:

```
$ kill %2
[2] + Terminated find / −name core −print>c.out &
$ find / −name core −print >c.out &
[2]   1453
$ jobs
[2] − Runningfind / −name core −print &
[1]    Runningsleep 1000 &
```

We can work on something else until we get the completion message.

```
[2] +Done     find / −name core −print>c.out &
```

Table 5.1: Job Control Commands

bg	put the current stopped job in the background
bg *%n*	put the stopped job *n* in the background
fg	move the current background job into the foreground
fg *%n*	move background job *n* into the foreground
jobs	display the status of all jobs
jobs −l	display the status of all jobs along with their process ids
jobs −p	display the process ids of all jobs
kill *%n*	kill job *n*
kill −l	list all valid signal names
kill *−signal %n*	send the specified signal to job *n*
set −m, set −o monitor	enable job control; execute background jobs in a separate process group, and report the exit status of background jobs
stty tostop	prevent background jobs from generating output
stty −tostop	allow background jobs to generate output (default)
wait	wait for all background jobs to complete
wait *%n*	wait for background job *n* to complete
Ctl-z	stop the current job

There are other ways to deal with job output. Jobs being executed in the background are prevented from generating output by setting **stty tostop**. Let's run the **find** job again with the **tostop** option enabled:

```
$ stty tostop
$ find / —name core —print &
[2]   1460
```

Now when the job has some output, we get this message:

```
[1] + Stopped(tty output) find / —name core —print &
```

The only way to see the **find** output is to bring the job back into the foreground.

```
$ fg
/usr/lbin/core
/home/anatole/bin/core
```

The **stty tostop** command can be put into your profile file so that background job output is by default disabled.

The **nohup** command can also be used to direct output from background jobs. It causes standard output *and* standard error to be automatically sent to **nohup.out**, or whatever file you give it. One added benefit: the **nohup** command will keep jobs running, even if you log out. Here we run the **find** job again using **nohup**. First we need to enable background job output:

```
$ stty —tostop
$ nohup find / —name core —print &
[2] 1469
$ wait
Sending output to 'nohup.out'
[2] + Done    nohup find / —name core —print &
```

The **find** job output is in **nohup.out**:

```
$ cat nohup.out
/usr/lbin/core
/home/anatole/bin/core
```

Job Names

Most people use the job number to refer to a job, because one number is easy to remember. However, jobs can be referred to in a number of other ways: by process id, current/previous job, or all or part of a job name. If we had these jobs:

```
$ jobs -l
[3]   + 466 Stopped        split -5000 hugefile
[2]   - 465 Running        find / -name  -print &
[1]     463 Running        sleep 25 &
```

then the **split** job could be referred to as **%3**, **%+**, **%%**, **466**, **%split**, or **%?sp**, the **find** job could be referred to as **%2**, **%−**, **465**, **%find**, or **%?f**, and the **sleep** could be referred to as **%1**, **463**, **%sleep**, or **%?sl**.

Table 5.2: Job Names

%*n*	job *n*
%+, **%%**	current job
%−	previous job
%*string*	job whose name begins with *string*
%?*string*	job that matches part or all of *string*

Leaving Stopped Jobs

The Korn shell displays a warning message if you try to exit from the
shell while jobs are stopped.

```
$ stty tostop
$ date &
[1]    541
[1] + Stopped(tty output)       date &
$ exit
You have stopped jobs
```

If you ignore this message and exit, the Korn shell will not attempt to
warn you again and any stopped jobs will be terminated.

Chapter 6: Performing Arithmetic

*The **let** Command*
The ((...)) Command
Declaring Integer Variables
Arithmetic Constants
Arithmetic Operators
Random Numbers

The Korn shell provides the ability to perform integer arithmetic in any base from two to thirty-six using built-in commands. It executes much faster than using the **expr** command, since it doesn't have to start another process. It can also be used instead of the **test** command for integer comparisons. In addition, all of the operators from the C programming language (except ++, −−, and **?:**) are now supported by the Korn shell.

The *let* Command

Integer arithmetic can be done with the **let** command and arithmetic expressions. The format for the **let** command is:

> **let** *"arithmetic-expression"*

where arithmetic-expressions can contain constants, operators, and Korn shell variables. Double quotes are used with arithmetic expressions that contain white space or operators that have special meaning to the Korn shell. For example, variable **X** can be set to the sum of 1+1 like this:

```
$ let "X=1 + 1"
$ print $X
2
```

then incremented:

```
$ let "X=X + 1"
$ print $X
3
```

Notice that in arithmetic expressions, regular variables can be referenced by name only, and do not have to be preceded by **$** for substitution to be performed. Both

```
$ let "X=X + 1"
```
and
```
$ let "X=$X + 1"
```

are equivalent. The first format is preferred because parameter expansion does not have to be performed. This causes it to be executed faster.

Table 6.1: Arithmetic Operators (in order of precedence)

−	unary minus
!	logical negation
~	bitwise negation
*, /, %	multiplication, division, remainder (modulo)
+, −	addition, subtraction
<<, >>	left shift, right shift
<=, <	less than or equal to, less than
>=, >	greater than or equal to, greater than
==	equal to
!=	not equal to
&	bitwise AND
^	bitwise exclusive OR
|	bitwise OR
&&	logical AND
||	logical OR
=	assignment
*=, /=, %=	multiply assign, divide assign, modulo assign
+=, −=	increment, decrement
<<=, >>=	left shift assign, right shift assign
&=, ^=, |=	bitwise AND assign, bitwise exclusive OR assign, bitwise OR assign
(...)	grouping (used to override precedence rules)

Arithmetic expressions are made up of constants, variables or any of the arithmetic operators in Table 6.1.

The ((...)) Command

The **((...))** command is equivalent to the **let** command, except that all characters between the ((and)) are treated as quoted arithmetic expressions. This is more convenient to use than **let**, because many of the arithmetic operators have special meaning to the Korn shell. The following commands are equivalent:

```
$ let "X=X + 1"
and
$ ((X=X + 1))
```

Before the Korn shell **let** and **((...))** commands, the only way to perform arithmetic was with **expr**. For example, to do the same increment **X** operation using **expr**:

```
$ X=`expr $X + 1`
```

In tests on a few systems, the **let** command performed the same operation 35-60 times faster! That is quite a difference.

Declaring Integer Variables

As with ordinary variables, integer variables need not be declared. A variable can simply be given an integer value, and then used in an arithmetic expression.

```
$ X=12
$ ((Y=X * 3))
$ print $Y
36
```

However, variables can be explicitly declared integer type by using the **typeset -i** command. The following example sets the **DAYS** and **MONTHS** variables to be integer type:

```
$ typeset -i DAYS MONTHS=12
```

There is also another command called **integer**, which is equivalent to **typeset -i**. It could be used to declare the **DAYS** and **MONTHS** variables like this:

```
$ integer DAYS MONTHS=12
```

Variables do not have to be explicitly declared integer type to be used in arithmetic expressions. It may improve performance, but what you really gain with declaring integer variables is stricter type checking on assignments. Integer variables cannot be assigned non-integer values:

```
$ integer I=abc
/bin/ksh: I: bad number
```

Another benefit to declaring integer variables is that arithmetic can be performed directly on integer variables without using the **let** or **((...))** commands, as long as the integer value is being assigned a value. In other words, you can do this:

```
$ integer DAYS="4 + 3"
instead of
$ ((DAYS=4 + 3))
or
$ let "DAYS=4 + 3"
```

This also means that **integer** variables can be assigned values using arithmetic expressions when declared. Let's try it with the **MONTHS** variable:

```
$ integer MONTHS="36 / 3"
$ print $MONTHS
12
```

Arithmetic Constants

The format for arithmetic constants is:

> *number*
> or
> *base#number*

where *base* is a whole number between **2** and **36**, and *number* is any non-negative integer. If not specified, the default base is **10**. The arithmetic base of a variable can be set with the **typeset −i***n* command, or by prepending *base#* to the value. In this example, variable **X** is set to **5** in base **2** using both formats:

```
$ typeset −i2 X=5
or
$ typeset −i X=2#101
```

When variable **X** is expanded, the value is written in base **2**:

```
$ print $X
2#101
```

If you want to display the value of **X** in another base, just reset the base with the **typeset –i***n* command. Here it is reset to base **3**:

```
$ typeset -i3 X
$ print $X
3#12
```

Arithmetic can be performed on numbers with different bases. Here is an example - **X** is set to **7** in base **2**:

```
$ typeset -i X=2#111
```

Y is set to **8** in base **5**:

```
$ typeset -i5 Y=8
```

and **Z** is set to base **16**:

```
$ typeset -i16 Z
```

Now, **X** and **Y** are added together and the result is put in **Z**:

```
$ Z=X+Y
$ print $Z
16#f
```

We could convert the result to octal by resetting the base of **Z** using the **typeset –i***n* command like this:

```
$ typeset -i8 Z
$ print $Z
8#17
```

Arithmetic Operators

The following sections contain examples for each of the arithmetic operators available to the Korn shell. Table 6.1 lists all of the arithmetic operators available to the Korn shell in order of precedence.

–expression (Unary Minus)

Evaluates to the negative value of *expression*.

```
$ ((X=-7))
$ ((Y=-X + 2))
$ print - "$X $Y"
-7 9
```

The **print** – command is used so that the negative sign is not interpreted as an argument.

!expression (Logical Negation)

The **!** operator returns **0** (true) for expressions that do not evaluate to zero, or **1** (false) if they do.

```
$ X=0
$ ((X=!X)); print "$X"
1
$ ((X=!X)); print "$X"
0
```

122

~expression (Bitwise Negation)

Evaluates to the bitwise negated value (one's complement) of
expression. It returns a value that contains a **1** in each bit position
where *expression* contains **0**, and a **0** in each bit position where
expression contains **1**.

```
$ X=2#011
$ ((X=~X)); print — "$X"
—2#100
```

expression1 * expression2 (Multiplication)
expression1 *= expression2 (Multiply Assign)

Evaluates to the product of *expression1* multiplied by *expression2*.
The second format assigned the result of the evaluation to
expression1.

```
$ ((X=5 * 4)); print "$X"
20
$ ((X=3 * 1 * 2 * 4)); print "$X"
24
$ ((X*=2)); print "$X"
48
```

expression1 / expression2 (Division)
expression1 /= expression2
(Divide Assign)

Evaluates to the quotient of *expression1* divided by *expression2*. The second format assigned the result of the evaluation to *expression1*.

```
$ Y=50
$ ((X=Y / 10)); print "$X"
5
$ ((X=21 / 5)); print "$X"
4
$ ((X/=2)); print "$X"
2
```

expression1 % expression2 (Modulo)
expression1 %= expression2
(Modulo Assign)

Evaluates to the remainder of *expression1* divided by *expression2*. The second format assigned the result of the evaluation to *expression1*.

```
$ ((X=20 % 7)); print "$X"
6
$ ((X=11 % 4)); print "$X"
3
$ ((X%=2)); print "$X"
1
```

expression1 + expression2 (Addition)
expression1 += expression2 (Increment)

Evaluates to the sum of *expression1* and *expression2*. The second
format assigned the result of the evaluation to *expression1*.

```
$ ((X=1 + 2)); print "$X"
3
$ ((X=4 + 1 + 3)); print "$X"
8
$ ((X+=1)); print "$X"
9
```

expression1 – expression2 (Subtraction)
expression1 –= expression2 (Decrement)

Evaluates to the difference of *expression1* and *expression2*. The
second format assigned the result of the evaluation to *expression1*.

```
$ ((X=3 – 1)); print "$X"
2
$ ((X=X – 1)); print "$X"
1
$ ((X–=1)); print "$X"
0
```

identifier=expression (Assignment)

Assigns *identifier* the value of *expression*.

```
$ ((X=12)); print "$X"
12
$ Y=7
$ ((X=Y)); print "$X"
2
```

expression1 << expression2 (Left shift)
expression1 <<= expression2
(Left Shift Assign)

Left shift *expression1* by the number of bits specified in *expression2*. The second format assigned the result of the evaluation to *expression1*.

```
$ typeset −i2 X
$ ((X=2#11 << 1)); print "$X"
2#110
$ ((X=2#110 << 2)); print "$X"
2#11000
$ ((X=2#11000 << 3)); print "$X"
2#11000000
```

expression1 >> expression2 (Right Shift)
expression1 >>= expression2
(Right Shift Assign)

Right shift *expression1* by the number of bits from *expression2*. The second format assigned the result of the evaluation to *expression1*.

```
$ typeset −i2 X
$ ((X=2#10101 >> 2)); print "$X"
2#101
```

```
$ ((X=2#101 >> 1)); print "$X"
2#10
$ ((X>>=1)); print "$X"
2#1
```

expression1 <= expression2
(Less Than or Equal)

Evaluates to **0** (true) if *expression1* is less than or equal to *expression2*, otherwise evaluates to **1** (false).

```
$ ((1 <= 2)) && print "1 is less than 2"
1 is less than 2
$ ((3 <= 2)) || print "3 is not less than 2"
3 is not less than 2
```

expression1 < expression2 (Less Than)

Evaluates to **0** (true) if *expression1* is less than *expression2*, otherwise evaluates to **1** (false).

```
$ ((1 < 2)); print "$?"
0
$ ((3 < 2)); print "$?"
1
```

expression1 >= expression2
(Greater Than Or Equal)

Evaluates to **0** (true) if *expression1* is greater than or equal to *expression2*, otherwise evaluates to **1** (false).

```
$ ((3 >= 2)) && print "3 is greater than 2"
3 is greater than 2
$ ((1 >= 2)) || print "1 is not greater than 2"
1 is not greater than 2
```

expression1 > expression2
(Greater Than)

Evaluates to **0** (true) if *expression1* is greater *expression2*, otherwise evaluates to **1** (false).

```
$ ((3 > 2)); print $?
0
$ ((1 > 2)); print $?
1
```

expression1 == *expression2* (Equal To)

Evaluates to **0** (true) if *expression1* is equal to *expression2*, otherwise evaluates to **1** (false).

```
$ ((3 == 3)) && print "3 is equal to 3"
3 is equal to 3
$ ((4 == 3)) || print "4 is not equal to 3"
4 is not equal to 3
```

expression1 != *expression2* (Not Equal To)

Evaluates to **0** (true) if *expression1* is not equal to *expression2*, otherwise evaluates to **1** (false).

```
$ ((4 != 3)); print "$?"
0
$ ((3 != 3 )); print "$?"
1
```

expression1 & *expression2* (Bitwise AND)
expression1 &= *expression2* (Bitwise AND Assign)

Returns a value that contains a **1** in each bit where there is a **1** in both expressions, and a **0** in every other bit. The second format assigned the result of the evaluation to *expression1*.

```
$ typeset —i2 X
$ ((X=2#11 & 2#10)); print "$X"
2#10
$ ((X=2#101 & 2#111)); print "$X"
2#101
$ ((X&=2#001)); print "$X"
2#1
```

expression1 ^*expression2* (Bitwise XOR)
expression1 ^= *expression2* (Bitwise XOR Assign)

Returns a value that contains a **1** in each bit where there is a **1** in only one of the expressions, and a **0** in every other bit. The second format assigned the result of the evaluation to *expression1*.

```
$ typeset —i2 X
$ ((X=2#11 ^ 2#10)); print "$X"
2#1
$ ((X=2#101 ^ 2#011)); print "$X"
2#110
$ ((X^=2#100)); print "$X"
2#10
```

expression1 | expression2 (Bitwise OR)
expression1 |= expression2
(Bitwise OR Assign)

Returns a value that contains a **1** in each bit where there is a **1** in either of the expressions, and a **0** in every other bit. The second format assigned the result of the evaluation to *expression1*.

```
$ typeset —i2 X
$ ((X=2#11 | 2#10)); print "$X"
2#11
$ ((X=2#101 | 2#011)); print "$X"
2#111
$ ((X|=2#1001)); print "$X"
2#1111
```

expression1 && expression2
(Logical AND)

If *expression1* evaluates to **0** (true), *expression2* is evaluated. The value of the entire expression is **0** (true) only if *expression1* and *expression2* are both true. Since both **X** and **Y** are equal to **1**, the entire expression returns **0**, and the **print** command is executed:

```
$ X=1 Y=1
$ ((X==1 && Y==1)) && print "X and Y equal 1"
X and Y equal 1
```

Now only **X** is equal to **1**, so the entire expression returns **1**, and the **print** command is not executed:

```
$ unset Y
$ ((X==1 && Y==1)) && print "X and Y equal 1"
$
```

expression1 || expression2 (Logical OR)

If *expression1* evaluates to non-zero (false), *expression2* is evaluated. The value of the entire expression is **0** (true) if either *expression1* or *expression2* are true. Since **X** is less than **2**, the entire expression returns **0**, and the **print** command is executed:

```
$ X=1 Y=2
$ ((X<2 || Y<5)) && print "X or Y less than 2"
X or Y less than 2
```

Now, neither **X** nor **Y** are less than **2**, so the entire expression returns **1**, and the **print** command is not executed:

```
$ X=2 Y=2
$ ((X<2 || Y<5)) && print "X or Y less than 2"
$
```

(expression) (Override Precedence)

The **()** operators are used to override precedence rules. In the next expression, normal precedence rules cause the **Y * Z** operation to be performed first:

```
$ X=1 Y=2 Z=3
$ ((TMP=X + Y * Z))
$ print $TMP
7
```

If the expression is rewritten using the precedence override operators, the **X + Y** operation is performed first:

```
$ ((TMP=(X + Y) * Z))
$ print $TMP
9
```

Random Numbers

The Korn shell provides a special variable, **RANDOM**, which is used to generate random numbers in the range from 0 to 32767. It generates a different random number each time it is referenced:

```
$ print $RANDOM
27291
$ print $RANDOM
5386
$ print $RANDOM
6884
```

You can also initialize a sequence of random numbers by setting **RANDOM** to a value. Here, **RANDOM** is set to 7. When subsequently accessed, the values **2726** and **18923** are returned:

```
$ RANDOM=7
$ print $RANDOM
2726
$ print $RANDOM
18923
```

When **RANDOM** is reset to **7** again, the same numbers are returned:

```
$ RANDOM=7
$ print $RANDOM
2726
$ print $RANDOM
18923
```

If **RANDOM** is unset, the special meaning is removed, even if reset.

Chapter 7:
The Environment

After You Log In
The Environment File
Environment Variables
Korn Shell Options
Aliases
Prompts
Subshells
Restricted Shell

Besides executing commands and being a programming language, the Korn shell also provides a number of commands, variables, and options that allow you to customize your working environment.

After You Log In

After you login, the Korn shell performs a number of actions before it displays the command prompt. Usually it first looks for **/etc/profile**. If it exists, it is read in and executed. The **/etc/profile** file contains system-wide environment settings, such as a basic **PATH** setting, a default **TERM** variable, the system **umask** value and more. The Korn shell then reads and executes **$HOME/.profile**. This file contains your local environment settings, such as your search path, execution options, local variables, aliases, and more. A sample profile file is included in **Appendix A**.

The Environment File

Once the profile files are processed, the Korn shell checks the environment file, which is specified by the **ENV** variable. The environment file usually contains aliases, functions, options, variables and other environment settings that you want available to subshells. Besides being processed at login, the environment file is processed each time a new Korn shell is invoked. There is no default value for **ENV**, so if not specifically set, this feature is not enabled. A sample environment file is included in **Appendix B**.

Because the environment file must be opened and read each time a new Korn shell is invoked, performance can be adversely affected by having a large environment file with lots of functions.

Environment Variables

There are a number of variables provided by the Korn shell that allow you to customize your working environment. Some are automatically set by the Korn shell, some have a default value if not set, while others have no value unless specifically set.

Table 7.1 lists some of the Korn shell variables. The following sections cover some of the important variables and how they affect your working environment. All the available variables are listed in the **Appendix E**.

The cd **Command**

New functionality has been added to the **cd** command. You can change back to your previous directory with:

```
$ cd -
```

It also causes the name of the new current directory to be displayed. Here, we start in **/home/anatole/bin**, then change directory to **/usr/spool/news/lib**:

```
$ cd /usr/spool/news/lib
```

Now we **cd** back to **/home/anatole/bin**:

```
$ cd -
/home/anatole/bin
```

Another **cd −**, and we are back in **/usr/spool/news/lib**:

```
$ cd -
/usr/spool/news/lib
```

You can also change directories by substituting parts of the current pathname with something else using this format:

```
cd string1 string2
```

where *string1* in the current pathname is substituted with *string2*. The new current working directory is displayed after the move. In this example, we start in **/usr/spool/uucp**:

```
$ pwd
/usr/spool/uucp
```

By substituting **uucp** with **cron**, we change directory to **/usr/spool/cron**:

```
$ cd uucp cron
/usr/spool/cron
```

CDPATH

The **CDPATH** variable is provided to make directory navigation easier. It contains a list of colon-separated directories to check when a full pathname is not given to the **cd** command. Each directory in **CDPATH** is searched from left-to-right for a directory that matches the **cd** argument. A : alone in **CDPATH** stands for the current directory. This **CDPATH**:

```
$ print $CDPATH
:/home/anatole:/usr/spool
```

indicates to check the current directory first, **/home/anatole**, then **/usr/spool** when **cd** is not given a full pathname. Instead of typing **cd /usr/spool/uucp**, you could just type **cd uucp**:

```
$ cd uucp
/usr/spool/uucp
```

Or to change directory to **/home/anatole/bin**, you could type **cd bin**:

```
$ cd bin
/home/anatole/bin
```

There is no default for **CDPATH**, so if it not specifically set, this feature is not enabled.

Make sure that only frequently used directories are included, because if **CDPATH** is too large, performance can be adversely affected by having to check so many directories each time **cd** is invoked.

PATH

The **PATH** variable contains a list of colon-separated directories to check when a command is invoked. Each directory in **PATH** is searched from left-to-right for a file whose name matches the command name. If not found, an error message is displayed. A **:** alone in **PATH** specifies to check the current directory. This **PATH** setting specifies to check the **/bin** directory first, then **/usr/bin**, **/usr/spool/news/bin**, and finally the current directory:

```
$ print $PATH
/bin:/usr/bin:/usr/spool/news/bin:
```

Don't let **PATH** get too large, because performance can be adversely affected by having to check so many directories each time a command is invoked.

If not set, the default value for **PATH** is **/bin:/usr/bin**.

TMOUT

The **TMOUT** variable specifies the number of seconds that the Korn shell will wait for input before displaying a 60-second warning message and exiting. If not set, the default used is **0**, which disables the timeout feature. To set a 10-minute timer, set **TMOUT** to **600**:

```
$ TMOUT=600
```

This variable is usually set by the system administrator in the **/etc/profile** file.

Mail

The Korn shell provides a number of variables that allow you to specify your mailbox file, how often to check for mail, what your mail notification message is, and a search path for mailbox files.

MAILCHECK

The **MAILCHECK** variable specifies how often, in seconds, to check for new mail. If not set, or set to zero, new mail is checked before each new prompt is displayed. Otherwise, the default setting is **600** seconds (10 minutes).

MAIL

The **MAIL** variable contains the name of a single mailbox file to check for new mail. It is not used if **MAILPATH** is set.

MAILPATH

The **MAILPATH** variable contains a colon-separated list of mailbox files to check for new mail and is used if you want to read multiple mailboxes. It overrides the **MAIL** variable if both are set. This **MAILPATH** setting specifies to check two mailbox files, **/home/anatole/mbox** and **/news/mbox**.

```
$ print $MAILPATH
MAILPATH=/home/anatole/mbox:/news/mbox
```

Just so you don't think you can go snooping around someone else's mailbox, this only works if you have read permission on the mailbox file.

If **MAILPATH** is not set, there is no default.

New Mail Notification Message

When you get new mail, the Korn shell displays this message on your terminal just before the prompt:

```
you have mail in mailbox-file
```

You can also create your own mail notification message by appending a **?** followed by your message to the mailbox files given in **MAILPATH**. If you wanted your message to be '**New mail alert**', then **MAILPATH** would be set like this:

```
$ MAILPATH=~anatole/mbox?'New mail alert'
```

What if you had two mailboxes set in **MAILPATH**? How would you know which one to read? For this reason, the Korn shell has the _ (underscore) variable. When given in the new mail notification message, it is substituted for the name of the mail box file. This **MAILPATH** setting:

```
$ MAILPATH=~anatole/mbox?'Check $_':\
/news/mbox?'Check $_'
```

would cause **"Check /home/anatole/mbox"** or **"Check /news/mbox"** to be displayed if new mail was received in either of the mailboxes.

TERM

The **TERM** variable specifies your terminal type, and is usually set by your system administrator in the global **/etc/profile** file. If it's not set there, then it's probably in your **~/.profile** file. You can tell if it's not set correctly by invoking **vi** on an existent file. If you get garbage on your screen or the **vi** commands are not working correctly, try resetting the **TERM** variable to something else:

```
$ typeset -x TERM=term-type
```

Then try running **vi** again and see what happens.

Korn Shell Options

The Korn shell has a number of options that specify your environment and control execution. There are options that cause background jobs to be run at a lower priority, prevent files from being overwritten with redirection operators, disable filename expansion, specify the **vi**-style

Table 7.1: Some Korn Shell Environment Variables

CDPATH	search path for **cd** when not given a full pathname (no default)
COLUMNS	window width for in-line edit mode and **select** command lists (default **80**)
EDITOR	pathname of the editor for in-line editing (default **/bin/ed**)
ENV	pathname of the environment file (no default)
HISTFILE	pathname of the history file (default **$HOME/.sh_history**)
HISTSIZE	number of commands to save in the command history file (default **128**)
HOME	home directory
IFS	internal field separator (default space, tab, newline)
LANG	locale
MAIL	name of mail file
MAILCHECK	specifies how often to check for mail (default **600** seconds)
MAILPATH	search path for mail files (no default)
PATH	search path for commands (default **/bin:/usr/bin:**)
PS1	primary prompt string (default **$, #**)
PS2	secondary prompt string (default **>**)
PS3	**select** command prompt (default **#?**)
PS4	debug prompt string (default **+**)
SHELL	pathname of the shell
TERM	specifies your terminal type (no default)
TMOUT	Korn shell timeout variable (default 0)
VISUAL	pathname of the editor for in-line editing

in-line command editor, and more.

Table 7.2 lists some of the Korn shell options, along with the default values (these may differ on your system). All of the options are listed in **Appendix E**.

Enabling/Disabling Options

Korn shell options are enabled with the **set** *−o*option or **set** *−option* command. For example, the **noglob** option disables file name substitution and can be set using either of these commands :

```
$ set −f
```
or
```
$ set −o noglob
```

Options can also be enabled by specifying them on the **ksh** command line. Here, a Korn subshell is started with the **emacs** option enabled:

```
$ ksh −o emacs
```

Options can be disabled with the **set +o** *option* or **set** *+option* command. In this example, the **noglob** option is disabled:

```
$ set +o noglob
```

The ignoreeof **Option**

If this option is enabled, you get this message when you try to log off using **Ctl-d**:

```
$ set —o ignoreeof
$ Ctl-d
Use 'exit' to terminate this shell
```

By default, this option is disabled.

The markdirs **Option**

When enabled, a trailing / is appended to directory names resulting from file name substitution. It's like the **ls —o** or **—F** options, except that you only see the results on file name substitution, not on directory listings. This means that / is added to directory names when you do this:

```
$ ls *
```

but not this:

```
$ ls
```

By default, the **markdirs** option is disabled.

The noclobber **Option**

The noclobber option prevents I/O redirection from truncating or *clobbering* existing files. Let's enable the option and give it a try:

```
$ set —o noclobber
$ ls>ls.out
$ ls>ls.out
/bin/ksh: ls.out: file already exists
```

If **noclobber** is enabled, and you really want to overwrite a file, use the >| operator:

```
$ ls>|ls.out
```

By default, this option is disabled.

The nounset Option

If the **nounset** option is disabled, then the Korn shell interprets unset variables as if their values were null.

```
$ unset X
$ print "X is set to: $X"
X is set to:
```

If enabled, the Korn shell displays an error message when it encounters unset variables and causes scripts to abort:

```
$ set —o nounset
$ unset X
$ print $X
/bin/ksh: X: parameter not set
```

Displaying the Current Settings

The setting of the current options is displayed with the **set —o** command. The first field is the option name, and the second field shows if the option is enabled or disabled:

Table 7.2: Some Korn Shell Options

set −a, set −o allexport
> automatically export variables when defined

set −o bgnice execute all background jobs at a lower priority

set −o emacs, set −o gmacs
> use **emacs/gmacs** in-line editor

set −o ignoreeof
> do not exit on end of file; use **exit** (default **Ctl-d**)

set −o markdirs
> display trailing / on directory names resulting from file name substitution

set −m, set −o monitor
> enable job control (system dependent)

set −n, set −o noexec
> read commands without executing them

set −o noclobber
> prevent I/O redirection from truncating existing files

set −f, set −o noglob
> disable file name expansion

set −u, set −o nounset
> return error on substitution of unset variables

set −h, set −o trackall
> make commands tracked aliases when first encountered

set −o vi use **vi**-style editor for in-line editing

set −x, set −o xtrace
> display commands and arguments as they are executed

```
$ set —o
allexport        off
bgnice           on
emacs            off
errexit          off
gmacs            off
ignoreeof        off
interactive      on
keyword          off
markdirs         off
monitor          on
noexec           off
noclobber        off
noglob           off
nolog            off
nounset          off
privileged       off
restricted       off
trackall         off
verbose          off
vi               on
viraw            on
xtrace           off
```

Command-line Options

Besides the options from the **set** command, the following options can also be specified on the **ksh** command line:

−c *string*	read and execute the commands from *string*
−i	execute in interactive mode
−r	run a restricted shell
−s	read commands from standard input

These cannot be enabled with the **set** command.

Aliases

Aliases are command name macros used as shorthand for other commands, especially frequently used ones. This saves a lot of typing time. Aliases are defined with the **alias** *name=value* command. For example, we could create an alias for the **print** command like this:

```
$ alias p=print
```

Whenever **p** is invoked, **print** is executed:

```
$ p Hello
Hello
```

Make sure to enclose the value in quotes if it contains whitespace. Here we create an alias **l** that is set to the **ls −Fac** command:

```
$ alias l="ls −Fac"
```

Now when you type in **l**, **ls −Fac** is executed:

```
$ l
./
../
compress.Z*
func.Z*
test/
uncompress.Z*
 . . .
```

Alias values can contain any text, including special characters, like wildcards, pipes, or I/O redirection operators. Let's change alias **l** so that the output is piped to the **more** command:

```
$ alias l="ls −Fac | more"
```

But what if you wanted to make this a global alias by setting it in the

/etc/profile file, and some people wanted to use **more**, while others wanted to use **pg**? We could add the **PAGER** variable to the **l** alias, and let each user set **PAGER** to whatever they wanted.

```
$ alias l="ls -Fac | ${PAGER:-/bin/pg}"
```

Notice that if **PAGER** is not set, the default **/bin/pg** will be used. One last point. Using double quotes causes alias values to be expanded only when the alias is set. This means that if we reset **PAGER** after **l** is defined, it would have no effect on the alias. To have the alias value expanded each time it is invoked, use single quotes like this:

```
$ alias l='ls -Fac | ${PAGER:-/bin/pg}'
```

Now whenever **PAGER** is redefined, the next time alias **l** is invoked, it uses the new value.

If an alias value ends with a blank, then the next word following the alias is also checked if it is an alias. Here we set two aliases: **p** and **h**. When invoked, we get **h** instead of **Hello**.

```
$ alias p='print' h=Hello
$ p h
h
```

After the **p** alias is reset with a trailing blank, **h** gets substituted in the next command correctly:

```
$ alias p='print ' h=Hello
$ p h
Hello
```

Displaying Current Aliases

A list of the current aliases is displayed using the **alias** command

Table 7.3: Preset Aliases

Alias	Value	Definition
autoload	typeset −fu	define an autoloading function
echo	print −	display arguments
functions	typeset −f	display list of functions
hash	alias −t −	display list of tracked aliases
history	fc −l	list commands from history file
integer	typeset −i	declare integer variable
r	fc −e −	re-execute previous command
stop	kill −STOP	suspend job
type	whence −v	display information about commands

without arguments:

```
$ alias
autoload=typeset —fu
cd=_cd
echo=print —
functions=typeset —f
h=Hello
hash=alias —t —
history=fc —l
integer=typeset —i
l=ls —Fac | more
ls=/usr/bin/ls
```

```
mv=/usr/bin/mv
nohup=nohup
p=print
r=fc -e -
rm=/usr/bin/rm
stop=kill -STOP
suspend=kill -STOP $$
type=whence -v
vi=SHELL=/bin/sh vi
```

Exported aliases are displayed using the **alias -x** command.

Tracked Aliases

Tracked aliases are used to associate an alias with the full pathname of a program. When a tracked alias is invoked, instead of searching each directory in **PATH**, the full pathname of the corresponding command is returned from the alias table. This speeds execution by eliminating the path search.

Most implementations of the Korn shell come with a few default tracked aliases. These are usually set to frequently used commands. Tracked aliases and their values can be displayed with the **alias -t** command. Let's see what we've got:

```
$ alias -t
ls=/usr/bin/ls
mv=/usr/bin/mv
rm=/usr/bin/rm
vi=/usr/ucb/vi
```

On this version of the Korn shell, the **ls**, **mv**, **rm**, and **vi** commands are standard tracked aliases. On other implementations, they may be different.

Tracked aliases are basically the same as normal aliases, except that they are defined using the following format:

```
alias -t name
```

Notice that a value is not given, as in normal **alias** *−name=value* syntax. This is because the Korn shell assigns a value automatically by doing a search on **PATH**. In the case of the tracked alias **ls**, the value is set to **/usr/bin/ls**, since **/usr/bin** is the first directory in **PATH** that contains **ls**.

We could set up a tracked alias for the **cp** command like this:

```
$ alias -t cp
```

If the **trackall** option is set (**set −h**, or **set −o trackall**), then the Korn shell attempts to generate tracked aliases for all commands that it encounters for the first time. By default, this option is usually disabled.

Tracked aliases become undefined if the **PATH** variable is unset. However, they continue to be tracked aliases. The next reference to the tracked alias causes the value to be reassigned.

Removing Aliases

Aliases are removed with the **unalias** command. Let's try it with the **l** alias:

```
$ unalias l
```

Now when invoked, it returns an error.

```
$ l
/bin/ksh: l:  not found
```

If you want to prevent an alias from being interpreted as one without having to delete it, just enclose it in single quotes. This is useful for when aliases are named after commands or functions. For example, on systems that alias **cd** to the **_cd** function, the real built-in **cd** command could be invoked like this:

```
$ 'cd'
```

Prompts

There are a number of prompt variables in the Korn shell: **PS1** and **PS2** are two of them. **PS1** contains your primary prompt string and is displayed by the Korn shell when it is ready to read a command. If not specified, the default is $ for regular users, and # for superusers.

PS2 specifies the secondary prompt string and is displayed whenever the Korn shell needs more input. For example, when you press <RETURN> before a complete command has been given, or continue a command onto the next line with the \ character, the **PS2** variable is displayed. If not specified, the default for **PS2** is the > character.

```
$ print "Here is
> another line"
Here is another line
```

Customizing Your Command Prompt

By default, the command prompt is set to the $ character. But you could set it to something else by simply reassigning a value to the **PS1** variable. For example, you could have the prompt give you a greeting message like this:

```
$ typeset -x PS1="Good morning "
```

As soon as you press the <RETURN> key, the prompt is reset.

```
Good morning: pwd
/home/anatole
Good morning:
```

The current command number can be displayed by putting a ! in the prompt variable **PS1** like this:

```
$ typeset -x PS1="!:Good morning:"
154: Good morning:
```

If you really want to display a ! in the prompt, use !!:

```
$ typeset -x PS1="Hello there!!"
Hello there!
```

Now let's make a fancy prompt that will display the command number and the current working directory. Besides ! for the command number, we'll need the **PWD** variable for the current working directory.

```
$ typeset -x PS1="!:$PWD> "
```

Just to make sure it works, let's change directories:

```
167:/home/anatole> cd /tmp
168:/tmp> cd /usr/spool/news/comp/sources
169:/usr/spool/news/comp/sources>
```

Don't go overboard with this. If you are using the in-line editor, remember that the prompt size affects the edit window width.

Subshells

Subshells are generated whenever you enclose commands in ()'s, perform command substitution, for background processes, and for co-processes (discussed later in **Chapter 8**). A subshell is a separate copy of the parent shell, so variables, functions, and aliases from the parent shell are available to the subshell. However, subshells cannot change the value of parent shell variables, functions, or aliases. So if we set **LOCALVAR** to a value in the current shell:

```
$ LOCALVAR="This is the original value"
```

then check the value in a subshell, we see that it is defined:

```
$ ( print $LOCALVAR )
This is the original value
```

If we set it in the subshell to another value:

```
$ ( LOCALVAR="This is the new value" )
```

then check the value in the parent shell, we see that **LOCALVAR** is still set to the original value:

```
$ print $LOCALVAR
This is the original value
```

By default, things like variables, aliases, and functions from the current environment are not available to separate invocations of the Korn shell unless explicitly exported or exported in the environment file. For example, variables are exported with the **typeset −x** command. Let's look at **LOCALVAR** again. It wasn't exported, so if we start a new Korn shell, **LOCALVAR** is not defined:

```
$ ksh
$ print $LOCALVAR
```

```
$ exit
```

Once exported, it is available to the new Korn shell:

```
$ typeset -x LOCALVAR
$ ksh
$ print $LOCALVAR
This is the original value
```

As with subshells, environment settings are not passed back to the parent Korn shell. If **LOCALVAR** is set to another value in the separate Korn shell:

```
$ LOCALVAR="This is the new value"
```

then we exit back to the parent shell, we see that **LOCALVAR** is still set to the original value:

```
$ exit
$ print $LOCALVAR
This is the original value
```

If the **allexport** option is enabled (**set -a**, or **set -o allexport**), variables are automatically exported when defined. By default, this option is disabled.

Aliases can also be exported to separate Korn shells with the **alias -x** command. If we wanted to use the **l** alias in a separate Korn shell, it would have to be exported like this:

```
$ alias -x l
```

Restricted Shell

This is a version of the shell that allows restricted access to Unix. Running under **rsh** is equivalent to **ksh**, except that the following is not allowed:

- changing directories
- setting the value of **ENV**, **PATH**, or **SHELL** variables
- specifying path or command names containing /
- redirecting output of a command with >, >|, <>, or >>

These restrictions apply only after the **.profile** and environment files have been processed.

Privileged Mode

Privileged mode allows execution of the environment and **.profile** files to be controlled. When enabled, the ~/**.profile** and environment files are not executed. Instead, **/etc/suid_profile** is read and executed.

The **/etc/suid_profile** file can be configured by the system administrator to control execution of setuid Korn shell scripts, track **su** invocations, set a default read only **PATH**, log commands, and more.

By default, privileged mode is disable, but is enabled whenever the real and effective user or group ids are not the same.

Chapter 8: Writing Korn Shell Scripts

Executing Korn Shell Scripts
The **((...))** Command
Control Commands
Input/Output Commands
Misc Programming Features

Besides providing a working environment and executing commands, the Korn shell is also a high-level programming language that can be used to write programs. In Korn shell terminology, these programs are called *scripts*. Korn shell scripts can contain anything that you enter at the command prompt: normal Unix commands, Korn shell commands, your own programs and scripts, or even commands from other Unix shells! Unlike many high-level programming languages, Korn shell scripts are interpreted, so they do not have to be compiled. This makes the Korn shell ideal for prototyping.

Executing Korn Shell Scripts

Let's make a Korn shell script out of the **print Hello world** command by putting it into a file like this:

```
$ print "print Hello world" >prhello
```

Before Korn shell scripts can be executed, they must be made executable by setting the execute and read bits with the **chmod** command:

```
$ chmod 755 prhello
or
$ chmod +rx prhello
```

Assuming that the current directory is in the search path **$PATH**, **prhello** can now be executed by simply invoking it by name:

```
$ prhello
Hello world
```

Korn shell scripts can also be executed by invoking them as the first argument to **ksh**:

```
$ ksh prhello
Hello world
```

Now we can use **prhello** like any other command. The output can be directed to a file:

```
$ prhello >p.out
$ cat p.out
Hello world
```

It can be used with a pipe:

```
$ prhello | wc
1        2       12
```

or with command substitution:

```
$ print "We always say \"$(prhello)\""
We always say "Hello world"
```

By default, Korn shell scripts are run in a separate environment. This means that variables from the current environment are not available to Korn shell scripts unless explicitly exported, and variables defined in Korn shell scripts are not passed back to the parent shell. Just to prove it, here is a demonstration. The **checkvar** Korn shell script does just one thing: it prints the value of **LOCALVAR**.

```
$ cat checkvar
print "LOCALVAR is set to: $LOCALVAR"
```

If **LOCALVAR** is set to something in the current environment, and **checkvar** is run, we see that **LOCALVAR** is not defined:

```
$ LOCALVAR="This is the original value"
$ checkvar
LOCALVAR is set to:
```

If we export **LOCALVAR**, then its value will be available to **checkvar**:

```
$ typeset -x LOCALVAR
$ checkvar
LOCALVAR is set to: This is the original value
```

To show that Korn shell script environments cannot modify variable values in the parent shell, we'll change **checkvar** to reassign a value to **LOCALVAR**.

```
$ cat checkvar
print "LOCALVAR is set to: $LOCALVAR"
LOCALVAR="This is a new value"
print "The new LOCALVAR is set to: $LOCALVAR"
```

Now when it is run, **LOCALVAR** is set to the new value:

```
$ checkvar
LOCALVAR is set to: This is the original value
The new LOCALVAR is set to: This is a new value
```

Meanwhile, back in the parent shell, **LOCALVAR** has not been affected.

```
$ print $LOCALVAR
This is the original value
```

If the **allexport** option is enabled (**set −a**, or **set −o allexport**), variables are automatically exported when defined. By default, this option is disabled.

Positional Parameters

Positional parameters are special variables used to keep track of arguments to the Korn shell, scripts, and functions. Positional parameter names contain only digits and cannot be set directly using *variable=value* syntax. By default, parameter zero (or **$0**) is set to the name of the shell, script or function.

```
$ print $0
/bin/ksh
```

The remaining parameters **1** to *n* are set to each of the arguments passed to the shell, script or function. For example, if you invoke a Korn shell script called **ptest** and pass the arguments **A**, **B**, and **C**,

Table 8.1: Positional Parameters

$0	name of script or function or pathname of Korn shell for **set**
$*n*	*n*th argument to script, function, or **set**
${*n*}	*n*th argument to script, function, or **set** when n is greater than 9
$#	number of positional parameters
$*, $@	all positional parameters separated with a blank
"$*"	all positional parameters enclosed in double quotes
${*:X}	all *X* to the last positional parameters
"${*:X}"	all *X* to the last positional parameters enclosed in double quotes
${*:X:n}	*n* positional parameters beginning with *X*th
"${*:X:n}"	*n* positional parameters beginning with *X*th enclosed in double quotes

then in the script **ptest**, **$0** would be set to **ptest**, **$1** to **A**, **$2** to **B**, and **$3** to **C**.

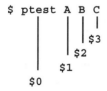

```
$ ptest A B C
```

There are three special Korn shell variables that provide information about the current positional parameters. The first is **$#**, and it contains the number of positional parameters. The other two are **$@** and **$***, and they both contain all the positional parameters. So in the above **ptest** example, **$#** would be **3**, and both **$*** and **$@** would be **A B C**. Here is a Korn shell script that manipulates positional parameters. It displays the name of the current script, the number of positional parameters, and the value of each of the positional parameters:

```
$ cat check_params
print "Script name:          $0"
print "Number of args passed:   $#"
print "Arguments passed:       $*"
print "Arg 1=$1, Arg 2=$2, Arg 3=$3"
```

If executed with no arguments, this is the output:

```
$ check_params
Script name:                check_params
Number of args passed:    0
Arguments passed:
Arg 1=, Arg 2=, Arg 3=
```

while if executed with the arguments **A** and **B**, the output is:

```
$ check_params A B
Script name:                check_params
Number of args passed:    2
Arguments passed:         A B
Arg 1=A, Arg 2=B, Arg 3=
```

Modifying Positional Parameters

By default, **$0** is set to the name of the shell, script or function. It cannot be set or modified. The remaining parameters from **$1** to **$***n* can be reassigned with the **shift** command.

The **shift** command, with no arguments, shifts positional parameters left once, so that **$1** takes the value of **$2**, **$2** takes the value of **$3**, and so on. The original value of **$1** is lost.

Let's change the **check_params** script so that it shifts the positional parameters left once:

```
$ cat check_params
print "Script name:              $0"
print "Number of args passed:    $#"
print "Arguments passed:         $*"
print "Arg 1=$1, Arg 2=$2, Arg 3=$3"
shift
print "Number of remaining args: $#"
print "Remaining args:           $*"
print "Arg 1=$1, Arg 2=$2, Arg 3=$3"
```

When we run it again with the arguments **A B**, we get:

```
$ check_params A B
Script name:                    check_params
Number of args passed:          2
Arguments passed:               A B
Arg 1=A, Arg 2=B, Arg 3=
Number of remaining args:       1
Remaining args:                 B
Arg 1=B, Arg 2=, Arg 3=
```

After the **shift** command, **$1** is set to **B** and **$2** is unset. The original value of **$1** is lost.

The positional parameters can be shifted left more than once by providing an integer argument to the **shift** command: **shift** *n*.

Now let's try something else with positional parameters. Here is a Korn shell script called **kuucp**. It uses **uucp** to copy a file to the public directory on the **rnihd** system.

```
$ cat kuucp
```

```
PUBDIR=${PUBDIR:-/usr/spool/uucppublic}
uucp $1 rnihd!$PUBDIR/$1
print "Copied $1 to rnihd!$PUBDIR/$1"
```

So instead of typing this long command line:

```
$ uucp n.out rnihd!/usr/spool/uucppublic/n.out
```

we can do this:

```
$ kuucp n.out
```

and in the script, **$1** gets substituted with **n.out** in both the source and target file arguments. We could extend this further to be able to **uucp** files to any system by having a system name given as another command-line argument. Now **$1** is used for the source and target file, and **$2** for the remote system name.

```
$ cat kuucp
PUBDIR=${PUBDIR:-/usr/spool/uucppublic}
uucp $1 $2!$PUBDIR/$1
print "Copied $1 to $2!$PUBDIR/$1"
```

To send the file **msg.c** to the **uucp** public directory on the **unisf** system, **kuucp** would be invoked like this:

```
$ kuucp msg.c unisf
```

$1 would be substituted with the **msg.c**, and **$2** with **unisf**. Notice that the destination directory is taken from **PUBDIR** variable. If it's not set, the default **uucp** public directory is used.

The exit **command**

In Chapter 2, we learned that Unix programs return an exit status. And that a zero exit status indicates successful execution, while a non-zero exit status indicates failure. The **exit** command allows you to terminate execution from anywhere in a Korn shell script and return an exit value using this format:

> **exit**
> or
> **exit** *n*

where *n* is the exit status to return. If *n* is not specified, the exit status of the previous command is used. If you don't use **exit**, then scripts finish after the last command is executed.

Take a look at the **kuucp** script again. What happens if an error occurs? For example, if the file argument is entered incorrectly, or it doesn't exist? The **uucp** command will fail, but the status message following will still get displayed. Here is a good place for **exit**. It could be used to terminate execution and return a non-zero exit status if for some reason the **uucp** command failed. To get the exit status, **$?** is checked after **uucp** is run. If it is non-zero, then we display our own error message and exit. Otherwise, the next command is executed and the script terminates successfully.

```
$ cat kuucp
PUBDIR=${PUBDIR:-/usr/spool/uucpublic}
uucp $1 $2!$PUBDIR/$1 2>&-
(($? != 0)) && {print "Got uucp error"; exit 1;}
print "Copied $1 to $2!$PUBDIR/$1"
```

By the way, the **2>&–** just traps the **uucp** error messages. We don't need to see them anymore, since **kuucp** is now doing its own error processing. Now when **kuucp** is run on a non-existent file, this is what happens:

```
$ kuucp nofile unisf
Got uucp error
$ print $?
1
```

The **exit** command does one more thing. If given at the command prompt, it terminates your login shell.

The [[...]] Command

The **[[...]]** command is used to evaluate conditional expressions with file attributes, strings, integers, and more. The basic format is:

[[*expression*]]

where *expression* is the condition you are evaluating. There must be whitespace after the opening brackets, and before the closing brackets. Whitespace must also separate the expression arguments and operators. For example, these are incorrect:

```
[[$X=$Y]]
[[$X = $Y]]
```

while this is correct:

```
[[ $X == $Y ]]
```

Notice that there is white space between **$X**, **$Y**, and the = operator.

If the expression evaluates to true, then a zero exit status is returned, otherwise the expression evaluates to false and a non-zero exit status is returned.

If you are familiar with the **test** and **[...]** commands, then you'll recognize that **[[...]]** is just a new and improved version of the same commands. It basically functions the same way, except that a number of new operators are available.

Table 8.2: [[...]] String Operators

−n *string*   true if length of *string* is not zero
−o *option*   true if *option* is set
−z *string*   true if length of *string* is zero
string1 = *string2*
               true if *string1* is equal to *string2*
string1 != *string2*
               true if *string1* is not equal to *string2*
string = *pattern*
               true if *string* matches *pattern*
string != *pattern*
               true if *string* does not match *pattern*
string1 < *string2*
               true if *string1* less than *string2*
string1 > *string2*
               true if *string1* greater than *string2*

Checking Strings

We could use the **[[...]]** command to check if a variable is set to a certain value. Here, variable **X** is assigned **abc**, then evaluated in this expression:

```
$ X=abc
$ [[ $X = abc ]] && print "X is set to abc"
X is set to abc
```

Using the **test** and **[...]** commands, the same command could be written as:

```
test "$X" = abc && print "X is set to abc"
or
[ "$X" = abc ] && print "X is set to abc"
```

To check if a variable is set to null, the **−z** option can be used:

```
[[ −z $VAR ]] && print "VAR is set to null"
```

or it could be compared to the null string like this:

```
[[ $VAR = "" ]] && "VAR is set to null"
```

Checking Patterns

The Korn shell also lets you compare strings to patterns. We could check if **X** begins with a **'a'** like this:

```
$ X=abc
$ [[ $X = a* ]] && print "$X matches a*"
abc matches a*
```

or if it's a three-character string:

```
$ [[ $X = ??? ]] && print "$X has exactly 3 \
characters"
abc has exactly 3 characters
```

Using the **+([0−9])** pattern, we could check if **X** is set to a number:

```
$ X=123
$ [[ $X = +([0−9]) ]] && print "$X is a number"
123 is a number
```

Table 8.2 lists the most commonly used **[[...]]** string operators.

170

Table 8.3: Some [[...]] File Operators

−**a** *file*	true if *file* exists.
−**d** *file*	true if *file* exists and is a directory.
−**f** *file*	true if *file* exists and is a regular file.
−**G** *file*	true if *file* exists and its group id matches the effective group id of the current process.
−**L** *file*	true if *file* exists and is a symbolic link.
−**O***file*	true if *file* exists and its user id matches the effective user id of the current process.
−**r** *file*	true if *file* exists and is readable.
−**s** *file*	true if *file* exists and its size is greater than zero.
−**S** *file*	true if *file* exists and is a socket.
−**u** *file*	true if *file* exists and its set user-id bit is set.
−**w** *file*	true if *file* exists and is writable.
−**x** *file*	true if *file* exists and is executable. If *file* is a directory, then true indicates that the directory is searchable.
file1 −**ef** *file2*	true if *file1* exists and is another name for *file2*.
file1 −**nt** *file2*	true if *file1* exists and is newer than *file2*.
file1 −**ot** *file2*	true if *file1* exists and is older than *file2*.

Checking File Attributes

Because manipulating files is so important in programming, the Korn shell provides a whole range of file operators. The most basic operation to perform on a file is to see if it exists, and that can be done using the **−a** operator. This is a new Korn shell file operator. Make sure you don't get it confused with the logical AND operator used by the **test** and **[...]** commands, which is also written as **−a**.

```
$ touch tmp
$ [[ −a tmp ]] && print "File tmp exists"
File tmp exists
```

This only indicates that it exists, but not much else. It may be a directory, or a symbolic link, but using this operator, that's all we know. If we wanted more information, the **−f** or **−d** operators could tell us if a file existed *and* was a normal file (**−f**) or if it was just a directory (**−d**). Let's try the **−f** operator on the **tmp** file:

```
$ [[ -f tmp ]] && print "File tmp exists and \
is a regular file"
File tmp exists and is a regular file
```

If we tried the **−d** operator on the **tmp** file, it would evaluate to false, because it isn't a directory:

```
$ [[ -d tmp ]] && print "File tmp exists and \
is a regular file"
$
```

While on a directory it would evaluate to true:

```
$ mkdir tmpdir
$ [[ -d tmpdir ]] && print "Directory tmp exists"
Directory tmp exists
```

This conditional command checks if **$FILE** is readable, and if not, prints an error message and exits:

```
[[ -r $FILE ]]||{ print $FILE not readable; exit 1; }
```

while this one checks if **$FILE** is writable:

```
[[ -w $FILE ]]||{ print $FILE not writable; exit 1; }
```

Here are a couple of new file operators: **−nt** and **−ot**. They compare two files and return true if *file1* is newer than (**−nt**) or older than (**−ot**) *file2*.

```
$ touch tfile2
$ touch tfile1
$ [[ tfile1 −nt tfile2 ]]&&print "tfile1 is \
newer than tfile2"
tfile1 is newer than tfile2
```

Let's switch the files in the expression and try the **−ot** operator:

```
$ [[ tfile2 −ot tfile1 ]]&&print "tfile2 is \
older than tfile1"
tfile2 is older than tfile1
```

Table 8.3 lists the most commonly used **[[...]]** file operators.

Checking Integer Attributes

The **[[...]]** command provides a few integer operators that allow integers to be compared. It is frequently used to check the number of command-line arguments. This expression evaluates to true if there are less than or equal to three positional parameters set:

```
[[ $# −le 3 ]] && print "3 or less args given"
```

The last expression is equivalent to checking if there are less than four positional parameters set:

```
[[ $# -lt 4 ]] && print "Less than 4 args given"
```

The number of users logged on could be checked like this:

```
$ [[ $(who | wc -l) -gt 10 ]] && print "More \
than 10 users are logged on"
More than 10 users are logged on
```

In many cases, the **[[...]]** integer operators may be sufficient for evaluating expressions that contain integers. To perform other arithmetic operations, use the **((...))** command (discussed in Chapter 6). It offers the same arithmetic comparison operators as the **[[...]]** command, plus many others. Besides offering more arithmetic operators, the **((...))** command provides substantial performance improvements over the **[[...]]** and **test** commands. The last command could also be given as:

```
(($(who | wc -l) > 10)) && print "More than \
10 users are logged on"
```

Using an arithmetic expression, the number of command-line arguments can be checked like this:

```
(($# < 4)) && print "Less than 4 args"
```

Table 8.4 lists the most commonly used **[[...]]** integer operators.

The ! Operator

The **!** operator negates the result of any **[[...]]** expression when used like this:

```
[[ ! expression ]]
```

For example, to check if **X** is *not* equal to **abc**:

```
$ X=xyz
$ [[ ! $X = abc ]] && print "$X not equals abc"
xyz not equals abc
```

or if a file doesn't exist:

```
$ rm tmp
$ [[ ! -f tmp ]] && print "tmp does NOT exist"
tmp does NOT exist
```

Table 8.4: [[...]] Integer Operators

exp1 **-eq** *exp2*	true if *exp1* is equal to *exp2*
exp1 **-ne** *exp2*	true if *exp1* is not equal to *exp2*
exp1 **-le** *exp2*	true if *exp1* is less than or equal to *exp2*
exp1 **-lt** *exp2*	true if *exp1* is less than *exp2*
exp1 **-ge** *exp2*	true if *exp1* is greater than or equal to *exp2*
exp1 **-gt** *exp2*	true if *exp1* is greater than *exp2*

There is one logical operator that can only be implemented with the **!** operator. There is no **[[...]]** file operator that will evaluate to true on a zero-length file.

```
$ >emptyfile
$ [[ ! -s emptyfile ]] && print "emptyfile is empty"
emptyfile is empty
```

Compound Expressions

Expressions can also be combined with the **&&** and || operators to form compound expressions.

&& - The AND Operator

The **&&** operator is used with the **[[...]]** command to test if multiple expressions are true using this format:

[[*expression1* **&&** *expression2*]]

We could check if two variables were set to specific values like this:

```
$ X=abc Y=def
$ [[ $X = abc && $Y = def ]] && print "X=abc  \
and Y=def"
X=abc and Y=def
```

This expression checks if the **noglob** and **noclobber** options are set:

```
[[ —o noglob && —o noclobber ]]
```

Multiple **&&** operators can also be given in one [[...]] command. We could check if three options were set like this:

```
[[ —o noglob && —o noclobber && —o bgnice ]]
```

In some versions of the Korn shell, multiple **&&** operators cannot be given in one [[...]] command unless grouped with parentheses.

Table 8.5: Other [[...]] Operators

[[*expression1* **&&** *expression2*]]
> true if both *expression1* and *expression2* are true

[[*expression1* || *expression2*]]
> true either *expression1* or *expression2* are true

[[(*expression*)]]
> true if *expression* evaluates to true. The ()'s are used to override the precedence rules.

[[!*expression*]]
> true if *expression* evaluates to false

|| - The OR Operator

The || operator is used with the **[[...]]** command to test if *expression1* OR *expression2* are true using this format:

> [[*expression1* || *expression2*]]

This expression checks if **$FILE** was readable or executable:

```
[[ -r $FILE || -w $FILE ]]
```

while this one checks if either variable was set to your name:

```
[[ $USER=$(whoami) || $LOGNAME=$(whoami) ]]
```

Multiple || operators can also be given in one [[...]] command. We could check if **$FILE** was readable, writable, or executable like this:

```
[[ -r $FILE || -w $FILE || -x $FILE ]]
```

As with the **&&** operator, in some versions of the Korn shell, multiple || operators cannot be given in one [[...]] command unless grouped with parentheses.

[[...]] vs test and [...]

The **[[...]]** command is preferred to **test** and **[...]**, since many of the errors associated with **test** and **[...]** do not occur. For example, when comparing two variables where one is set to null or unset, the **test** and **[...]** commands return a syntax error if the variable is not surrounded in double quotes. Here, **X** is unset, while **Y** is set to **1**:

```
$ unset X
$ Y=1
```

Without double quotes around the variable names, the **test** and **[...]** commands return a syntax error:

```
$ test $X = $Y && print "X and Y are equal"
/bin/ksh: test: argument expected
or
$ [ $X = $Y ] && print "X and Y are equal"
/bin/ksh: test: argument expected
```

while the **[[...]]** command does not (unless the **nounset** option is enabled):

```
$ [[ $X = $Y ]] && print "X and Y are equal"
X and Y are equal
```

Checking File Descriptors

On systems that support the **/dev/fd** directory for naming open files, the *files* argument in expressions can be given as **/dev/fd/**n so that the test is applied to the open file associated with file descriptor n. This command checks to see if standard input (file descriptor 0) is readable:

```
$ [[ -r /dev/fd/0 ]] && print "Stdin is readable"
Stdin is readable
```

Control Commands

The Korn shell provides a number of control-flow commands typically found in high-level programming languages. The following sections cover these special commands.

The case **Command**

The **case** command provides multiple-branch capability. It is used to compare a single value against a number of other values. Commands associated with that value are executed when a match is made. The syntax for the **case** command is:

```
case value in
        pattern1 )          command
                            command ;;

        pattern2 )          command
                            command ;;

        . . .

        patternn )          command
                            command ;;

esac
```

where *value* is compared to *pattern1, pattern2, ... patternn*. When a match is found, the commands associated with that pattern up to the double semi-colons are executed.

The following Korn shell script demonstrates a simple **case** statement. It successively compares the command-line argument given to −**a**, −**b**, or −**c** and then prints out which flag was given. First, it checks to make sure that at least one command-line argument is given:

```
$ cat checkargs
(($#<1)) && { print Not enough args; exit 1; }

case $1 in
        −a )    print − "−a flag given" ;;
        −b )    print − "−b flag given" ;;
        −c )    print − "−c flag given" ;;
esac
$ checkargs −b
−b flag given
$ checkargs −a
−a flag given
```

The −**d** argument is given in the next invocation. It doesn't match any of the patterns, so nothing is printed:

```
$ checkargs −d
$
```

Specifying Patterns with case

The same patterns used in file name substitution can also be used in **case** statements to match patterns. For example, the * pattern is frequently used to specify a default pattern. It will always match if no other match is made. Another pattern, **@([1–9])*([0–9])**, will match any number **1–9999999***. Let's expand the **checkargs** script to match on any type of argument using some special pattern-matching characters.

```
$ cat checkargs
case $1 in
    -@([a-z]) )
            print "Lowercase argument given: $1" ;;
    -@([A-Z]) )
            print "Uppercase argument given: $1" ;;
    @([1-9])*([0-9]) )
            print "Integer argument given: $1" ;;
    "" )    print "No argument given" ;;
    * )     print "Invalid argument given" ;;
esac
```

Here is sample output:

```
$ checkargs -a
Lowercase argument given: -a
$ checkargs 99
Integer argument given: 99
$ checkargs -C
Uppercase argument given: -C
$ checkargs 0
Invalid argument given
$ checkargs
No argument given
```

Notice that the **-@(a-z)** and **-@(A-Z)** patterns cause a − followed by only one character to be matched. An argument like **-axyz** would cause the invalid argument message to be printed:

```
$ checkargs -axyz
Invalid argument given!
```

The −+([A−z]) **case** pattern would allow for multiple characters to follow the − character. Multiple **case** patterns can be given, as long as they are separated with a | character. For example, the pattern

```
-a | -b | -c
```

would match −**a**, −**b**, or −**c**. The new Korn shell pattern matching formats also allow multiple **case** patterns to be given like this:

```
?(pattern1 | pattern2 | ... | patternn)
```
      matches zero or one occurrence of any pattern

```
*(pattern1 | pattern2 | ... | patternn)
```
      matches zero or more occurrences of any pattern

```
@(pattern1 | pattern2 | ... | patternn)
```
      matches exactly one occurrence of any pattern

```
+(pattern1 | pattern2 | ... | patternn)
```
      matches one or more occurrence of any pattern

```
!(pattern1 | pattern2 | ... | patternn)
```
      matches all strings except those that match any pattern

The for Command

The **for** command is used to execute commands a specified number of times. In programming terminology, this iterative execution of commands is called a *loop*, so you may also hear the **for** command referred to as a **for** loop. The basic syntax for the **for** command is:

for *variable* **in** *word1 word2 . . . wordn*
do
      commands
done

The *commands* are executed once for each *word*, and for each execution, *variable* is set to *word*. So if there were three words, the *commands* would be executed three times, with *variable* set to *word1* in the first execution, *word2* in the second execution, and *word3* in the third and last execution. Here is a simple **for** loop:

```
$ cat floop
integer LOOPNUM=1
for X in A B C
do
        print "Loop $LOOPNUM: X=$X"
        ((LOOPNUM+=1))
done
```

When executed, it prints out the loop number and the value of **X** for each loop.

```
$ floop
Loop 1: X=A
Loop 2: X=B
Loop 3: X=C
```

Remember the **kuucp** script that we wrote earlier in this chapter? We could use it with a **for** loop to **uucp** multiple files to a remote system like this:

```
$ for FILE in chap1 chap2 chap3
> do
>       print "Copying $FILE to ukas"
>       kuucp $FILE ukas
> done
Copying chap1 to ukas
Copying chap2 to ukas
Copying chap3 to ukas
```

Notice that this **for** loop was run from the prompt, and not from a script. Korn shell control commands are like any other commands, and can be entered at the command prompt. This is useful when you want to run something quickly without having to edit a file.

File name substitution, command substitution, and variable substitution can also be used to generate a list of word arguments for the **for** command. The first line of the previous command could have been given as:

```
for FILE in chap[1-3]
or
for FILE in $(ls chap[1-3])
or
CHAPS=$(ls chap[1-3])
for FILE in $CHAPS
```

The **$*** and **$@** variables can be used to loop on command-line arguments like this:

> **for** *variable* **in $***
> **do**
> > *commands*
>
> **done**

This is the same as:

> **for** *variable* **in $1 $2 $3 . . .**
> **do**
> > *commands*
>
> **done**

This idea could be used to make a Korn shell script that **uucp**'s a variable number of files to **ukas**:

```
$ cat myuucp
```

184

```
for FILE in $*
do
        print "Copying $FILE to ukas"
        kuucp $FILE ukas
done
```

Now to **uucp** just one file to **ukas**:

```
$ myuucp chap1
Copying chap1 to ukas
```

or all the **chap** files to **ukas**:

```
$ myuucp chap*
Copying chap1 to ukas
Copying chap2 to ukas
Copying chap3 to ukas
. . .
```

With no argument, nothing is displayed:

```
$ myuucp
$
```

Other for Syntax

The **for** command can also be used without the list of word arguments:

> **for** *variable*
> **do**
> > *commands*
> **done**

The *commands* are executed once for each positional parameter, and *variable* is set to each successive positional parameter. It is equivalent to:

> **for** *variable* **in** "$@"
> **do**
>   *commands*
> **done**

The **myuucp** script could be modified to use this format and still do the same thing.

```
$ cat myuucp
for FILE
do
        print "Copying $FILE to ukas"
        kuucp $FILE ukas
done
```

Use this format to enter the **for** command on one line:

> **for** *var* **in** *word1 word2 . . . wordn* **; do** *commands* **; done**
> or
> **for** *var* **; do** *commands* **; done**

Notice the **;** character before the **do** and **done** commands. This is needed so that the **do** and **done** commands are separated from the previous commands.

The if Command

The **if** command is used to execute commands if a given condition is true. The basic syntax of the **if** command is:

> **if** *command1*
> **then**
> > *commands*
> **fi**

If *command1* returns a zero exit status, then the commands between **then** and **fi** are executed. Otherwise, the commands are skipped. For example, if **ANSWER** is set to **YES**, then the **print** command is executed.

```
if [[ $ANSWER = YES ]]
then
        print "Ok, the answer is $ANSWER"
fi
```

Here is a Korn shell script that uses the **if** command to check if a file exists, before trying to copy it.

```
$ cat fileck
FILE=$1

if [[ -f $FILE ]]
then
        print "Copying $FILE to PUBDIR"
        cp $FILE /usr/spool/uucppublic
fi
```

We could add another **if** command to check the number of arguments. If there is less than one command-line argument, a usage message is printed and the script exits.

```
$ cat fileck
if (($# < 1))
then
        print "Usage: $0 file"
        exit 1
fi
FILE=$1
if [[ -f $FILE ]]
then
        print "Copying $FILE to PUBDIR"
        cp $FILE /usr/spool/uucppublic
fi
```

The command-line argument check in **fileck** could have been written using the **&&** operator like this:

```
(($# < 1)) && {print "Usage:$0 file"; exit 1;}
```

This version is more compact, albeit less readable than the previous one using the **if** command.

Use this format if you want to give an **if** command on one line:

if *command1* ; **then** *command2* ; **fi**

The **;** characters are needed to separate **then** and **fi** from the previous commands.

Other if Syntax: else

This form of the **if** command is used to execute one set of commands if a condition is true, or another set of commands if the condition is not true.

```
if command1
then
        commands
else
        commands
fi
```

If *command1* returns a zero exit status, then the commands between **then** and **else** are executed. If *command1* returns a non-zero exit status, then commands between **else** and **fi** are executed. In this example, if **ANSWER** is **YES**, then the **print** command is executed. Otherwise, it exits:

```
if [[ $ANSWER = YES ]]
then
        print "Ok, the answer is $ANSWER"
else
        exit 1
fi
```

We could add the **else** part to the **if** command in **fileck** to make sure the file existed before it was copied:

```
$ cat fileck
if (($# < 1))
then
        print "Usage: $0 file"
        exit 1
fi
FILE=$1

if [[ -f $FILE ]]
then
        print "Copying $FILE to PUBDIR"
        cp $FILE /usr/spool/uucppublic
else
        print "$FILE non-existent"
        exit 2
fi
```

189

Here is some sample output:

```
$ fileck
Usage: fileck file
$ fileck nofile
nofile non-existent
$ fileck log.out
Copying log.out to PUBDIR
```

Notice that **exit 1** was used for a usage error, while **exit 2** was used for the non-existent file error. In Korn shell scripts, especially large ones, it's a good idea to use different exit codes for different types of error conditions. It can be helpful in debugging.

```
$ fileck; print $?
Usage: fileck file
1
$ fileck nofile; print $?
nofile non-existent
2
$ fileck log.out; print $?
Copying log.out to PUBDIR
0
```

Other if Syntax: elif

This form of the **if** command is used to execute one set of commands if one condition is true, another set of commands if another condition is true, and so on, or else execute a set of commands if none of the conditions are true. The syntax for this **if** command is:

> **if** *command1*
> **then**
>   *commands*
> **elif** *command2*
> **then**

commands
. . .
elif *commandn*
then
commands
else
commands
fi

If *command1* returns a zero exit status, or *command2* returns a zero exit status, or *commandn* returns a zero exit status, then execute the commands corresponding to the **if/elif** that returned a zero exit status. Otherwise, if all the **if/elif** commands return a non-zero exit status, execute the commands between **else** and **fi**. This **if** format is much easier to explain with an example. The following Korn shell script checks how many users are logged on, and prints the appropriate message:

```
$ cat whonu
USERS=$(who | wc -l)
if ((USERS == 1))
then
      print "There is 1 user logged on."
elif ((USERS == 2))
then
      print "There are 2 users logged on."
elif ((USERS == 3))
then
      print "There are 3 users logged on."
else
      print "More than 4 users are logged on."
fi
```

If **USERS** equals **1**, **2**, or **3**, then the corresponding **if/elif..then** clause is executed:

```
$ whonu
There are 3 users logged on.
```

Otherwise, the **else** clause is executed:

```
$ whonu
More than 4 users are logged on.
```

if/elif **vs** case

When there are more than a few conditions to check, the **case** statement should be considered instead of **if/elif**. Not only is it more readable, but less code is actually needed. The **whonu** script could be written using a **case** statement like this:

```
USERS=$(who | wc -1)
case $USERS in
        1 )     print "There is 1 user logged on" ;;
        2 )     print "There are 2 users logged on" ;;
        3 )     print "There are 3 users logged on" ;;
        * )     print "There are 4 or more users \
                logged on" ;;
esac
```

The **whonu** script had thirteen lines of code using **if/elif/else**, and only seven lines of code using a **case** statement.

The while Command

Here is another type of looping command. The syntax for the **while** command is:

```
while command1
do
        commands
done
```

where *command1* is executed, and if the exit status is zero, the *commands* between **do** and **done** are executed. *Command1* is executed again, and if the exit status is zero, the *commands* between **do** and **done** are also executed again. This continues until *command1* returns a non-zero exit status. The **listargs** script loops on the command-line arguments. For each loop, the positional parameter **$1** is displayed, then the positional parameters are shifted. This continues until the number of positional parameters is **0**.

```
$ cat listargs
while (($# != 0))
do
        print $1
        shift
done
```

In the first loop, $# equals **4**, so the value of **$1** is printed and the positional parameters are shifted left once. In the second loop, $# equals **3** and the loop commands are executed again. This continues until the fourth loop, where after the **print** command, **shift** sets $# to **0**. Back at the top of the loop on the fifth try, $# is now **0**, so the *commands* between **do** and **done** are skipped. Execution continues with commands following **done**.

```
$ listargs A B C D
A
B
C
D
```

The following **while** command loops until there is no **LOCKFILE**.
Every 30 seconds, it wakes up to check if it's still there.

```
$ while [[ -f LOCKFILE ]]
> do
>     print "LOCKFILE still exists"
>     sleep 30
> done
LOCKFILE still exists
LOCKFILE still exists
. . .
```

You've heard the term "stuck in an endless loop". Well, here is one for
you. This command will loop forever, since the **true** command always
returns a zero exit status:

```
$ while true
> do
>     print "Looping forever..."
> done
Looping forever...
Looping forever...
Looping forever...
. . .
```

To give the **while** command on one line, use this format:

while *command1* **; do** *commands* **; done**

Just like with **if** and **for** command on-line formats, the **;** characters are needed to separate **do** and **done** from the previous commands.

The until **Command**

The **until** command is another looping command. It's like the **while** command, except that instead of looping while the condition is true, it loops while the condition is false. So you can think of it as the opposite of the **while** command. The syntax for the **until** command is:

> **until** *command1*
> **do**
>   *commands*
> **done**

where *commands* are executed until *command1* returns a zero exit status. To demonstrate the differences between the **until** and **while** commands, let's rewrite the **listargs** script. In this version that uses the **until** command, **$#** is checked if it equals **0** before looping. This is in contrast to the **while** version that checked if **$#** was *not* equal to **0** before looping.

```
$ cat listargs
until (($# == 0))
do
  print $1
  shift
done
```

Here is sample output:

```
$ listargs A B
A
B
```

Just to prove that almost any **while** loop can be rewritten using **until**, let's take the second example from the **while** section and rewrite it. Now instead of looping while **LOCKFILE** exists, we loop until it is non-existent:

```
$ until [[ ! -f LOCKFILE ]]
> do
>       print "LOCKFILE still exists"
>       sleep 30
> done
LOCKFILE still exists
LOCKFILE still exists
. . .
```

Even the forever loop can be rewritten using **until**:

```
$ until false
> do
>       print "Looping forever..."
> done
Looping forever...
Looping forever...
Looping forever...
. . .
```

Nested Loops

There is another type of loop that is used to loop inside of another loop. In programming terms, this is called a *nested loop*. For example, in this script, the loops work together to count from 10 to 35 in increments of 5. The **for i in 1 2 3** is called the *outer loop*, and the **for j in 0 5** is called the *inner loop*.

```
$ cat nloop
for i in 1 2 3
do
        for j in 0 5
        do
                print "$i$j"
        done
done
```

For each outer loop, the inner loop is executed twice. So, the first inner loop sets **j** to **0**, and the second inner loop sets **j** to **5**. This is repeated for each outer loop. The output explains this much better.

```
$ nloop
10
15
20
25
30
35
```

Breaking Out of Loops

You may want to exit from a loop before the loop condition is satisfied. This is where the **break** command comes in. It causes an exit from a loop-type command, but not from the entire script. Once you **break** from a loop, execution continues with the next command following the loop. For example, we could change the **listargs** script so that if a character argument was not given, the **while** loop would be terminated.

```
$ cat listargs
while (($# != 0))
do
        if [[ $1 = +([A-z]) ]]
        then
```

```
                       print "$1: arg ok"
                       shift
              else
                       print "$1: Invalid argument!"
                       break
              fi
      done
      print "Finished with args"
      . . .
```

Here is sample output. Notice that the command following the **while** loop is executed after the **break**. If you wanted to terminate the entire script, **exit** would have to be used instead of **break**.

```
$ listargs A 1 B
A: arg ok
1: Invalid argument!
Finished with args
```

The **break** command can also be used to exit from a nested loop using this format:

break *n*

where *n* specifies the *nth* enclosing loop to exit from. Here is a new version of the **nloop** script that breaks out of both loops if **i** equals **2** and **j** equals **0**:

```
$ cat nloop
for i in 1 2 3
do
       for j in 0 5
       do
              if (( i == 2 && j == 0 ))
              then
                     break 2
              else
                     print "$i$j"
              fi
       done
done
```

Now the output would be:

```
$ nloop
10
15
```

If **break** was used instead of **break 2**, then only the inner **for** loop would have been terminated, and execution would have continued with **i** set to **3** in the outer loop, and **j** set to **0** in the inner loop.

The continue **Command**

The **continue** command causes execution to continue at the top of the current loop. It's like the **break** command, except instead of exiting from the loop completely, only the remaining commands in the current loop are skipped. Let's change the **listargs** script so that instead of exiting on an invalid argument, it just prints out the error message, but continues execution.

```
$ cat listargs
while (($# != 0))
do
        if [[ $1 = +([A-z]) ]]
        then
                print "$1: arg ok"
                shift
        else
                print "$1: Invalid argument!"
                shift
                continue
        fi
done
print "Finished with args"
. . .
```

Here is more sample output. Notice that this time, even though an invalid argument was given, the next command-line argument was processed.

```
$ listargs A 1 B
A: arg ok
1: Invalid argument!
B: arg ok
Finished with args
```

Like with the **break** command, an integer argument can be given to the **continue** command to skip commands from nested loops.

The select **Command**

This is the last loop command we'll talk about. The **select** command is used to display a simple menu that contains numbered items, and a prompt message. The syntax for the **select** command is:

> **select** *variable* **in** *word1 word2 . . . wordn*
> **do**
> > *commands*
> **done**

where *word1* through *wordn* are displayed as numbered menu choices followed by a prompt (default **#?**). If the response is in the range **1** through *n*, then *variable* is set to the corresponding word, **REPLY** is set to the response, and the *commands* are executed. Execution continues until a **break**, **exit**, **return**, or EOF is encountered. Here is a simple **select** command that displays three numbered choices: **Choice-A**, **Choice-B**, and **Choice-C**.

```
$ cat stest
select i in Choice-A Choice-B Choice-C
do
        print "You picked selection $REPLY: $i"
done
```

At the first prompt, selection **1** is entered, so **REPLY** is set to **1**, **i** is set to **Choice-A** and the value is printed. At the next prompt, selection **3** is entered, so **REPLY** is set to **3**, **i** is set to **Choice-C** and the value of **i** is displayed again.

```
$ stest
1) Choice-A
2) Choice-B
3) Choice-C
#? 1
You picked selection 1: Choice-A
#? 3
You picked selection 3: Choice-C
```

Here the <RETURN> key is pressed, so the menu is just redisplayed:

```
#? <RETURN>
1) Choice-A
2) Choice-B
3) Choice-C
```

What if we enter an invalid choice?

```
1) Choice-A
2) Choice-B
3) Choice-C
#? 5
You picked selection 5:
#?
```

The **print** command was still run, but because an invalid choice was given, **i** was not set to anything. Let's add an **if** command to check the value inside the loop.

```
$ cat stest
select i in Choice-A Choice-B Choice-C
do
        if [[ $i = Choice-[A-C] ]]
        then
                print "You picked selection $REPLY: $i"
        else
                print "$REPLY: Invalid choice!"
                continue
        fi
done
```

Now it works!

```
$ stest
1) Choice-A
2) Choice-B
3) Choice-C
#? 2
You picked selection 2: Choice-B
#? 5
5: Invalid choice!
#? 1
You picked selection 1: Choice-A
```

A different prompt can be used by setting the **PS3** variable like this:

```
$ typeset -x PS3="Enter selection>"
```

Now when **stest** is run again, the new message prompt is displayed:

```
$ stest
1) Choice-A
2) Choice-B
3) Choice-C
Enter selection>3
You picked selection 3: Choice-C
```

The **select** and **case** commands are used in this Korn shell script to provide a simple menu interface to a few Unix commands. Notice that the **LIST FILES** portion runs in a subshell so that the prompt (**PS3**) can be changed without having to reset it each time for the rest of the script.

```
$ cat smenu
PS3="Enter selection>"
select CMD in "CURRENT DIRECTORY NAME" \
"LIST FILES" MAIL DONE
do
     case $CMD in
         CURRENT* )
               pwd ;;
         LIST* )
               (  PS3="List which directory?"
               select DIR in HOME PUBDIR TOOLS DONE
               do
                    case $DIR in
                      HOME )
                              ls $HOME ;;
                      PUBDIR)
                              ls $PUBDIR ;;
                      TOOLS )
                              ls ~/tools ;;
                      DONE ) break ;;
                      * )     print "Bad choice"
                              break ;;
                    esac
               done  ) ;;
         MAIL )
               mail ;;
         DONE )
               break ;;
         * )  print "Invalid choice"
               break ;;
     esac

done
```

The first menu displays three numbered choices: **CURRENT DIRECTORY NAME**, **LIST FILES**, **MAIL**, and **DONE**. If you enter **1**, **pwd** is executed:

```
$ smenu
1) CURRENT DIRECTORY NAME
2) LIST FILES
3) MAIL
4) DONE
Enter selection>1
/home/anatole/tbin
```

If **2** is given, then another menu is displayed that gives you four numbered choices: **HOME**, **PUBDIR**, **TOOLS**, and **DONE**. Choices **1** through **3** cause contents of a directory to be listed, while choice **4** takes you back to the main menu.

```
1) CURRENT DIRECTORY NAME
2) LIST FILES
3) MAIL
4) DONE
Enter selection>2
1) HOME
2) PUBDIR
3) TOOLS
4) DONE
List which directory?1
NEWS    dialins              nohup.out    proc.doc
asp            mail          pc           tools
bin            newauto.bat                pers
List which directory?4
1) CURRENT DIRECTORY NAME
2) LIST FILES
3) MAIL
4) DONE
Enter selection>
```

If **3** is entered, **mail** is invoked, and if **4** is entered, we exit from the script:

```
Enter selection>3
No mail.
1) CURRENT DIRECTORY NAME
2) LIST FILES
3) MAIL
4) DONE
Enter selection>4
$
```

Other select Syntax

The **select** command can also be used without the list of *word* arguments:

> **select** *variable*
> **do**
> > *commands*
> **done**

It functions the same way as the previous **select** syntax, except that the positional parameters are displayed as numbered menu choices from 1 to *n*, instead of the words from the word list. It is equivalent to:

> **select** *variable* **in** "$@"
> **do**
> > *commands*
> **done**

The select **Menu Format**

The format of the **select** menu can be controlled by assigning values to the **LINES** and **COLUMNS** variables. The **LINES** variable specifies the number of lines to use for the menu. The menu choices are displayed vertically until about two-thirds of lines specified by **LINES** are filled. The **COLUMNS** variable specifies the menu width. This example displays how the **COLUMNS** and **LINES** variables affect a **select** menu. With the default setting, the **stest** menu is displayed like this:

```
$ stest
1) Choice-A
2) Choice-B
3) Choice-C
Enter selection>
```

If **LINES** is set to **2**, the menu choices are displayed on one line:

```
$ typeset -x LINES=2
$ stest
1) Choice-A           2) Choice-B      3) Choice-C
Enter selection>
```

while if **COLUMNS** is set to **50**, the menu choices are displayed closer together on one line:

```
$ typeset -x COLUMNS=50
$ stest
1) Choice-A  2) Choice-B  3) Choice-C
Enter selection>
```

If these variables are not explicitly set, the default used is **80** for **COLUMNS**, and **24** for **LINES**.

Comments

Comments are used in Korn shell scripts for debugging and documentation purposes. They provide a way to include text that is not executed. Good commenting makes it easier for you or someone else to read your scripts. Words beginning with # up to end of the current line are treated as comments and ignored. The **listargs** script could be commented like this:

```
$ cat listargs
#       listargs — List arguments

# Loop on each argument
while (($# != 0))
do

        # Make sure argument is alphanumeric
        if [[ $1 = +([A-z]) ]]
        then
                print "$1: arg ok"
                shift
        else
                print "$1: Invalid argument!"
                shift
                continue
        fi
done
```

The # character can also be used to make your Korn shell scripts compatible with other shells. Any Korn shell script that begins with:

> #!*interpreter*

is run by the given interpreter. So, for the C and Bourne shell users on your system, if you want your shell scripts to be run by the Korn shell (assuming it is installed in **/bin**), make sure they start with this:

```
#!/bin/ksh
```

Input/Output Commands

The Korn shell provides a number of input/output commands, which are covered in the following sections.

The print **Command**

You've already seen this command a hundred times since it was introduced in Chapter 3, but here it is again. This is a more formal definition of the command that describes the other things it can be used for. The **print** command displays *arguments* according to *options* with this format:

> **print** [*options*] *arguments*

Without options, special characters, or quotes, each argument is displayed separated with a space, and all the arguments are terminated with a newline:

```
$ print X           Y           Z
X Y Z
```

Notice that all the extra whitespace between the arguments was truncated. We could keep the whitespace by enclosing the arguments in quotes like this:

```
$ print "X          Y           Z"
X           Y           Z
```

Escape Characters

There are a number of special escape characters that allow you to format the **print** arguments. For example, to display arguments on separate lines, instead of using multiple **print** commands:

```
$ print X; print Y; print Z
X
Y
Z
```

Table 8.6: print **Escape Characters**

\a	bell character
\b	backspace
\c	line without ending newline (remaining arguments ignored)
\f	formfeed
\n	newline
\r	return
\t	tab
\v	vertical tab
****	backslash
\0x	8-bit character whose ASCII code is the 1-, 2-, or 3-digit octal number x

the arguments could be separated with the newline escape character
\n:

```
$ print "X\nY\nZ"
X
Y
Z
```

The **print** arguments could be double-spaced like this:

```
$ print "X\n\nY\n\nZ"
X

Y

Z
```

Make sure escape characters are enclosed in quotes. Otherwise they
are not interpreted correctly. Here, without the quotes, **\n** is
interpreted as an escaped **'n'**, and not as the newline escape character:

```
$ print X\nY\nZ
XnYnZ
```

The \ character can also be used to quote the escape characters:

```
$ print X\\nY\\nZ
X
Y
Z
```

A tab can be displayed with the **\t** escape character:

```
$ print "X\tY\tZ"
X       Y       Z
```

The **\c** escape character causes the trailing newline to be dropped
from the output. It is often used to create prompts.

```
$ print "Enter choice: \c"
Enter choice: $
```

Notice that the command prompt was displayed following the argument, and not on the next line.

The **\r** escape character causes a carriage return without line feed to be displayed and can be used to format non-fixed length data. This command prints an **R** on the right side, then the **\r** escape character moves the cursor back to the beginning of the same line and prints an **L** on the left side followed by **TEXT**:

```
$ print     '                     R\rLTEXT'
LTEXT           R
$ print '                 R\rL       TEXT'
L           TEXTR
```

Notice that the **L** and **R** characters are lined up, while **TEXT** is in a different position in both commands. In the Bourne shell, this is the easiest way to display non-fixed-length data in a fixed-length format. In the Korn shell, the same display could be created by using a fixed-length variable. First, variable **X** is set to ten-character wide, left-justified with a value of **TEXT**. Notice that {}'s must be given to delimit the variable name **X**:

```
$ typeset −L10 X=TEXT
$ print "L${X}R"
LTEXT           R
```

To right-justify the value of **X**, the right-justify attribute is set:

```
$ typeset −R10 X
$ print "L${X}R"
L                TEXTR
```

This **print** command displays a message and beeps:

```
$ print "Unexpected error!\a"
Unexpected error!<BEEP>
```

Using octal codes, the previous command could be given like this:

```
$ print "Unexpected error!\007"
Unexpected error!<BEEP>
```

print **Options**

The **print** command has a number of options that affect the way its arguments are interpreted. The − option is used if you want to **print** arguments that begin with a − character. In the next command, without the − argument, **−Z** is interpreted as an option and causes an error to be returned:

```
$ print −Z
/bin/ksh: print: bad options(s)
$ print − −Z
−Z
```

The **−n** option is used when you don't want the trailing newline to be printed:

```
$ print −n "Enter choice:"
Enter choice:$
```

This is equivalent to:

Table 8.7: print **Options**

–	treat everything following – as an argument, even if it begins with –.
–n	do not add a ending newline to the output.
–p	redirect the given arguments to a co-process.
–r	ignore the \ escape conventions.
–R	ignore the \ escape conventions; do not interpret –arguments as options (except **–n**).
–s	redirect the given arguments to the history file.
–un	redirect arguments to file descriptor n. If the file descriptor is greater than **2**, it must first be opened with the **exec** command. If n is not specified, the default file descriptor is **1**.

```
$ print "Enter choice:\c"
Enter choice:$
```

The **–r** option causes the special escape characters to be ignored. Here, \t is printed without interpretation as the tab character:

```
$ print -r 'a\tb'
a\tb
```

The **–R** option is the same as **–r**, except that it also causes arguments beginning with – (except **–n**) to be interpreted as regular arguments and not as options.

```
$ print -R - '-a\tb'
- -a\tb
```

The **–s** option redirects the given arguments to the history file.

```
$ print -s "This is a history entry"
$ history -2
165    This is a history entry
166    history -2
```

The **–u** option is used to redirect arguments to a specific file descriptor. Instead of displaying a message to standard error like this:

```
$ print "This is going to standard error >&2
This is going to standard error
```

the **print –u2** command can be used.

```
$ print -u2 "This is going to standard error"
This is going to standard error
```

The echo **Command**

The **echo** command displays its arguments on standard output and is provided for compatibility with the Bourne shell. In the Korn shell, **echo** is an exported alias set to "**print –**".

The exec **Command**

The **exec** command is used to perform I/O redirection with file descriptors **0** through **9** using this format:

> **exec** *I/O-redirection-command*

The I/O redirection performed by the **exec** command stays in effect until specifically closed, changed, or if the script or shell terminates. We could use this idea to direct standard output to a file. First, let's start a subshell. You know that **1>std.out** directs standard output to **std.out**. So if we put the **exec** command in front of it, *all* subsequent standard output will be redirected.

```
$ ksh
$ exec 1>std.out
```

Now anything that goes to standard output is redirected to **std.out** until file descriptor 1 is specifically reset.

```
$ pwd
$ whoami
$ print "Where is this going?"
```

Notice that standard error is still attached to your terminal:

```
$ print —u2 "This is going to standard error"
This is going to standard error
```

Let's exit from the subshell, and take a look at the output file:

```
$ exit
$ cat std.out
/home/anatole/bin
anatole
Where is this going?
```

Here, file **redir.out** is opened as file descriptor 5 for reading and writing:

```
$ exec 5<>redir.out
```

Now the **print** command writes something to file descriptor 5:

```
$ print -u5 "This is going to fd 5"
```

and the **cat** command reads from it:

```
$ cat <&5
This is going to fd 5
```

To finish up, we use another **exec** to close file descriptor 5:

```
$ exec 5<&-
```

Any subsequent attempts to write to it or read from it would generate this error message:

```
$ print -u5 "Trying to write to fd 5 again"
/bin/ksh:  5: bad file unit number
```

Standard input can be taken from a file like this:

```
exec 0<file
```

Commands could be read in from file, and it would be almost as if you typed them at your terminal.

The **exec** command can also be used to replace the current program with a new one. For example, you know that if you wanted to run the C shell, you could invoke it as a subshell like this:

```
$ csh
{aspd:1}
```

But why have the extra parent shell process hanging around if you don't need it? In this case, the **exec** command could be used to *replace* the current shell with the C shell:

```
$ exec csh
{aspd:1}
```

Now if you exited from the C shell, you would be logged out.

Here is another application. Remember the **smenu** script from the **select** command section? You could make a full-blown UNIX interface menu out of it by adding some more commands. If you wanted to set it up as a login shell, this would need to be added to a **.profile** file:

```
exec smenu
```

and execution would be restricted to **smenu**.

The read **Command**

The **read** command is used to read input from a terminal or file. The basic format for the **read** command is:

> **read** *variables*

where a line is read from standard input. Each word in the input is assigned to a corresponding variable, so the first variable gets the first word, the second variable the second word, and so on. Here, "**This is output**" is read in to the variables **X**, **Y**, and **Z**. The first word of the input is **This**, so it is assigned to the first variable **X**. The second word is **is**, so it is assigned to the second variable **Y**. The third word is **output**, so it is assigned to **Z**.

```
$ print "This is output" | read X Y Z
$ print $X
This
$ print $Y
is
$ print $Z
output
```

If there aren't enough variables for all the words in the input, the last variable gets all the remaining words. This command is the same as the last one, except that an extra string "**again**" is given.

```
$ print "This is output again " | read X Y Z
$ print $X
This
$ print $Y
is
```

Because there are four strings, but only three variables, **Z** gets the remaining unassigned words:

rocess

continuation

the command

escriptor *n*. If

ter than **2**, it

ith the **exec**

specified, the

If one variable argument is given to the **read** command, it gets assigned the entire line. Here, the variable **LINE** is set to the entire line:

```
$ print "This is output again" | read LINE
$ print $LINE
This is output again
```

The **kuucp** script could be modified so that it prompted for a source file and target system. This is just a bare-bones script that demonstrates the use of the **read** command. A usable version is included in Appendix D.

```
$ cat kuucp
PUBDIR=${PUBDIR:-/usr/spool/uucpublic}

# Prompt for source file
print -n "Enter source file: "
read SOURCE

# Prompt for remote system name
print -n "Enter remote system name: "
read RSYS

print "Copying $SOURCE to $RSYS!$PUBDIR/$SOURCE"
uucp $SOURCE $RSYS!$PUBDIR/$SOURCE
```

Here is some sample output:

```
$ kuucp
Enter source file: rt.c
Enter remote system name: mhhd
Copying rt.c to mhhd!/usr/spool/uucppublic/rt.c
```

Reading Input from Files

Besides reading input from your terminal, the **read** command is also used to read input from a file. The **read** command by itself will only read one line of input, so you need a looping command with it. To read in the contents of a file, use this format:

> **exec 0<***file*
> **while read** *variable*
> **do**
> > *commands*
> **done**

The **exec** command opens *file* for standard input, and the **while** command causes input to be read a line at a time until there is no more input. If the **exec** open on *file* fails, the script will exit with this error message:

> *script-name*: *file*: **cannot open**

Here is a stripped-down version of **kcat**. It is a simple version of the UNIX **cat** command. It displays the given file on standard output one line at a time.

```
$ cat kcat
exec 0<$1
while read LINE
do
        print $LINE
done
```

In terms of performance, it is about 3-4 times slower than the UNIX **cat** command, but it will do for demonstration purposes. Here is sample output:

```
$ kcat test.input
1: All work and no play makes Jack a dull boy.
2: All work and no play makes Jack a dull boy.
3: All work and no play makes Jack a dull boy.
. . .
```

The real version of the **kcat** command is listed in **Appendix D**.

Here is an alternate format that will also work for reading input from files:

> **cat** *file* | **while read** *variable*
> **do**
>   *commands*
> **done**

On the systems tested, the **exec** format for reading input from files was about 40-60 times faster than the last version above. It may be different on your system, but that's still a significant performance improvement.

The IFS **Variable**

The **read** command normally uses the **IFS** (Internal Field Separator) variable as the word separators. The default for **IFS** is space, tab, or newline character, in that order, but it can be set to something else. It is useful for when you want to read data that is not separated with whitespace. In this example, **IFS** is set to a comma:

```
$ IFS=,
```

then the **print** arguments are separated with the new word separator for **read**:

```
$ print 'This,is,output' | read WORD1 WORD2 WORD3
$ print $WORD1 $WORD2 $WORD3
This is output
```

By setting **IFS** to **:**, the fields in the **/etc/passwd** file could be read into separate variables.

```
$ cat ifs_test
IFS=:
exec 0</etc/passwd
while read -r NAME PASS UID GID COMM HOME   SHELL
do
        print "Account name=    $NAME
Home directory=     $HOME
Login Shell= $SHELL"
done
```

Here is sample output:

```
$ ifs_test
Account name=root
Home directory=      /
Login Shell= /bin/ksh
Account name=anatole
Home directory=        /home/anatole
Login Shell= /bin/ksh
. . .
```

More with read

Another format for the **read** command is:

> **read** *options* [*variables*]

where input is read and assigned to *variables* according to the given options. The **−u** option is used to read input from a specific file descriptor. If the file descriptor is greater than **2**, then it must first be opened with the **exec** command. Let's look at the stripped-down version of **kcat** again. It could be changed to prompt to continue before displaying the next line like this:

```
$ cat kcat
exec 0<$1
while read LINE
do
        print $LINE
        print −n "Do you want to continue?"
        read ANSWER
        [[ $ANSWER = @([Nn])* ]] && exit 1
done
```

Here is the **test.input** file again:

```
$ cat test.input
1: All work and no play makes Jack a dull boy.
2: All work and no play makes Jack a dull boy.
3: All work and no play makes Jack a dull boy.
. . .
```

When the new version of **kcat** is run, the output looks strange. Can you figure out the problem? The reason is that we redirected standard input from **test.input**, but we are also expecting the input to **ANSWER** from standard input. In the first loop, line 1 from **test.input** is assigned to **LINE**. The next **read** command, which is inside the loop, reads the next line into **ANSWER**. In the second loop, we're up to line 3, so it gets assigned to **LINE**, and so on.

```
$ kcat test.input
1: All work and no play makes Jack a dull boy.
Do you want to continue?3: All work and no play
makes Jack a dull boy.
Do you want to continue?
. . .
```

Instead of redirecting standard input (file descriptor **0**) from **test.input**, we could redirect it from another file descriptor and read it using the **−u** option. Then it wouldn't interfere with **read ANSWER** which is expecting input from standard input. Here is the new and improved version:

```
$ cat kcat
exec 4<$1
while read -u4 LINE
do
        print $LINE
        print −n "Do you want to continue?"
        read ANSWER
        [[ $ANSWER = @([Nn])* ]] && exit 1
done
```

Now it works.

```
$ kcat test.input
1: All work and no play makes Jack a dull boy.
Do you want to continue?<RETURN>
2: All work and no play makes Jack a dull boy.
Do you want to continue?<RETURN>
3: All work and no play makes Jack a dull boy.
Do you want to continue?n
$
```

The **–s** option saves a copy of the input in the history file. Here is an example:

```
$ print "This is a history entry" | read -s HVAR
```

Just to make sure, let's look at both the history file:

```
$ history -2
170     This is a history entry
171     history -2
```

and **HVAR**:

```
$ print $HVAR
This is a history entry
```

Reading Input Interactively

The **read** command allows input to be read interactively using this format:

> **read** *name?prompt*

where *prompt* is displayed on standard error and the response is read into *name*. So instead of using two commands to display a prompt and read the input:

```
$ print -n "Enter anything: "
$ read ANSWER
```

The same thing can be done with one command.

```
$ read ANSWER?"Enter anything: "
Enter anything: ANYTHING
```

Here is **ANSWER**:

```
$ print $ANSWER
ANYTHING
```

Let's change the **kuucp** script (again) so that this format of the read command was used:

```
$ cat kuucp
PUBDIR=${PUBDIR:-/usr/spool/uucpublic}

read SOURCE?"Enter source file: "
read RSYS?"Enter remote system name: "

print "Copying $SOURCE to $RSYS!$PUBDIR/$SOURCE"
uucp $SOURCE $RSYS!$PUBDIR/$SOURCE
```

The REPLY variable

If no variables are given to the **read** command, the input is automatically assigned to the **REPLY** variable. Here, **ANYTHING** is read into **REPLY**:

```
$ print ANYTHING | read
$ print $REPLY
ANYTHING
```

Miscellaneous Programming Features

The next sections cover some miscellaneous programming features.

The . Command

The **.** command reads in a complete file, then executes the commands in it as if they were typed in at the prompt. This is done in the current shell, so any variable, alias, or function settings stay in effect. It is typically used to read in and execute a profile, environment, alias, or functions file. Here the **.profile** file is read in and executed:

```
$ . .profile
```

The following example illustrates the difference between executing files as Korn shell scripts and reading/executing them using the **.** command. The **.test** file sets the variable **X**:

```
$ cat .test
X=ABC
```

When the **.test** file is executed as a Korn shell script, variable **X** is not defined in the current environment, because scripts are run in a subshell:

```
$ ksh .test
$ print $X

$
```

After the **.test** file is read in and executed using the **.** command, notice that the variable **X** is still defined:

```
$ . .test
```

```
$ print $X
ABC
```

The standard search path, **PATH**, is checked if the file is not in the current directory.

Functions

Functions are a form of commands like aliases, scripts, and programs. They differ from Korn shell scripts, in that they do not have to be read in from the disk each time they are referenced, so they execute faster. Functions differ from aliases, in that functions can take arguments. They provide a way to organize scripts into routines in the same way as in other high-level programming languages. Since functions can have local variables, recursion is possible. Functions are most efficient for commands with arguments that are invoked fairly often, and are defined with the following format:

> **function** *name* {
> > *commands*
>
> }

To maintain compatibility with the Bourne shell, functions can also be declared with this POSIX-style format:

> *function-name*() {
> > *commands*
>
> }

These types of functions have many limitations compared to Korn shell style functions, such as no support for local variables.

Here is a function called **md** that makes a directory and **cd**'s to it:

```
$ cat md
function md {
        (($# < 1)) && { print "$0: dir"; exit 1; }
        mkdir $1 && cd $1
        pwd
}
```

To be able to execute a function, it must first be read in. This is done with the **.** command:

```
$ . md
```

Now the **md** function can be invoked. Here, we try it with the **dtmp** directory:

```
$ md dtmp
/home/anatole/dtmp
```

Functions are executed in the current environment, so any variables and option settings are available to them.

Returning Function Exit Status

The **return** command is used to return from a function to the invoking Korn shell script and pass back an exit value. The syntax for the **return** command is:

> **return**
> or
> **return** *n*

where *n* is a return value to pass back to the invoking Korn shell script or shell. If a return value is not given, the exit status of the last command is used. To exit from a function and the invoking Korn shell script, use the **exit** command from inside the function.

Scope and Availability

By default, functions are not available to subshells. This means that a regular function that was read in your working environment, **.profile** file, or environment file would not be available in a Korn shell script. To export a function, use the **typeset –fx** command:

> **typeset –fx** *function-name*

To make a function available across separate invocations of the Korn shell, include the **typeset –fx** *function-name* command in the environment file.

Using Functions in Korn Shell Scripts

Functions are very useful in Korn shell scripts. Not only because you can organize scripts into routines, but they also provide a way to consolidate redundant sequences of commands. For example, instead printing out an error message and exiting each time an error condition is encountered, an all-purpose error function can be created. The arguments passed to it are the message to display and the exit code:

```
$ cat error
function error {
        print ${1:-"unexplained error encountered"}
        exit ${2:-1}
}
```

If function **error** is called without arguments, then you get the default error message "**unexplained error encountered**" and a default exit code of 1. Now on a non-existent file error, function **error** could be called like this:

```
error "$FILE:non-existent or not accessible" 3
```

It can save quite a bit of code, and it's easier to maintain. One more thing: because functions need to be read in before they can be invoked, it's a good idea to put all function definitions at the top of Korn shell scripts.

Function Variables

All function variables, except those explicitly declared locally within the function with the **typeset** command, are inherited and shared by the calling Korn shell script. In this example, the **X**, **Y**, and **Z** variables are set within and outside of the function **f**:

```
$ cat ftest
X=1
function f {
        Y=2
        typeset Z=4
        print "In function f, X=$X, Y=$Y, Z=$Z"
        X=3
}
f
print "Outside function f, X=$X, Y=$Y, Z=$Z"
```

Notice that when executed, all the variable values are shared between the function and calling script, except for variable **Z**, because it is explicitly set to a local function variable using the **typeset** command. The value is not passed back to the calling Korn shell script:

```
$ ftest
In function f, X=1, Y=2, Z=4
Outside function f, X=3, Y=2, Z=
```

The current working directory, aliases, functions, traps, and open files from the invoking script or current environment are also shared with functions.

Displaying Current Functions

The list of currently available functions are displayed using the **typeset –f** command:

```
$ typeset -f
function _cd
{
        'cd' $1
        PS1="$PS0$PWD> "
}
function md
{
        mkdir $1 && 'cd' $1
}
```

Autoloading Functions

To improve performance, functions can be specified to autoload. This causes the function to be read in when invoked, instead of each time a Korn shell script is invoked, and is used with functions that are not invoked frequently. To define an autoloading function, use the **typeset –fu** *function-name* command. Here, **lsf** is made an autoloading function:

```
$ typeset -fu lsf
```

The **autoload** alias can also be used to define an autoloading function. On most systems, it is preset to **typeset –fu**.

The **FPATH** variable which contains the pathnames to search for autoloading functions must be set and have at least one directory for autoloading functions to work.

Discipline Functions

Discipline functions are a new feature in KornShell 93. They are a special type of function used to manipulate variables. They are defined but not specifically called. Rather, they are called whenever the variable associated with the function is accessed.

There are some specific rules as to how discipline functions are named and accessed. First of all, discipline functions are named using this syntax:

name.function

Notice the function has two parts separated with a dot. The first part corresponds to the name of a variable, and the second part must be **get**, **set**, or **unset**. These correspond to the following operations on the variable:

get whenever the base discipline variable is accessed
set whenever the base discipline variable is set
unset whenever the base discipline variable is unset

For example, the discipline function **LBIN.get**, **LBIN.set**, **LBIN.unset** is called whenever the variable **LBIN** is accessed, set, or unset.

All three discipline functions are optional, so not all need to be specified.

Within a discipline function, the following special reserved variables can be used:

.sh.name name of current variable
.sh.value value of the current variable
.sh.subscript name of the subscript (if array variable)

From a practical perspective, discipline functions are often used to help debug by tracing the setting and current value of variables in running scripts. Here is a function that can be used to trace setting the value of **X**:

```
function X.set {
        print "DEBUG: ${.sh.name} = ${.sh.value}"
}
```

Discipline functions are also a good place to centralize your variable assignment validation rules. Here is a function that checks to make sure that X it set to a number between 3 and 10:

```
function X.set {
    if (( .sh.value<3 || .sh.value >10 ))
    then
        print "Bad value for ${.sh.name}: ${.sh.value}"
    fi
}
```

Note that **builtin** functions can also be used as additional discipline functions.

FPATH

The **FPATH** variable contains a list of colon-separated directories to check when an autoloading function is invoked. It is analogous to **PATH** and **CDPATH**, except that the Korn shell checks for function files, instead of commands or directories. Each directory in **FPATH** is searched from left-to-right for a file whose name matches the name of the function. Once found, it is read in and executed in the current environment. With the following **FPATH** setting, if an autoloading function **lsf** was invoked, the Korn shell would check for a file called **lsf** in **/home/anatole/.fdir**, then **/etc/.functions**, and if existent, read and execute it:

```
$ print $FPATH
/home/anatole/.fdir:/etc/.functions
```

There is no default value for **FPATH**, so if not specifically set, this feature is not enabled.

Removing Function Definitions

Functions are removed by using the **unset −f** command. Here, the **rd** function is removed:

```
$ unset −f rd
```

and when invoked, it is now undefined:

```
$ rd
/bin/ksh: not found
```

Multiple function names can also be given to the **unset −f** command.

Traps

The **trap** command is used to execute commands when the specified signals are received.

> **trap** *commands signals*

Trap commands are useful in controlling side effects from Korn shell scripts. For example, if you have a script that creates a number of temporary files, and you hit the <Break> or <Delete> key in the middle of execution, you may inadvertently leave the temporary files. By setting a **trap** command, the temporary files can be cleaned up on an error or interrupt.

The **trap_test** script creates some files, then removes them when an interrupt is received. Notice that the **trap** command is surrounded in single quotes. This is so that the **FILES** variable is evaluated when the signal is received, not when the **trap** is set.

```
$ cat trap_test
trap 'print "$0 interrupted - removing temp  files" ;\
rm —rf $FILES; exit 1' 1 2
FILES="a b c d e f"
touch $FILES
sleep 100
$ trap_test
Ctl-c
trap_test interrupted - removing temp files
```

If an invalid **trap** is set, an error is generated.

Ignoring Signals

The **trap** command can be used to ignore signals by specifying null as the command argument:

    trap "" *signals*

This could be used to make all or part of a Korn shell script uninterruptable using normal interrupt keys like **Ctl-c**. This **trap** command causes signals 2 and 3 to be ignored:

```
$ trap "" 2 3
```

The "" argument must be in this type of **trap** command, otherwise the trap is reset.

Resetting Traps

The **trap** command can also be used to reset traps to their default action by omitting the command argument:

> **trap** – *signals*
> or
> **trap** *signals*

Exit and Function Traps

A **trap** can be set to execute when a Korn shell script exits. This is done by using a **0** or **EXIT** as the signals argument to the **trap** command:

> **trap** '*commands*' **0**
> or
> **trap** '*commands*' **EXIT**

This could be used to consolidate Korn shell script cleanup functions into one place. The **trap_test** script contains a **trap** command that causes a message to be printed out when the script finishes executing:

```
$ cat trap_test
trap 'print exit trap being executed' EXIT
print "This is just a test"
$ trap_test
This is just a test
exit trap being executed
```

If set within a function, the commands are executed when the function returns to the invoking script. This feature is used to implement the C shell **logout** function in **Appendix C**.

Debugging with trap

The **trap** command can be helpful in debugging Korn shell scripts. The special signal arguments **DEBUG** and **ERR** are provided to execute **trap** commands after each command or only when commands in a script fail. This is discussed in the next section.

Trap Signal Precedence

If multiple traps are set, the order of precedence is:

- **DEBUG**
- **ERR**
- Signal Number
- **EXIT**

Trapping Keyboard Signals

The Korn shell traps **KEYBD** signals (sent when you type a character) and automatically assigns the following reserved variables:

.sh.edchar	contains last character of key sequence
.sh.edtext	contains current input line
.sh.edmode	contains NULL character (or escape character

Table 8.9: Korn Shell Debugging Options

set −e, set −o errexit
        execute **ERR** trap (if set) on non-zero exit status from any commands

set −n, set −o noexec
        read commands without executing them

set −v, set −o verbose
        display input lines as they are read

set −x, set −o xtrace
        display commands and arguments as they are executed

typeset −ft *function*
        display the commands and arguments from *function* as they are executed

---

        if user in command mode)

.sh.edcol   contains position within the current line

Debugging Korn Shell Scripts

The Korn shell provides a number of options that are useful in debugging scripts: **noexec**, **verbose**, and **xtrace**. The **noexec** option causes commands to be read without being executed. It is used to check for syntax errors in Korn shell scripts. The **verbose** option causes the input to be displayed as it is read. The **xtrace** option causes the commands in a script to be displayed as they are executed. This is the most useful, general debugging option.

Enabling Debug Options

These options are enabled in the same way other options are enabled.
You can invoke the script with the option enabled:

```
$ ksh —option script
```

invoke a subshell with the option enabled:

```
$ ksh —option
$ script
```

set the option globally before invoking the script:

```
$ set —option
$ script
```

or set the option within the script.

```
$ cat script
. . .
set —option
. . .
```

Debugging Example

Here is a Korn shell script called **dbtest**. It sets variable **X** to **ABC**,
then checks the value and prints a message. Notice that there is an
unmatched double quote on line 2:

```
$ cat dbtest
X=ABC
if [ $X" = "foo" ]
then
        print "X is set to ABC"
fi
```

When run with the **noexec** option, the syntax error is flagged:

```
$ ksh -n dbtest
dbtest[2]: syntax error at line 2: `"' unmatched
```

When an error is detected while executing a Korn shell script, the name of the script or function, the error message, and the line number enclosed in []'s are displayed. For functions, the line number relative to the beginning of the function is displayed. The **dbtest** script is fixed and run again with the **noexec** option:

```
$ ksh -n dbtest
$
```

No error is flagged this time, but also notice that no output is generated. This is because the **noexec** option causes the commands to be read, but not executed. Now, the **dbtest** script is run with the **xtrace** option:

```
$ ksh -x dbtest
+ alias -x echo=print -
+ alias -x vi=SHELL=/bin/sh vi
+ PS0=!:
+ PS1=!:/home/anatole/bin>
+ typeset -fx cd md
+ typeset -x EDITOR=vi
+ X=ABC
+ [ X = ABC ]
+ print X is set to ABC
X is set to ABC
```

Now there is a lot of output, most of which is execution trace output from processing of the environment file. The value of **PS4** is displayed in front of each line of execution trace. If not explicitly reset, the default is the + character. The line number can also be included in the debug prompt by including **LINENO** in the **PS4** setting.

```
$ typeset —x PS4='[$LINENO] '
```

Now the line number is displayed in brackets in the trace output:

```
$ ksh —x dbtest
[11] alias —x echo=print —
[12] alias —x vi=SHELL=/bin/sh vi
[13] PS0=!:
[14]  PS1=!:/home/anatole/bin>
[15] typeset —fx cd md
[16] typeset —x EDITOR=vi
[1] X=ABC
[2] [ X = ABC ]
[4] print X is set to ABC
X is set to ABC
```

When the **dbtest** script is run without any debugging options, this is the output:

```
$ dbtest
X is set to ABC
```

Debugging with trap

The **trap** command can also be helpful in debugging Korn shell scripts. The syntax for this type of **trap** command is:

Table 8.10: Some Frequently-Used Signals

0	shell exit	**3**	quit
1	hangup	**15**	terminate
2	interrupt		

> **trap** *commands* **DEBUG**
> or
> **trap** *commands* **ERR**

If the **trap** command is set with **DEBUG**, then the trap commands are executed after each command in the script is executed. The following **trap** command causes **pwd** to be executed after each command if the variable **DB_MODE** is set to **yes**, otherwise a normal trap is executed.

```
if [[ $DB_MODE = yes ]]
then
        trap "pwd" DEBUG
else
        trap "rm -rf $TMPFILE; exit 1" 1 2 15
fi
```

If set with **ERR** and the **errexit** (−e) option is enabled, the trap is executed after commands that have a non-zero (unsuccessful) exit status. This **case** statement causes a different trap to be set, depending on the debug flag. If the debug flag is **0**, then a normal trap is set, which removes some temporary files on normal or abnormal termination. If the debug flag is **1**, then an **ERR** trap is set, which causes the line number to be displayed when an error occurs. If the debug flag is **2**, then a **DEBUG** trap is set, which causes the line number and current working directory to be displayed.

```
case $DB_FLAG in
        0 )     # Default trap - perform cleanup
                trap "rm —rf $FILES; exit 1" 0 1 2 15 ;;

        1 )     # Execute trap for failed commands only
                set —o errexit
                trap 'print Error at $LINENO' ERR ;;

        2 )     # Execute trap for all commands
                trap 'print At $LINENO; pwd' DEBUG ;;

        * )     # Invalid debug flag
                print "Invalid debug flag" ; exit 1 ;;
    esac
```

Parsing Command-line Arguments

Here is an alternative to using **case** to parse command-line arguments: the **getopts** command. It works with the **OPTARG** and **OPTIND** variables to parse command-line arguments using this format:

> **getopts** *optstring name args*
> or
> **getopts** *optstring name*

where *optstring* contains the list of legal options, *name* is the variable that will contain the given option letter, and *args* is the list of arguments to check. If not given, the positional parameters are checked instead. If an option begins with a +, then + is prepended to *name*. In all other cases, *name* is set to the option letter only.

There are some requirements on option format with the **getopts** command. Options must begin with a + or −, and option arguments can be separated from the options with or without whitespace. This **getopts** command specifies that **a**, **b**, and **c** are valid options, and **OPT** will be set to the given option:

> **getopts abc OPT**

A **:** after an option in *optstring* indicates that the option needs an argument, and **OPTARG** is set to the option argument. This **getopts** command specifies that the **a**, **b**, and **c** are valid options, and that options **a** and **c** have arguments:

> **getopts a:bc: OPT**

If *optstring* begins with a **:**, then **OPTARG** is set to any invalid options given, and *name* is set to **?**. If an option argument is missing, *name* is set to "**:**". In the following Korn shell script, the **getopts** command is used in conjunction with the **case** command to process options and their arguments. The "**:a:bc:**" options string specifies that options **a** and **c** need arguments, and that invalid options are processed.

```
$ cat getopts_test
while getopts :a:bc: OPT
do
      case $OPT in
            a|+a ) print "$OPT received" ;;
            b|+b ) print "$OPT received" ;;
            c|+c ) print "$OPT received" ;;
            : )    print "$OPTARG needs arg" \exit ;;
            \? )   print "$OPTARG:bad option"exit ;;
      esac
done
```

Here the **+b** and **−b** options are given:

```
$ getopts_test +b −b
+b received
b received
```

The **c** option needs an argument, so an error message is displayed:

```
$ getopts_test -c
c needs arg
```

Here, an invalid option is given:

```
$ getopts_test -x
x: bad option
```

The **OPTIND** variable is set by the **getopts** command to the index of the next argument. It is initialized to **1** when a new function, Korn shell, or script is invoked.

More with Here Documents

The here document feature is also used in shareware software distribution. Multiple here documents are put into one file, and when executed, generate all the modules separately. Here is an example Korn shell archive file called **archive_test**:

```
$ cat archive_test
print "Extracting a"
cat >a <<-END
      This is file a.
END
print "Extracting b"
cat >b <<-END
      This is file b.
END
print "Extracting c"
cat >c <<-END
      This is file c.
END
```

When executed, it generates three files: **a**, **b**, and **c**.

```
$ ls
archive_test
$ archive_test
Extracting a
Extracting b
Extracting c
```

This feature also allows you to edit a file from within a Korn shell script. The **htest** script edits the file **tmp** and inserts one line:

```
$ cat htest
ed — tmp <<EOF
a
This is a new line
.
w
q
EOF
```

After the **htest** Korn shell script is run, here is the result:

```
$ htest
$ cat tmp
This is a new line
```

The <<– operator is the same as <<, except that leading tab characters from each standard input line including the line with *word* are ignored. This is used to improve program readability by allowing the here document to be indented along with the rest of the code in Korn shell scripts.

The here document feature is also useful for generating form letters. The **hmail** script shows how to send a mail message to multiple users using this feature.

```
$ cat hmail
for i in terry larry mary
do
        mail $i <<-END
                $(date)
                Have a good holiday $i!
        END
done
```

Co-Processes

Co-processes are commands that are terminated with a |**&** character. They are executed in the background, but have their standard input and output attached to the current shell. The **print −p** command is used to write to the standard input of a co-process, while **read −p** is used to read from the standard output of a co-process. Here, the output of the **date** command is read into the **DATE** variable using the **read −p** command:

```
$ date |&
[2] 241
$ read −p DATE
$ print $DATE
Thu Jul 18 12:23:57 PST 1996
```

Co-processes can be used to edit a file from within a Korn shell script. In this example, we start with file **co.text**:

```
$ cat co.text
This is line 1
This is line 2
This is line 3
```

It is edited using a co-process, so the job number and process id are returned:

Table 8.11: Co-Processes

command |**&**	execute *command* in the background with the standard input and output attached to the shell.
n<**&p**	redirect input from co-process to file descriptor *n*. If *n* is not specified, use standard input.
n>**&p**	redirect output of co-process to file descriptor *n*. If *n* is not specified, use standard output.
print −p	write to the standard input of a co-process.
read −p	read from the standard output of a co-process.

```
$ ed — co.text |&
[3] 244
```

The command (display line 3) is written to the co-process using **print −p**. The output of the **ed** command is then read into the **LINE** variable using **read LINE**:

```
$ print −p 3p
$ read —p LINE
$ print $LINE
This is line 3
```

The next commands delete line 2, then send the write and quit commands to **ed** via the co-process:

```
$ print -p 2d
$ print -p w
$ print -p q
[3] + Done            ed - co.text |&
```

After editing from the co-process, **co.text** file looks like this:

```
$ cat co.text
This is line 1
This is line 3
```

Chapter 9: Miscellaneous Commands

The following sections cover miscellaneous Korn shell commands. Many of these are used in Korn shell scripts. The rest work with your environment and system resources.

The : Command

The : command is the null command. If specified, arguments are expanded. It is typically used as a no-op, to check if a variable is set, or for endless loops. The : command here is used to check if **LBIN** is set.

```
$ : ${LBIN:?}
LBIN: parameter null or not set
```

If given in a Korn shell script, it would cause it to exit with an error if **LBIN** was not set.

This example counts the number of lines in the file **ftext**, then prints the total. The : command is used as a no-op, since we only want to print the total number of lines after the entire file has been read, not after each line.

```
$ integer NUM=0
$ exec 0<ftext && while read LINE && ((NUM+=1))
> do
>       :
> done; print $NUM
7
```

In the following Korn shell script, the : command is used to loop continuously until **fred** is logged on.

```
$ cat fred_test
while :
do
        FRED=$(who | grep fred)
        if [[ $FRED != "" ]]
        then
                print "Fred is here!"
                exit
        else
                sleep 30
        fi
done
```

The eval Command

The **eval** command reads and executes commands using the following format:

eval *commands*

It causes *commands* to be expanded twice. For simple commands, there is no difference in execution with or without **eval**:

```
$ eval print ~
/home/anatole
```

Here is a more complicated command that illustrates the use of **eval**. We want the contents of the **stext** file redirected when variable **X** is accessed.

```
$ cat stext
She sells seashells by the seashore.
```

First, variable **X** is set to "**<stext**":

```
$ X="<stext"
```

When the value of **X** is printed using simple variable expansion, it generates an error:

```
$ cat $X
<stext: No such file or directory
```

Using the **eval** command, **X** is first expanded to **<stext**, then the command **cat <stext** is executed. This causes the contents of **stext** to be displayed:

```
$ eval cat $X
She sells seashells by the seashore.
```

In this Korn shell script, the **eval** command is used to display the last command-line argument:

```
$ cat eval_test
print "Total command-line arguments is $#"
print "The last argument is $$#"
```

What you want is $# to be expanded first to the number of arguments, then $*n* to be expanded to the value of the last argument. Without the **eval** command, this is the output of **eval_test**:

```
$ eval_test a b c
Total command-line arguments is 3
The last argument is 581#
```

The output **581#** is generated because **$$** is first expanded to the process id. Using the **eval** command to expand the **print** command twice, we get the correct result.

```
$ cat eval_test
print "Total command-line arguments is $#"
print "The last argument is $(eval print \$$#)"
$ eval_test1 a b c
The number of command-line arguments is 3
The last argument is c
```

The \ is needed so that the **$** character is ignored on the first expansion. After the first expansion, the **$(eval print \$$#)** command becomes **$(print $3)**. This is then expanded to **c**.

The export **Command**

The **export** command sets and/or exports variables to the environment. It is equivalent to **typeset –x**, except when used within functions. Here, the **PATH** variable is set and exported:

```
$ export PATH=$PATH:/usr/5bin
```

Multiple variables can be given to the **export** command. In this example, the variables **A**, **B**, **C**, and **D** are set and/or exported:

```
$ export A B=1 C D=2
```

If no arguments are specified, the **export** command lists the names and values of exported variables:

```
$ export
EDITOR=vi
HOME=/home/anatole
LOGNAME=anatole
PATH=/usr/bin:/usr/ucb:/usr/etc:/usr/5bin:
PWD=/home/anatole/asp/pubs/ksh/v2
SHELL=/bin/ksh
TERM=sun
USER=anatole
```

The false **Command**

The **false** command returns a non-zero exit status. That's all. It is often used to generate infinite **until** loops. In some versions of the Korn shell, **false** is a preset alias **let 0**. In either case, it does the same thing.

The *newgrp* **Command**

The **newgrp** command changes the group id and is equivalent to '**exec /bin/newgrp** *group*'. In this example, the group id is changed from **users** to **networks**:

```
$ id
uid=100(anatole)  gid=101(users)
$ newgrp networks
uid=100(anatole)  gid=12(networks)
```

Without arguments, **newgrp** resets the group-id to the default:

```
$ newgrp
uid=100(anatole)  gid=101(users)
```

The *pwd* **Command**

The **pwd** command prints the current working directory. It is a Korn shell built-in command and is equivalent to the **print −r −** **$PWD** command.

The *readonly* **Command**

The **readonly** command sets the value and/or **readonly** attribute of variables. It is equivalent to the **typeset −r** command, except that when used within a function, a local variable is not created. This command sets **X** to readonly and assigns it a value of **1**:

256

```
$ readonly X=1
```

This is equivalent to:

```
$ typeset —r X=1
```

Multiple variables can be given to the **readonly** command.

```
$ readonly X Y=1 Z=2
```

If no arguments are given, a list of readonly variables and their values
is displayed:

```
$ readonly
Z=1
Y=1
Z=2
PPID=175
```

The set Command

Besides manipulating Korn shell options, the**set** command can be used
to display a list of your local and exported variables.

```
$ set
EDITOR=vi
ENV=${HOME:—.}/.env
FCEDIT=/bin/ed
HOME=/home/anatole
LOGNAME=anatole
MAILCHECK=600
PATH=:/usr/bin:/usr/ucb:/usr/5bin
PPID=180
. . .
```

It can also be used to "manually" reset positional parameters. For example:

```
$ set X Y Z
```

would set **$1** to **X**, **$2** to **Y**, **$3** to **Z**, and **$#** to **3**:

```
$ print $1 $2 $3 $#
X Y Z 3
```

The positional parameters **$@** and **$*** would be set **X Y Z**:

```
$ print $*
X Y Z
$ print $@
X Y Z
```

The **$*** and **$@** parameters are basically the same, except for the way they are expanded when surrounded with double quotes. The positional parameters in **$@** are interpreted as separate strings, while in the **$***, they are interpreted as a single string. Using **$@**, the **wc** command counts three separate strings

```
$ print "$@" | wc —w
3
```

while with **$***, only one string is counted:

```
$ print "$*" | wc —w
1
```

To manually set positional parameters that begin with the – character, use the **set –** command.

```
$ set − −X −Y −Z
$ print − $*
−X −Y −Z
```

All the positional parameters can be unset with the **set ——** command:

```
$ set A B C
$ print $*
A B C
$ set − −
$ print $*

$
```

The *time* **Command**

The **time** command is a built-in command in the Korn shell and functions the same as the Unix **times** command. Here, the **ls** command is timed. It indicates the amount of elapsed, user, and system time spent executing the **ls** command:

```
$ time ls /usr/spool/uucppublic
mail

real    0m0.33s
user    0m0.05s
sys     0m0.18s
```

The times *Command*

The **times** command displays the amount of time the current Korn shell and child processes. The first line shows the total user and system time (in hundredths of a second) for the current Korn shell, while the second line shows the totals for the child processes.

The true *Command*

The **true** command does one thing: return a zero exit status. It is often used to generate infinite loops for argument-processing. In some versions of the Korn shell, **true** is a preset alias ":". It also returns a zero exit status.

The ulimit *Command*

The **ulimit** command manipulates system resource limits for current and child processes using the following format:

> **ulimit** [*options*]
> or
> **ulimit** [*options*] *n*

where *n* indicates to set a resource limit to *n* (except with the **−a** option). If *n* is not given, the specified resource limit is displayed. If no option is given, the default **−f** (file size limit) is used. Here, all the current resource limits are displayed:

Table 9.1: ulimit **Options**

−a	displays all the current resource limits
−c *n*	set the core dump size limit to *n* 512-byte blocks
−d *n*	set the data area size limit to *n* kilobytes
−f *n*	set the child process file write limit to *n* 512-byte blocks (default)
−m *n*	set the physical memory size limit to *n* kilobytes
−s *n*	set the stack area size limit to *n* kilobytes
−t *n*	set the process time limit to *n* seconds

```
$ ulimit −a
time(seconds)      unlimited
memory(kbytes)     unlimited
data(kbytes)       4294901761
stack(kbytes)      2048
file(blocks)       unlimited
coredump(blocks)   unlimited
```

This command sets the core dump size limit to 500 blocks:

```
$ ulimit −c 500
```

To disable generation of core dumps, the dump size should be set to 0 blocks:

```
$ ulimit -c 0
```

To display the current file size write limit, use **ulimit** without arguments:

```
$ ulimit
unlimited
```

Table 9.1 lists the **ulimit** options. If a size argument is not given, the current limit is displayed.

The **ulimit** command is system dependent. Some systems may have different resource limits, and some may not allow changing resource limits. Check your local system documentation for discrepancies.

The umask *Command*

The **umask** command sets the file-creation mask using this format:

umask *mask*

where *mask* is an octal number or symbolic value that correspond to the permissions to be disabled. Here, the write and execute permissions for group and others are removed:

```
$ umask 033
$ touch tmp
$ ls -l tmp
-rw-r--r--  1 root   9 Sep  2 11:18 tmp
```

This **umask** command adds write permission to the group:

```
$ umask 013
$ touch tmp1
$ ls -l tmp1
-rw-rw-r--  1 root  9 Sep  2 11:19 tmp1
```

To remove read permission for other using symbolic format:

```
$ umask o-r
$ touch tmp2
-rw-rw----  1 root  9 Sep  2 11:23 tmp2
```

With no arguments, **umask** displays the current value. This **umask** is set to remove write permission for group and others:

```
$ umask
022
```

The whence *Command*

The **whence** command is used to display information about a command, like if it is an alias, built-in Korn shell command, function, reserved Korn shell word, or just a normal Unix command. The format for the **whence** command is:

> **whence** *name*
> or
> **whence −v** *name*

where *name* is the command or whatever you want to get information about. Here, the **whence** command shows that **history** is set to **fc −l**:

```
$ whence history
fc -l
```

The **-v** option causes more information to be provided about the command. Now we see that **history** is an exported alias:

```
$ whence -v history
history is an exported alias for fc -l
```

and **until** is a keyword:

```
$ whence -v until
until is a keyword
```

For compatibility with the Bourne shell, a preset alias **type** is set to **whence -v**.

```
$ type md
md is an exported function
```

Appendix A: Sample .profile File

This appendix contains a sample **.profile** file. Notice that the environment variables are set and exported with one **typeset** command. This speeds up processing of the **.profile** file.

```
#
#       Sample .profile File
#

# Set/export environment variables
typeset -x CDPATH=:$HOME:/usr/spool \
      EDITOR=vi \
      ENV=${HOME:-.}/.env \
      HISTFILE=$HOME/.history \
      HISTSIZE=200 \
      HOME=/home/anatole \
      LOGNAME=anatole \
      MAILCHECK=300 \
      MAILPATH=~/inbox:/usr/spool/mail/$LOGNAME \
      PAGER=$(whence more) \
```

```
        PATH=${PATH#:}:/usr/etc:$NEWS/bin:  \
        PS1='!:$PWD> '  \
        PS4='[$LINENO]+ '  \
        SHELL=/bin/ksh  \
        TERM=sun  \
        TMOUT=600  \
        USER=$LOGNAME

# Set global options
set -o noclobber -o markdirs +o bgnice

# Execute commands from the ~/.logout file on exit
trap '. ~/.logout' EXIT
```

Appendix B: Sample Environment File

This appendix contains a sample environment file. It sets the global functions, aliases, and prompt variable.

```
#
#       Sample env File
#

# Function md - make a directory and _cd to it
function md {
        mkdir $1 && _cd $1
}

# Set up the echo alias
alias -x echo='print -'

# Set temporary prompt variable to the command number
# followed by a colon
PS0='!:'
```

```
# Function _cd - changes directories, then sets the
# command prompt to: "command-number:pathname>"
function _cd {

        if (($# == 0))
        then
                'cd'
                PS1="$PS0$PWD> "
        fi

        if (($# == 1))
        then
                'cd' $1
                PS1="$PS0$PWD> "
        fi

        if (($# == 2))
        then
                'cd' $1 $2
                PS1="$PS0$PWD> "
        fi
}

# Alias the cd command to the _cd function
alias -x cd=_cd

# Export the _cd and md functions
typeset -fx _cd md
```

Appendix C: C Shell Functionality

Directory Functions

Miscellaneous Commands

This appendix contains the source code listings for the C Shell directory management functions, and other miscellaneous C Shell commands.

Directory Functions

These Korn shell functions implement the C shell directory management commands: **dirs**, **popd**, and **pushd**. They can be put into a separate **cshfuncs** file and read in with the **.** command when necessary. Their basic functionality is:

dirs	display directory stack
popd	remove directory stack entry and **cd** to it
pushd	add directory stack entry and **cd** to it

The **dirs** function lists the current directory stack.

With no argument, the **popd** function removes the top entry (previous working directory) from the directory stack and changes directory to it. If a +*n* argument is given, then the *nth* directory stack entry (*nth* previous working directory) is removed.

With no argument, the **pushd** function switches the top two entries (current and previous working directory) and changes directory to the previous working directory. This is equivalent to "**cd −**". If a directory argument is given, **pushd** puts the directory on the top of the directory stack and changes directory to it. If a +*n* argument is given, **pushd** puts the *nth* directory stack entry (*nth* previous working directory) on the top of the stack and changes directory to it.

```
#
#       Sample C Shell Directory Management Functions
#

# Function fcd - verify accessibility before changing
# to target directory
function fcd
{
        # Make sure directory exists
        if [[ ! -d $1 ]]
        then
                print "$1: No such file or directory"
                return 1
        else
                # Make sure directory is searchable
                if [[ ! -x $1 ]]
                then
                        print "$1: Permission denied"
                        return 1
                fi
        fi

        # Otherwise change directory to it
        cd $1
        return 0
}
```

```
# Function dirs - display directory stack
function dirs
{
      # Display current directory and directory stack
      print "$PWD ${DSTACK[*]}"
}


# Function pushd - add entry to directory stack
function pushd
{
      # Set stack depth (number of stack entries)
      integer DEPTH=${#DSTACK[*]}

      case $1 in

      "" )# No argument - switch top 2 stack elements
            if ((${#DSTACK[*]} < 1))
            then
                    print "$0: Only one stack entry."
                    return 1
            else
                    fcd ${DSTACK[0]} || return
                    DSTACK[0]=$OLDPWD
                    dirs
            fi
            ;;


      +@([1-9])*([0-9]) )
            # Number argument 1-999* - move entry to top
            # of directory stack and cd to it
            integer ENTRY=${1#+}
            if ((${#DSTACK[*]} < $ENTRY))
            then
                    print "$0: Directory stack not that deep"
                    return 1
            else
                    fcd ${DSTACK[ENTRY-1]} || return
                    DSTACK[ENTRY-1]=$OLDPWD
                    dirs
            fi
            ;;
```

```
        * )     # Directory argument - verify argument
                # before changing directory and adjusting
                # rest of directory stack
                fcd $1 || return
                until ((DEPTH == 0))
                do
                        DSTACK[DEPTH]=${DSTACK[DEPTH-1]}
                        ((DEPTH-=1))
                done
                DSTACK[DEPTH]=$OLDPWD
                dirs
                ;;
        esac
}


# Function popd - remove entry from directory stack
function popd
{
        # Set stack depth (number of stack entries)
        integer i=0 DEPTH=${#DSTACK[*]} ENTRY=${1#+}
        case $1 in

        "" )
                # No argument - discard top stack entry
                if ((${#DSTACK[*]} < 1))
                then
                        print "$0: Directory stack empty."
                        return 1
                else
                        fcd ${DSTACK[0]} ||  return
                        while ((i < (DEPTH-1)))
                        do
                                DSTACK[i]=${DSTACK[i+1]}
                                ((i+=1))
                        done
                        unset DSTACK[i]
                        dirs
                fi
                ;;

        +@([1-9])*([0-9]) )
                # Number argument 1-999* - discard nth
                # stack entry
                if ((${#DSTACK[*]} < ENTRY))
```

```
        then
                print "$0: Directory stack not that deep"
                return 1
        else
                while ((ENTRY < DEPTH))
                do
                        DSTACK[ENTRY-1]=${DSTACK[ENTRY]}
                        ((ENTRY+=1))
                done
                unset DSTACK[ENTRY-1]
                dirs
        fi
        ;;

# Invalid argument given
*  )    print "$0: Invalid argument."
        return 1
        ;;

esac
}
```

Miscellaneous Commands

The following sections contain Korn shell equivalents of some
miscellaneous C shell commands and functions.

The .logout File

In the C shell, commands in the ~/.logout file are executed on
exit. If the following command is added to the ~/.profile file,
then the same thing will happen in the Korn shell:

```
trap '. ~/.logout' EXIT
```

The chdir **Command**

The C shell **chdir** command changes to the specified directory and can be set to a Korn shell alias like this:

```
alias chdir='cd'
```

The logout **Command**

The C shell **logout** command is equivalent to the **exit** command. It can be set to a Korn shell alias:

```
alias logout='exit 0'
```

The setenv **Command**

The C shell **setenv** command is used to set/display variables and can be invoked like this:

setenv   display a list of variables
setenv *variable*
                   set *variable* to null
setenv *variable value*
                   set *variable* to *value*, then export it

It can be set to a Korn shell function like this:

```
function setenv {
      set -o allexport
      typeset TMP="$1=$2"
      eval $(print ${1+$TMP})
      typeset -x $1
}
```

The source **Command**

The C shell **source** reads and executes a file in the current environment. It can be aliased to the Korn shell . command:

```
alias source=.
```

Appendix D: Sample Korn Shell Scripts

Display Files - **kcat**
Interactive **uucp** - **kuucp**
Basename - **kbasename**
Dirname - **kdirname**
Display Files with Line Numbers - **knl**
Find Words - **match**
Simple Calculator - **kcalc**
Search for Patterns in Files - **kgrep**
Calendar Program - **kcal**

This appendix contains listings for some Korn shell scripts. The source for these scripts can also be downloaded from our Web site listed in the Preface.

Display Files - kcat

Here is a simple Korn shell version of the Unix **cat** command. It is only 3-4 times slower than the Unix version (on a 100-line file), because it uses the **exec** command for the file I/O.

```
#!/bin/ksh
#
#       kcat - Korn shell version of cat
#

# Check usage
if (($# < 1))
then
        print "Usage: $0 file ..."
        exit 1
fi

# Process each file
while (($# > 0))
do
        # Make sure file exists
        if [[ ! -f $1 ]]
        then
                print "$1: non-existent or not accessible"
        else
                # Open file for input
                exec 0<$1
                while read LINE
                do
                        # Display output
                        print $LINE
                done
        fi

        # Get next file argument
        shift
done
```

Interactive uucp - kuucp

Here is an interactive version of the **uucp** command. Instead of looking for a system name in the uucp systems file using **grep**, the remote system name is verified by using file I/O substitution and Korn shell patterns.

```ksh
#!/bin/ksh
#
#      kuucp - Korn shell interactive uucp
#

# Check usage
if (($# > 0))
then
      print "Usage: $0"
      exit 1
fi

# Set variables
PUBDIR=${PUBDIR:-/usr/spool/uucpublic}

# This sets UUSYS to the contents of the HDB-UUCP
# Systems file.  It may be different on your system.
UUSYS=$(</usr/lib/uucp/Systems)

# Get source file
read SOURCE?"Enter source file: "

# Check source file
if [[ ! -f $SOURCE ]]
then
      print "$SOURCE: non-existent or not accessible"
      exit 2
fi

# Get remote system name
read RSYS?"Enter remote system name: "

# Check remote system name.  It looks for a pattern
# match on the system name in the UUSYS file
#
```

```
# For the Bourne shell or older versions
# of Korn shell, this could be given as:
#       if [[ $(grep ^$RSYS $UUSYS) != "" ]]
if [[ $UUSYS != *$RSYS* ]]
then
        print "$RSYS: Invalid system name"
        exit 2
fi

print "Copying $SOURCE to $RSYS!$PUBDIR/$SOURCE"
uucp $SOURCE $RSYS!$PUBDIR/$SOURCE
```

Basename - *kbasename*

This is the Korn shell version of the Unix **basename** command. It is
used to return the last part of a pathname. A suffix can also be given
to be stripped from the resulting base directory. The substring feature
is used to get the basename and strip off the suffix.

```
#!/bin/ksh
#
#       kbasename - Korn shell basename
#

# Check arguments
if (($# == 0 || $# > 2))
then
        print "Usage: $0 string [suffix]"
        exit 1
fi

# Get the basename
BASE=${1##*/}

# See if suffix arg was given
if (($# > 1))
then
        # Display basename without suffix
        print ${BASE%$2}
```

```
else
        # Display basename
        print $BASE
fi
```

Dirname - kdirname

Here is the Korn shell version of the Unix **dirname** command. It returns a pathname minus the last directory. As in **kbasename**, the substring feature does all the work.

```
#!/bin/ksh
#
#       kdirname - Korn shell dirname
#

# Check arguments
if (($# == 0 || $# > 1))
then
        print "Usage: $0 string"
        exit 1
fi

# Get the dirname
print ${1%/*}
```

Display Files with Line Numbers - knl

This is a simple Korn shell version of the Unix **nl** command. It displays line-numbered output.

```
#!/bin/ksh
#
#       knl - Korn Shell line-numbering filter
#

# Initialize line number counter
integer LNUM=1

# Check usage
if (($# == 0))
then
        print "Usage: $0 file . . ."
        exit 1
fi

# Process each file
for FILE
do
        # Make sure file exists
        if [[ ! -f $FILE ]]
        then
                print "$FILE: non-existent or not readable"
                exit 1
        else
                # Open file for reading
                exec 0<$FILE

                # Read each line, print out with line number
                while read -r LINE
                do
                        print "$LNUM: $LINE"
                        ((LNUM+=1))
                done
        fi

        # Reset line number counter
        LNUM=1
done
```

Find Words - match

The **match** command uses Korn shell pattern-matching characters to find words in a dictionary. It can be used to help with crossword puzzles, or test your patterns.

```
#!/bin/ksh
#
#       match - Korn shell word-finder
#

# Check usage
if (($# < 1 || $# > 2))
then
      print "Usage: $0 pattern [file]"
      exit 1
fi


# Check/set DICT to word dictionary
: ${DICT:=${2:-/usr/dict/words}}

# Open $DICT for input
exec 0<$DICT

# Read each word into WORD
while read WORD
do
      # This command didn't work on all systems.  If
      # it doesn't on yours, use this instead of
      # exec 0<$DICT:
      #     cat $DICT | while read WORD
      #
      # If WORD matches the given pattern,
      # print the match
      [[ $WORD = $1 ]] && print - $WORD
done
```

Simple Calculator - *kcalc*

This Korn shell script implements a simple **expr**-like command. Arithmetic expressions are passed in as arguments, and the result is displayed. Parentheses for grouping must be escaped.

```
#!/bin/ksh
#
#       kcalc - Korn Shell calculator
#

# Initialize expression
integer EXPR

# Check usage
if (($# == 0))
then
        print "$0: Must provide expression arguments."
        exit 1
fi

# Set/evaluate EXPR
((EXPR=$*))

# Print result
print $EXPR
```

Searching for Patterns in Files - *kgrep*

This is the Korn shell version of the Unix **grep** command. The **−b** option is not supported, and the **−i** flag causes multi-character expressions to be matched in both all upper-case or all lower-case (**kgrep −i AbC test** matches **AbC**, **abc**, or **ABC** in **test**, but not **aBc** or other permutations). Here are the supported options:

      −c   display the number of lines that contain
                          the given pattern

−i	ignore case of letters during comparison (see above)
−l	display only names of files with matching lines once
−n	display the output with line numbers
−s	do not display error messages
−v	display all lines, except those that match the given expression

```ksh
#!/bin/ksh
#
#       kgrep - Korn Shell grep program
#

# Declare default flags
CFLAG= IFLAG= LFLAG= NFLAG= SFLAG= VFLAG=
integer LNUM=0 COUNT=0 TOT_COUNT=0

# Disable file name generation
set -f

# Check usage
if (($# < 2))
then
      print "Usage: $0 [options] expression files"
      exit 1
fi

# Parse command-line options
while true
do
      case $1 in
            -b* )  print "b option not supported" ;;
            -c* )  CFLAG=1 ;;
            -i* )  IFLAG=1 ;;
            -l* )  LFLAG=1 ;;
            -n* )  NFLAG=1 ;;
            -s* )  SFLAG=1 ;;
            -v* )  VFLAG=1 ;;
            -* )          print "$0: unknown flag $1"
                          exit 2 ;;
```

```
                    * )                 PATTERN=$1
                                        shift
                                        break ;;
        esac
        shift
done

# Set no-print flags
NOPRINT=$VFLAG$CFLAG$LFLAG
V_NOPRINT=$CFLAG$LFLAG

# Set upper/lower pattern
typeset -u UCPATTERN=$PATTERN
typeset -l LCPATTERN=$PATTERN

# Check for file arg
if (($# == 0))
then
        print "Must have file argument"
        exit 1
fi

# Process files
for FILE
do
     # Open file for standard input
     exec 0<$FILE

     # Read each line in file
     while read -r LINE
     do
             # Increment line number counter
             ((LNUM+=1))

             # Check each line for the pattern
             case $LINE in

                 # See if PATTERN matches input
                 *$PATTERN* )
                         if [[ $VFLAG = "" ]]
                         then
                                 [[ $NOPRINT = "" ]] && \
print -r "${NFLAG:+$LNUM:}$LINE"
                                 ((COUNT+=1))
                         fi ;;
```

```
                    # For -i option: See if
                    # upper/lowercase patterns match
                    *$UCPATTERN* | *$LCPATTERN* )
                         if [[ $IFLAG != "" ]]
                         then
                              if [[ $VFLAG = "" ]]
                              then
                                 [[ $NOPRINT = "" ]] && \
print -r "${NFLAG:+$LNUM:}$LINE"
                                 ((COUNT+=1))
                              fi
                         else
                              if [[ $VFLAG != "" ]]
                              then
                                 [[ $V_NOPRINT = "" ]] && \
 print -r "${NFLAG:+$LNUM:}$LINE"
                                 ((COUNT+=1))
                              fi
                         fi ;;
                    # For -v option: See if
                    # pattern doesn't match
                    !(*$PATTERN*) )
                         if [[ $VFLAG != "" ]]
                         then
                              [[ $V_NOPRINT = "" ]] && \
print -r "${NFLAG:+$LNUM:}$LINE"
                              ((COUNT+=1))
                         fi ;;
            esac
       done

       # Process -l flag
       # Display just the filename
       # if there are matches in this file
       if [[ $LFLAG != "" ]] && ((COUNT))
       then
            print - $FILE
       fi

       # Increment the total match counter
       # for when kgrep'ing multiple files
       ((TOT_COUNT+=COUNT))

       # Reset the line number counter for the next file
       LNUM=0
```

```
        # Reset the match counter for the next file
        COUNT=0
done

# Process -c flag
# Display the total number of matches found
[[ $CFLAG != "" ]] && print $TOT_COUNT

# Exit successfully
exit 0
```

Calendar Program - *kcal*

This is a Korn shell script that implements a menu-driven calendar
program. It supports addition, deletion, modification, and listing of
calendar entries. It also provides the ability to find the calendar entry
for the current day and list all calendar entries.

```
#!/bin/ksh
#
#       kcal - Korn Shell calendar program
#

# Process errors
function error {
        print ${1:-"unexplained error encountered"}
        exit ${2}
}

# Check arguments
if (($# > 0))
then
        error "Usage: $0" 1
fi

# Use environment variable setting or default
: ${CALFILE:=$HOME/.calfile}
```

```
# Create calendar file if non-existent; flag
# creation error
if [[ ! -f $CALFILE ]]
then
       print "Creating default $HOME/.calfile"
       > $HOME/.calfile || error "$HOME/.calfile: \
       cannot create" 1
fi

# Variable declaration/assignment
typeset DATE= LINE= ENTRY= REPLY="yes" \
PAGER=$(whence more)  CLEAR=$(whence clear)

# Set trap to not allow interrupts
trap '$CLEAR; print "\aInterrupt ignored - use \
menu to quit.  Press <Return> to continue."; \
read TMP; $CLEAR' INT QUIT

# Set EXIT trap - perform cleanup
trap 'rm -rf /tmp/.FOUND$$ /tmp/.CHANGE$$ \
/tmp/.DEL$$' EXIT

# Check the date
function checkdate {
     while true
     do
          # Prompt for date
          read DATE?"Enter date in mmdd[yy] format (default
today):"
          case $DATE in

               # Default - use todays date
               "" ) DATE=$(date +%m-%d-%y)
                   break ;;

               # Check the given date
               +([0-9]) )
                   case ${#DATE} in
                        4|6)# Set month to first 2 chars
                        typeset -L2 MO=$DATE
```

```
                    # Check length for year;
                    # 4 = mmdd, 6 = mmddyy
                    if (($ {#DATE} == 6))
                    then
                           # Set TMP to get date
                           typeset -L4 TMP=$DATE

                           # Get day
                           typeset -R2 DA=$TMP

                           # Get year
                           typeset -R2 YR=$DATE
                    else
                           # Get day
                           typeset -R2 DA=$DATE

                           # Set to current year
                           YR=$(date +%y)
                           DATE=$DATE$YR
                    fi

                    # Now check indiv values
                    # Day must be in range 01-31
                    if ((DA < 01 || DA > 31))
                    then
                           print "$DA: invalid day \
                           format - try again"
                           continue
                    fi
                           # Month must be 01-12
                           if ((MO < 01 || MO > 12))
                           then
                              print "$MO: invalid \
                              month format - try again"
                              continue
                           fi

                           # Set date format mm-dd-yy
                           DATE=$MO-$DA-$YR
                           break ;;

              * )   # Invalid format
                    print "$DATE: invalid date \
                    format - try again" ;;

        esac ;;
```

```
        # Invalid date given
        * ) print "$DATE: invalid format - try again" ;;

        esac
        done
}

# Add new calendar entry
function addentry {
        $CLEAR
        ENTRY="$DATE"

        # For existent entry, just add more data
        COUNT=$(grep -c "^$DATE" $CALFILE)
        if ((COUNT > 0))
        then
                changeentry
                return
        fi

        # Prompt for input
        print "Enter info for $DATE: (enter <Return> by itself
when finished)"
        while true
        do
                read LINE?"=>"
                if [[ -n $LINE ]]
                then
                        ENTRY="$ENTRY,$LINE"
                else
                        break
                fi
        done

        # Append to calendar file
        print $ENTRY>>$CALFILE

        # Sort the calendar file
        sort -o $CALFILE $CALFILE
}
```

```
function formatentry {
      $CLEAR

      typeset IFS="," \
      BORDER="**************************************" \
      BORDER1="*                              *" \
      FILE=$1

      if [[ -s $FILE ]]
      then

              # Open calendar file for reading, and
              # format output
              (exec 0<$FILE
              while read -r ENTRY
              do
                      print "$BORDER\n$BORDER1"
                      set $ENTRY
                      typeset -L35 LINE="DATE: $1"
                      print "* $LINE*"
                      shift
                      print "$BORDER1"
                      for i
                      do
                              LINE="$i"
                              print "* $LINE*"
                      done
                      print "$BORDER1"
              done
              print "$BORDER"
              ) | $PAGER
      else
              print "No entries found."
      fi

      # Prompt to continue
      until [[ $REPLY = "" ]]
      do
              read REPLY?"Enter <Return> to continue..."
      done
}
```

```
# Find specific entry
function findentry {
      $CLEAR
      # Check for entry - put it in temp found file
      grep $DATE $CALFILE >/tmp/.FOUND$$

      # Format found entries
      formatentry /tmp/.FOUND$$
}

# Change an entry
function changeentry {

      # Find specific entry - put it in temp found file
      grep $DATE $CALFILE | tr ',' '\012'>/tmp/.FOUND$$

      # Return if no entry was found
      if [[ ! -s /tmp/.FOUND$$ ]]
      then
            $CLEAR
            read TMP?"Entry for $DATE not found - press
<Return> to continue"
            return
      fi

      # Prompt again for change
      while [[ $REPLY != "" ]]
      do
            read REPLY?"Change/Add to entry for <$DATE>?"
            case $REPLY in

                  [yY]* | "" )
                        break ;;
                  [nN]* )      print "Ok, aborting entry
change"
                        return ;;

                  * ) print "Invalid reply - try again." ;;

            esac
      done

      # Edit the temporary found file
      ${EDITOR:-vi} /tmp/.FOUND$$
```

```
        # Remove the specified original entry
        grep -v $DATE $CALFILE > /tmp/.CHANGE$$

        # Put back new change in record format.
        # Add trailing \n
        (cat /tmp/.FOUND$$ | tr '\012' ',' ; print  ) \
        >>/tmp/.CHANGE$$

        # Put back new file
        cat /tmp/.CHANGE$$ > $CALFILE

        # Clean up tmp files
        rm -rf /tmp/.CHANGE$$ /tmp/.FOUND$$
}

# Remove specific entry
function delentry {

        # Look for entry
        grep $DATE $CALFILE >/tmp/.FOUND$$

        # Return if not found
        if [[ ! -s /tmp/.FOUND$$ ]]
        then
                $CLEAR
                read TMP?"Entry for $DATE not found - press
<Return> to continue"
                return
        fi

        # Prompt to delete
        while [[ $REPLY != "" ]]
        do
                read REPLY?"Delete entry for <$DATE>?"
                case $REPLY in

                        [yY]* | "" )
                                break ;;

                        [nN]* )
                                print "ok, aborting delete";
return ;;

                        * )    print "Invalid reply - try again."
;;
```

```
        esac
done
# Merge changes - put them in temporary file
grep -v $DATE $CALFILE > /tmp/.DEL$$

# Put back new file
cat /tmp/.DEL$$ > $CALFILE

# Clean up tmp files
rm -rf /tmp/.DEL$$ /tmp/.FOUND$$
}


 Set menu selection prompt
PS3="Enter selection or <Return> for default menu:"

# Display menu
while true
do
    $CLEAR
    select i in "Add calendar entry" "Delete calendar
entry" "Change calendar entry" "Find calendar entry" "List
all calendar entries" "List todays calendar entry" "Exit"
    do
        case $i in

                "Add calendar entry")
                    checkdate
                    addentry
                    $CLEAR ;;
                "Delete calendar entry")
                    checkdate
                    delentry
                    $CLEAR ;;
                "Change calendar entry")
                    checkdate
                    changeentry
                    $CLEAR ;;
                "Find calendar entry")
                    checkdate
                    findentry
                    $CLEAR ;;
                "List all calendar entries")
                    formatentry $CALFILE
                    $CLEAR ;;
```

```
                        "List todays calendar entry")
                                DATE=$(date +%m-%d-%y)
                                findentry
                                $CLEAR ;;
                        "Exit")
                                exit ;;
                        * )     print "\aInvalid selection \c"
                                read TMP?"- press <Return> to
continue"

                                $CLEAR
                                continue ;;

                esac
        done
done
```

Appendix E: Korn Shell Man Page

ksh, **rsh** - Korn shell, a standard/restricted command and programming language

Synopsis

ksh [+/–**abcefhikmnoprstuvxCD**] [–**R**] [+/–**o** *option*] [–][*arg*]

rsh [+/–**abcefhikmnoprstuvxCD**] [–**R**] [+/–**o** *option*] [–][*arg*]

Description

Ksh is a command and programming language that executes commands read from a terminal or a file. **Rsh** is a restricted version of the standard command interpreter **ksh**; it is used to set up login names and execution environments whose capabilities are more controlled than those of the standard Korn shell. See **Invocation** below for the meaning of arguments to the shell.

Korn Shell User and Programming Manual

Definitions

A metacharacter is one of the following characters:

; & ( ) | < > new-line space tab

A *blank* is a **tab** or a **space**. An *identifier* is a sequence of letters, digits, or underscores starting with a letter or underscore. Identifiers are used as components of *variable* names. A *vname* is a sequence of one or more identifiers separated by a **.** and optionally preceded by a **..** Vnames are used as function and variable names. A *word* is a sequence of *characters* from the character set defined by the current locale, excluding non-quoted *metacharacters*.

A command is a sequence of characters in the syntax of the shell language. The shell reads each command and carries out the desired action either directly or by invoking separate utilities. A built-in command is a command that is carried out by the shell without creating a separate process. Some commands are built-in purely for convenience and are not documented here. Built-ins that cause side effects in the shell environment and built-ins that are found before performing a path search (see **Execution** below) are documented here. For historical reasons, some of these built-ins behave differently than other built-ins and are called *special built-ins*.

Commands

A *simple-command* is a list of variable assignments (see *Variable* Assignments below) or a sequence of *blank* separated words which may be preceded by a list of variable assignments (see *Environment* below). The first word specifies the name of the command to be executed. Except as specified below, the remaining words are passed as arguments to the invoked command. The command name is passed as argument 0 (see *exec*(2)). The *value* of a simple-command is its exit status; 0-255 if it terminates normally; 256+*signum* if it terminates abnormally (the name of the signal corresponding to the exit status can be obtained via the **-l** option of the **kill** built-in utility).

A pipeline is a sequence of one or more commands separated by |. The standard output of each command but the last is connected by a pipe(2) to the standard input of the next command. Each command, except possibly the last, is run as a separate process; the shell waits for the last command to terminate. The exit status of a pipeline is the exit status of the last command. Each pipeline can be preceded by the reserved word **!** which causes the exit status of the pipeline to become 0 if the exit status of the last command is non-zero, and 1 if the exit status of the last command is 0.

A list is a sequence of one or more pipelines separated by **;**, **&**, **|&**, **&&**, or **||**, and optionally terminated by **;**, **&**, or **|&**. Of these five symbols, **;**, **&**, and **|&** have equal precedence, which is lower than that of **&&** and **||**. The symbols **&&** and **||** also have equal precedence. A semicolon (**;**) causes sequential execution of the preceding pipeline; an ampersand (**&**) causes asynchronous execution of the preceding pipeline (i.e., the shell does not wait for that pipeline to finish). The symbol **|&** causes asynchronous execution of the preceding pipeline with a two-way pipe established to the parent shell; the standard input and output of the spawned pipeline can be written to and read from by the parent shell by applying the redirection operators **<&** and **>&** with arg **p** to commands and by using **-p** option of the built-in commands **read** and **print** described later. The symbol **&&** (**||**) causes the list following it to be executed only if the preceding pipeline returns a zero (non-zero) value. One or more new-lines may appear in a list instead of a semicolon, to delimit a command.

A command is either a simple-command or one of the following. Unless otherwise stated, the value returned by a command is that of the last simple-command executed in the command.

for *identifier* [**in** *word* ...] ; **do** *list* ; **done**
> Each time a **for** command is executed, *identifier* is set to the next *word* taken from the in *word* list. If **in** *word* ... is omitted, then the **for** command executes the **do** *list* once for each positional parameter that is set (see **Parameter Substitution** below). Execution ends when there are no more words in the list.

for (([*expr1*] ; [*expr2*] ; [*expr3*])) ;do *list* ;**done**
> The arithmetic expression *expr1* is evaluated first (see **Arithmetic Evaluation** below). The arithmetic expression *expr2* is repeatedly evaluated until it evaluates to zero and when non-zero, *list* is executed and the arithmetic expression *expr3* evaluated. If any expression is omitted, then it behaves as if it evaluated to 1.

select *identifier* [**in** *word* ...] ; **do** *list* ; **done**
> A **select** command prints on standard error (file descriptor 2), the set of *words*, each preceded by a number. If **in** *word* ... is omitted, then the positional parameters are used instead (see **Parameter Substitution** below). The **PS3** prompt is printed and a line is read from the standard input. If this line consists of the number of one of the listed *words*, then the value of the parameter identifier is set to the *word* corresponding to this number. If this line is empty the selection list is printed again. Otherwise the value of the parameter identifier is set to null. The contents of the line read from standard input is saved in the parameter **REPLY**. The list is executed for each selection until a **break** or end-of-file is encountered.

case *word* **in** [[(]*pattern* [| *pattern*] ...) *list* ;; ... **esac**
> A **case** command executes the *list* associated with the

first*pattern*that matches*word*. The form of the patterns is the same as that used for file-name generation (see **File Name Generation** below).

if *list* **; then** *list* **elif** *list* **; then** *list* **...** **; else** *list* **; fi**

The *list* following **if** is executed and, if it returns a zero exit status, the *list* following the first **then** is executed. Otherwise, the *list* following **elif** is executed and, if its value is zero, the *list* following the next **then** is executed. Failing that, the **else** list is executed. If no **else** *list* or **then** *list* is executed, then the **if** command returns a zero exit status.

while *list* **; do** *list* **; done**
until *list* **; do** *list* **; done**

A **while** command repeatedly executes the **while** *list* and, if the exit status of the last command in the list is zero, executes the do*list*; otherwise the loop terminates. If no commands in the **do** *list* are executed, then the **while** command returns a zero exit status; **until** may be used in place of **while** to negate the loop termination test.

(*list***)** Execute*list*in a separate environment. Note, that if two adjacent open parentheses are needed for nesting, a space must be inserted to avoid arithmetic evaluation as described below.

{*list***;}** *list* is simply executed. Note that unlike the metacharacters (and), { and } are reserved words and must at the beginning of a line or after a **;** in order to be recognized.

[[*expression* **]]**

Evaluates*expression*and returns a zero exit status when

expression is true. See **Conditional Expressions** later in this appendix, for a description of *expression*.

function *identifier {list;}*
identifier () *{list;}*

> Define a **function** which is referenced by *identifier*. The body of the **function** is the *list* of commands between { and }. (See**Functions**later in this appendix).

time *pipeline*

> The *pipeline* is executed and the elapsed time as well as the user and system time are printed on standard error.

The following reserved words are only recognized as the first word of a command and when not quoted:

**if then else elif fi case esac for while until do done { }
function select time [[ ]] !**

Variable Assignments

One or more variable assignments can start a simple command or can be arguments to the**typeset**, **export**, or **readonly** special built-in commands. The syntax for an*assignment*is of the form:

varname =word
varname [*word*]=*word*

> No space is permitted between *varname* and the = or between = and *word*.

varname =(assign_list)

> No space is permitted between *varname* and the =. An *assign_list* can be one of the following:

word ...

> Indexed array assignment.

[*word*]=*word* **. . .**

> Associative array assignment.

assignment . . .

Nested variable assignment.

typeset [*options* **]** *assignment* **. . .**

Nested variable assignment. Multiple assignments can be specified by separating each of them with a ;.

Comments

A word beginning with # causes that word and all the following characters up to a new-line to be ignored.

Aliasing

The first word of each command is replaced by the text of an **alias** if an **alias** for this word has been defined. An **alias** name consists of any number of characters excluding metacharacters, quoting characters, file expansion characters, parameter expansion and command substitution characters, and =. The replacement string can contain any valid shell script including the metacharacters listed above. The first word of each command in the replaced text, other than any that are in the process of being replaced, will be tested for aliases. If the last character of the alias value is a *blank* then the word following the alias will also be checked for alias substitution. Aliases can be used to redefine built-in commands but cannot be used to redefine the reserved words listed above. Aliases can be created and listed with the **alias** command and can be removed with the **unalias** command.

Aliasing is performed when scripts are read, not while they are executed. Therefore, for an alias to take effect, the **alias** definition command has to be executed before the command which references the alias is read.

The following aliases are compiled into the shell but can be unset or redefined:

autoload='typeset -fu'

```
command='command '
fc=hist
float='typeset -E'
functions='typeset -f'
hash='alias -t - -'
history='hist -l'
integer='typeset -i'
nameref='typeset -n'
nohup='nohup '
r='hist -s'
redirect='command exec'
stop='kill -s STOP'
suspend='kill -s STOP $$'
times='{ { time;} 2>&1;}'
type='whence -v'
```

Tilde Substitution

After alias substitution is performed, each word is checked to see if it begins with an unquoted ~. For tilde substitution, *word* also refers to the *word* portion of parameter expansion (see **Parameter Expansion** below). If it does, then the word up to a / is checked to see if it matches a user name in the password database (often the **/etc/passwd** file). If a match is found, the ~ and the matched login name are replaced by the login directory of the matched user. If no match is found, the original text is left unchanged. A ~ by itself, or in front of a /, is replaced by **$HOME**. A ~ followed by a + or - is replaced by the value of **$PWD** and **$OLDPWD** respectively.

In addition, when expanding a variable assignment, tilde substitution is attempted when the value of the assignment begins with a ~, and when a ~ appears after a :. The : also terminates a ~ login name.

Command Substitution

The standard output from a command enclosed in parentheses preceded by a dollar sign (**$( )**) or a pair of grave accents (` `` `) may be used as part or all of a word; trailing new-lines are removed. In the second (obsolete) form, the string between the quotes is processed for special quoting characters before the command is executed (see **Quoting** below). The command substitution **$(cat file)** can be replaced by the equivalent but faster **$(<file)** .

Arithmetic Substitution

An arithmetic expression enclosed in double parentheses preceded by a dollar sign (**$(( ))**) is replaced by the value of the arithmetic expression within the double parentheses.

Process Substitution

This feature is only available on versions of the Unix operating system that support the **/dev/fd** directory for naming open files. Each command argument of the form **<(**_list_**)** or **>(**_list_**)** will run process list asynchronously connected to some file in **/dev/fd**. The name of this file will become the argument to the command. If the form with **>** is selected then writing on this file will provide input for list. If **<** is used, then the file passed as an argument will contain the output of the list process. For example,

paste <(cut −f _file1_**) <(cut −f3** _file2_ **) | tee >(**_process1_**) >(**_process2_**)**

cuts fields 1 and 3 from the files _file1_ and _file2_ respectively, pastes the results together, and sends it to the processes _process1_ and _process2_, as well as putting it onto the standard output. Note that the file, which is passed as an argument to the command, is a Unix system **pipe(2)** so programs that expect to **lseek(2)** on the file will not work.

Parameter Expansion

A *parameter* is a *variable*, one or more digits, or any of the characters *, @, #, ?, -, $, and !\ . A *variable* is denoted by a *vname*. To create a variable whose *vname* contains a ., a variable whose *vname* consists of everything before the last . must already exist. A *variable* has a *value* and zero or more *attributes*. *Variables* can be assigned *values* and *attributes* by using the **typeset** special built-in command. The attributes supported by the shell are described later with the **typeset** special built-in command. Exported variables pass values and attributes to the environment.

The shell supports both indexed and associative arrays. An element of an array variable is referenced by a *subscript*. A *subscript* for an indexed array is denoted by an *arithmetic*expression (see **Arithmetic Evaluation** later in this appendix) between a [and a]. To assign values to an indexed array, use **set -A** *vname value* . . . . The value of all subscripts must be in the range of 0 through 4095. Indexed arrays need not be declared. Any reference to a variable with a valid subscript is legal and an array will be created if necessary.

An associative array is created with the **-A** option to **typeset**. A subscript for an associative array is denoted by a string enclosed between [and].

Referencing any array without a subscript is equivalent to referencing the array with subscript 0.

The *value* of a *variable* may be assigned by writing:

vname=value [vname=value] . . .
or
vname[subscript]=value [vname[subscript]=value] . . .

Note that no space is allowed before or after the =.

A *nameref* is a variable that is a reference to another variable. A nameref is created with the **-n** attribute of **typeset**. The value of the variable at the time of the **typeset** command becomes the variable that will be referenced whenever the nameref variable is used. The name of a nameref cannot contain a **..** When a variable or function name contains a **.**, and the portion of the name up to the first **.** matches the name of a nameref, the variable referred to is obtained by replacing the nameref portion with the name of the variable referenced by the nameref. A nameref provides a convenient way to refer to the variable inside a function whose name is passed as an argument to a function. For example, if the name of a variable is passed as the first argument to a function, the command

typeset -n var=$1

inside the function causes references and assignments to **var** to be references and assignments to the variable whose name has been passed to the function.

If either of the floating point attributes, **-E**, or **-F**, or the integer attribute, **-i**, is set for vname, then the value is subject to arithmetic evaluation as described below.

Positional parameters, parameters denoted by a number, may be assigned values with the **set** special built-in command.

Parameter **$0** is set from argument zero when the shell is invoked.

The character **$** is used to introduce substitutable parameters.

${*parameter* }
>   The shell reads all the characters from **${** to the matching **}** as part of the same word even if it contains braces or metacharacters. The value, if any, of the

parameter is substituted. The braces are required when *parameter* is followed by a letter, digit, or underscore that is not to be interpreted as part of its name, when the variable name contains a **.**, or when a variable is subscripted. If *parameter* is one or more digits then it is a positional parameter. A positional parameter of more than one digit must be enclosed in braces. If *parameter* is * or @, then all the positional parameters, starting with **$1**, are substituted (separated by a field separator character). If an array vname with subscript * or @ is used, then the value for each of the elements is substituted, separated by the first character of the value of **IFS**.

${#*parameter* }

If *parameter* is * or @, the number of positional parameters is substituted. Otherwise, the length of the value of the *parameter* is substituted.

${#*vname*[*]}
${#*vname*[@]}

The number of elements in the array *vname* is substituted.

${!*vname* }

Expands to the name of the variable referred to by *vname*. This will be *vname* except when *vname* is a name reference.

${!*vname* [*subscript*]}

Expands to name of the subscript unless *subscript* is * or @. When *subscript* is *, the list of array subscripts for *vname* is generated. For a variable that is not an array, the value is 0 if the variable is set. Otherwise it is null. When *subscript* is @, same as above, except that when used in double quotes, each array subscript yields a separate argument.

${!*prefix* *}

Expands to the names of the variables whose names begin with *prefix*.

${*parameter* :-*word* }

> If *parameter* is set and is non-null then substitute its value; otherwise substitute *word*.

${*parameter* :=*word* }

> If *parameter* is not set or is null then set it to *word*; the value of the *parameter* is then substituted. Positional parameters may not be assigned to in this way.

${*parameter* :?*word* }

> If *parameter* is set and is non-null then substitute its value; otherwise, print *word* and exit from the shell (if not interactive). If *word* is omitted then a standard message is printed.

${*parameter* :+*word* }

> If *parameter* is set and is non-null then substitute *word*; otherwise substitute nothing.

${*parameter* :*offset* :*length* }

${*parameter* :*offset* }

Expands to the portion of the value of *parameter* starting at the character (counting from **0**) determined by expanding offset as an arithmetic expression and consisting of the number of characters determined by the arithmetic expression defined by length. In the second form, the remainder of the *value* is used. If parameter is * or @, or is an array name indexed by * or @, then offset and length refer to the array index and number of elements respectively.

${*parameter* #*pattern* }

${*parameter* ##*pattern* }

> If the shell *pattern* matches the beginning of the value of *parameter*, then the value of this expansion is the value of the *parameter* with the matched portion deleted; otherwise the value of this *parameter* is substituted. In the first form the smallest matching *pattern* is deleted and in the second form the largest matching *pattern* is deleted. When *parameter* is @, *, or an array variable with subscript @ or *, the substring operation is applied to each element in turn.

${*parameter %pattern* }
${*parameter %%pattern* }

> If the shell *pattern* matches the end of the value of *parameter*, then the value of this expansion is the value of the *parameter* with the matched part deleted; otherwise substitute the value of *parameter*. In the first form the smallest matching *pattern* is deleted and in the second form the largest matching *pattern* is deleted. When *parameter* is @, *, or an array variable with subscript @ or *, the substring operation is applied to each element in turn.

${*parameter /pattern /string* }
${*parameter //pattern /string* }
${*parameter /#pattern /string* }
${*parameter /%pattern /string* }

> Expands *parameter* and replaces the longest match of *pattern* with the given string. Each occurrence of \n in *string* is replaced by the portion of *parameter* that matches the *n* -th sub-pattern. In the first form, only the first occurrence of *pattern* is replaced. In the second form, each match for *pattern* is replaced by the given *string*. The third form restricts the *pattern* match to the beginning of the *string* while the fourth form restricts the pattern match to the end of the *string*. When *string* is null, the *pattern* will be deleted and the / in front of *string* may be omitted. When *parameter* is @, *, or an array variable with subscript @ or *, the substitution operation is applied to each element in turn.

In the above, *word* is not evaluated unless it is to be used as the substituted string, so that, in the following example, **pwd** is executed only if **d** is not set or is null:

print ${d:- $(pwd) }

If the colon (**:**) is omitted from the above expressions, then the shell only checks whether *parameter* is set or not.

The following parameters are automatically set by the shell:

\#   The number of positional parameters in decimal.

-        Options supplied to the shell on invocation or by the **set** command.

?   The decimal value returned by the last executed command.

\$ The process number of this shell.

_   Initially, the value of _ is an absolute pathname of the shell or script being executed as passed in the *environment*. Subsequently it is assigned the last argument of the previous command. This parameter is not set for commands which are asynchronous. This parameter is also used to hold the name of the matching **MAIL** file when checking for mail.

!   The process number of the last background command invoked.

.sh.edchar

This variable contains the value of the keyboard character (or sequence of characters if the first character is an ESC, ascii **033**) that has been entered when processing a **KEYBD** trap (see *KeyBindings* below). If the value is changed as part of the trap action, then the new value replaces the key (or key sequence) that caused the trap.

.sh.edcol

The character position of the cursor at the time of the most recent **KEYBD** trap.

.sh.edmode

The value is set to ESC when processing a **KEYBD** trap while in **vi** insert mode. (See **Vi Editing Mode** later in this appendix.) Otherwise, **.sh.edmode** is null when processing a **KEYBD** trap.

.sh.edtext

The characters in the input buffer at the time of the

most recent **KEYBD** trap. The value is null when not processing a **KEYBD** trap.

.sh.name

Set to the name of the variable at the time that a discipline function is invoked.

.sh.subscript

Set to the name subscript of the variable at the time that a discipline function is invoked.

.sh.value

Set to the value of the variable at the time that the **set** discipline function is invoked.

.sh.version

Set to a value that identifies the version of this shell.

LINENO

The current line number within the script or function being executed.

OLDPWD

The previous working directory set by the **cd** command.

OPTARG

The value of the last option argument processed by the **getopts** built-in command.

OPTIND

The index of the last option argument processed by the **getopts** built-in command.

PPID The process number of the parent of the shell.

PWD The present working directory set by the **cd** command.

RANDOM

Each time this variable is referenced, a random integer, uniformly distributed between 0 and 32767, is generated. The sequence of random numbers can be initialized by assigning a numeric value to **RANDOM**.

REPLY

This variable is set by the **select** statement and by the **read** built-in command when no arguments are supplied.

SECONDS

Each time this variable is referenced, the number of seconds since shell invocation is returned. If this variable is assigned a value, then the value returned upon reference will be the value that was assigned plus the number of seconds since the assignment.

The following variables are used by the shell:

CDPATH

The search path for the **cd** command.

COLUMNS

If this variable is set, the value is used to define the width of the edit window for the shell edit modes and for printing **select** lists.

EDITOR

If the value of this variable ends in **emacs**, **gmacs**, or **vi** and the **VISUAL** variable is not set, then the corresponding option will be turned on. See the **set** command later in this appendix.

ENV If this variable is set, then parameter expansion, command substitution, and arithmetic substitution are performed on the value to generate the pathname of the script that will be executed when the shell is invoked (see **Invocation** section later in this appendix). This file is typically used for **alias** and **function** definitions.

FCEDIT

Obsolete name for the default editor name for the **hist** command. **FCEDIT** is not used when **HISTEDIT** is set.

FIGNORE

A pattern that defines the set of filenames that will be ignored when performing filename matching.

FPATH

The search path for function definitions. This path is searched for a file with the same name as the function or command when a function with the **-u** attribute is referenced and when a command is not found. If an executable file with the name of that command is found, then it is read and executed in the current environment.

HISTCMD

Number of the current command in the history file.

HISTEDIT

Name for the default editor name for the **hist** command.

HISTFILE

If this variable is set when the shell is invoked, then the value is the pathname of the file that will be used to store the command history (see **Command Re-entry** later in this appendix).

HISTSIZE

If this variable is set when the shell is invoked, then the number of previously entered commands that are accessible by this shell will be greater than or equal to this number. The default is 128.

HOME

The default argument (home directory) for the **cd** command.

IFS   Internal field separators, normally **space**, **tab**, and **new-line** that are used to separate the results of command substitution or parameter expansion and to separate fields with the built-in command **read**. The first character of the **IFS** variable is used to separate arguments for the "**$***" substitution (see **Quoting** later in this appendix). Each single occurrence of an **IFS** character in the string to be split, that is not in the isspace character class, and any adjacent characters in **IFS** that are in the isspace character class, delimit a field. One or more characters in **IFS** that belong to the isspace character class, delimit a field. In addition, if the same isspace character appears consecutively inside **IFS**, this character is treated as if it were not in the isspace class, so that if **IFS** consists of two **tab** characters, then two adjacent **tab** characters delimit a null field.

LANG This variable determines the locale category for any category not specifically selected with a variable starting with **LC_** or **LANG**.

LC_ALL

This variable overrides the value of the **LANG** variable and any other **LC_** variable.

LC_COLLATE

This variable determines the locale category for character collation information.

LC_CTYPE

This variable determines the locale category for character handling functions. It determines the character classes for pattern matching (see **File Name Generation** later in this appendix).

LC_NUMERIC

This variable determines the locale category for the decimal point character.

LINES

If this variable is set, the value is used to determine the column length for printing **select** lists. Select lists will print vertically until about two-thirds of **LINES** lines are filled.

MAIL

If this variable is set to the name of a mail file and the **MAILPATH** variable is not set, then the shell informs the user of arrival of mail in the specified file.

MAILCHECK

This variable specifies how often (in seconds) the shell will check for changes in the modification time of any of the files specified by the **MAILPATH** or **MAIL** variables. The default value is 600 seconds. When the time has elapsed the shell will check before issuing the next prompt.

MAILPATH

A colon (:) separated list of file names. If this variable is set, then the shell informs the user of any modifications to the specified files that have occurred within the last **MAILCHECK** seconds. Each file name can be followed by a **?** and a message that will be printed. The message will undergo parameter expansion, command substitution, and arithmetic substitution with the variable **$_** defined as the name of the file that has changed. The default message is "**you have mailin $_** ".

PATH

The search path for commands (see **Execution** later in this appendix). The user may not change **PATH** if executing under **rsh** (except in **.profile**).

PS1   The value of this variable is expanded for parameter expansion, command substitution, and arithmetic substitution to define the primary prompt string which by default is "**$** ". The character **!** in the primary prompt string is replaced by the command number (see **Command Re-entry** later in this appendix). Two successive occurrences of **!** will produce a single **!** when the prompt string is printed.

PS2   Secondary prompt string, by default "**>** ".

PS3   Selection prompt string used within a **select** loop, by default "**#?** ".

PS4   The value of this variable is expanded for parameter evaluation, command substitution, and arithmetic substitution and precedes each line of an execution trace. By default, **PS4** is "**+** ". In addition when **PS4** is unset, the execution trace prompt is also "**+** ".

SHELL

The pathname of the shell is kept in the environment. At invocation, if the basename of this variable is **rsh**, **rksh**, or **krsh**, then the shell becomes restricted.

TMOUT

> If set to a value greater than zero, **TMOUT** will be the default timeout value for the **read** built-in command. The **select** compound command terminates after **TMOUT** seconds when input is from a terminal. Otherwise, the shell will terminate if a line is not entered within the prescribed number of seconds while reading from a terminal. (Note that the shell can be compiled with a maximum bound for this value which cannot be exceeded.)

VISUAL

> If the value of this variable ends in emacs, gmacs, or vi then the corresponding option (see **set** command later in this appendix) will be turned on. The value of **VISUAL** overrides the value of **EDITOR.**

The shell gives default values to **PATH, PS1, PS2, PS3, PS4, MAILCHECK, FCEDIT, TMOUT** and **IFS**, while **HOME, SHELL, ENV**, and **MAIL** are not set at all by the shell (although **HOME** is set by **login**(1)). On some systems **MAIL** and **SHELL** are also set by **login**(1).

Field Splitting

After parameter expansion and command substitution, the results of substitutions are scanned for the field separator characters (those found in **IFS**) and split into distinct fields where such characters are found. Explicit null fields (" " or ' ') are retained. Implicit null fields (those resulting from *parameters* that have no values or command substitutions with no output) are removed.

File Name Generation

Following splitting, each field is scanned for the characters *, ?, (, and [unless the **-f** option has been set. If one of these characters appears, then the word is regarded as a *pattern*. Each file name component that contains any pattern character is replaced with a lexicographically sorted set of names that matches the pattern from that directory. If no file name is found that matches the pattern, then that component of the filename is left unchanged. If **FIGNORE** is set, then each file name component that matches the pattern defined by the value of **FIGNORE** is ignored when generating the matching filenames. The names **.** and **..** are also ignored. If **FIGNORE** is not set, the character **.** at the start of each file name component will be ignored unless the first character of the pattern corresponding to this component is the character **.** itself. Note, that for other uses of pattern matching the / and **.** are not treated specially.

*   Matches any string, including the null string.
?   Matches any single character.
[...]

Matches any one of the enclosed characters. A pair of characters separated by - matches any character lexically between the pair, inclusive. If the first character following the opening [is a ! then any character not enclosed is matched. A - can be included in the character set by putting it as the first or last character.

Within [and] , character classes can be specified with the syntax [:*class*:] where class is one of the following classes defined in the ANSI-C standard:

alnum alpha blank cntrl digit graph lower print punct space upper xdigit

Within [and] , an equivalence class can be specified with the syntax [=*c*=] which matches all characters with the same primary collation weight (as defined by the current locale) as the character *c*. Within [and] , [.*symbol*.] matches the collating symbol *symbol*.

A *pattern-list* is a list of one or more patterns separated from each other with a **&** or |. A **&** signifies that all patterns must be matched whereas | requires that only one pattern be matched. Composite patterns can be formed with one or more of the following sub-patterns:

?(*pattern-list*)
>	Optionally matches any one of the given patterns.

*(*pattern-list*)
>	Matches zero or more occurrences of the given patterns.

+(*pattern-list*)
>	Matches one or more occurrences of the given patterns.

@(*pattern-list*)
>	Matches exactly one of the given patterns.

!(*pattern-list*)
>	Matches anything except one of the given patterns.

Each sub-pattern in a composite pattern is numbered, starting at 1, by the location of the **(** within the pattern. The sequence \\$n$, where n is a single digit and \\$n$ comes after the n-th. sub-pattern, matches the same string as the sub-pattern itself.

Quoting

Each of the *metacharacters* listed above (See **Definitions** earlier in this appendix) has a special meaning to the Korn shell and causes termination of a word unless quoted. A character may be quoted (i.e., made to stand for itself) by preceding it with a \\. The pair \\new-line is ignored. All characters enclosed between a pair of single quote marks ("), are quoted. A single quote cannot appear within single quotes. Inside double quote marks (""), parameter and command substitution occurs and \\ quotes the characters \\, `, " , and $. The meaning of $* and $@ is identical when not quoted or when used as a parameter assignment value or as a file name.

However, when used as a command argument, "$*" is equivalent to "$1*d$2*d..." , where *d* is the first character of the **IFS** parameter, whereas "$@" is equivalent to "$1" "$2" .... Inside grave quote marks (``) \ quotes the characters \, `, and $. If the grave quotes occur within double quotes then \ also quotes the character ".

The special meaning of reserved words or aliases can be removed by quoting any character of the reserved word. The recognition of function names or special command names listed below cannot be altered by quoting them.

Arithmetic Evaluation

The shell performs arithmetic evaluation for arithmetic substitution, to evaluate an arithmetic command, to evaluate an indexed array subscript, and to evaluate arguments to the built-in commands **shift** and **let**. Evaluations are performed using double precision floating point arithmetic. Floating point constants follow the ANSI-C programming language conventions. Integer constants are of the form [*base#*]*n* where *base* is a decimal number between two and sixty-four representing the arithmetic base and *n* is a number in that base. The digits above 9 are represented by the lower case letters, the upper case letters, @, and _ respectively. For bases less than or equal to 36, upper and lower case characters can be used interchangeably. If *base* is omitted, then base 10 is used.

An arithmetic expression uses the same syntax, precedence, and associativity of expression as the C language. All the C language operators that apply to floating point quantities can be used. In addition, when the value of an arithmetic variable or sub-expression can be represented as a long integer, all C language integer arithmetic operations can be performed. Variables can be referenced by name within an arithmetic expression without using the parameter expansion syntax. When a variable is referenced, its value is evaluated as an arithmetic expression.

The following math library functions can be used with an arithmetic expression:

abs acos asin atan cos cosh exp int log sin sinh sqrt tan tanh

An internal representation of a *variable* as a double precision floating point can be specified with the **-E** [*n*] or **-F** [*n*] option of the **typeset** special built-in command. The **-E** option causes the expansion of the value to be represented using scientific notation when it is expanded. The optional option argument *n* defines the number of significant figures. The **-F** option causes the expansion to be represented as a floating decimal number when it is expanded. The optional option argument *n* defines the number of places after the decimal point in this case.

An internal integer representation of a *variable* can be specified with the **-i** [*n*] option of the **typeset** special built-in command. The optional option argument *n* specifies an arithmetic base to be used when expanding the variable. If you do not specify an arithmetic base, the first assignment to the variable determines the arithmetic base.

Arithmetic evaluation is performed on the value of each assignment to a variable with the **-E**, **-F**, or **-i** attribute. Assigning a floating point number to a variable whose type is an integer causes the fractional part to be truncated.

Prompting

When used interactively, the shell prompts with the value of **PS1** after expanding it for parameter expansion, command substitution, and arithmetic substitution, before reading a command. In addition, each single **!** in the prompt is replaced by the command number. A **!!** is required to place **!** in the prompt. If at any time a new-line is typed and further input is needed to complete a command, then the secondary prompt (i.e., the value of **PS2**) is issued.

Conditional Expressions

A *conditional expression* is used with the **[[** compound command to test attributes of files and to compare strings. Field splitting and file name generation are not performed on the words between **[[** and **]]**. Each expression can be constructed from one or more of the following unary or binary expressions:

string	True, if *string* is not null.
-a *file*	Same as **-e** below. This is obsolete.
-b *file*	True, if *file* exists and is a block special file.
-c *file*	True, if *file* exists and is a character special file.
-d *file*	True, if *file* exists and is a directory.
-e *file*	True, if *file* exists.
-f *file*	True, if *file* exists and is an ordinary file.
-g *file*	True, if *file* exists and it has its setgid bit set.
-k *file*	True, if *file* exists and it has its sticky bit set.
-n *string*	True, if length of *string* is non-zero.
-o *option*	True, if option named *option* is on.
-p *file*	True, if *file* exists and is a fifo special file or a pipe.
-r *file*	True, if *file* exists and is readable by current process.
-s *file*	True, if *file* exists and has size greater than zero.
-t *fildes*	True, if file descriptor number *fildes* is open and associated with a terminal device.
-u *file*	True, if *file* exists and it has its setuid bit set.
-w *file*	True, if *file* exists and is writable by current process.
-x *file*	True, if *file* exists and is executable by current process. If *file* exists and is a directory, then true if the current process has permission to search in the directory.
-z *string*	True, if length of *string* is zero.
-L *file*	True, if *file* exists and is a symbolic link.
-O *file*	True, if *file* exists and is owned by the effective user id of this process.

322

-G *file*   True, if *file* exists and its group matches the effective group id of this process.

-S *file*   True, if *file* exists and is a socket.

file1 **-nt** file2

      True, if *file1* exists and *file2* does not, or *file1* is newer than *file2*.

file1 **-ot** *file2*

      True, if *file2* exists and *file1* does not, or *file1* is older than *file2*.

file1 **-ef** *file2*

      True, if *file1* and *file2* exist and refer to the same file.

string == *pattern*

      True, if *string* matches *pattern*. Any part of *pattern* can be quoted to cause it to be matched as a string.

string = *pattern*

      Same as == above, but is obsolete.

string != *pattern*

      True, if *string* does not match *pattern*.

string1 < *string2*

      True, if *string1* comes before *string2* based on ASCII value of their characters.

string1 > *string2*

      True, if *string1* comes after *string2* based on ASCII value of their characters.

The following obsolete arithmetic comparisons are also permitted:

exp1 **-eq** *exp2*

      True, if *exp1* is equal to *exp2*.

exp1 **-ne** *exp2*

      True, if *exp1* is not equal to *exp2*.

exp1 **-lt** *exp2*

      True, if *exp1* is less than *exp2*.

exp1 **-gt** *exp2*
> True, if *exp1* is greater than *exp2*.

exp1 **-le** *exp2*
> True, if *exp1* is less than or equal to *exp2*.

exp1 **-ge** *exp2*
> True, if *exp1* is greater than or equal to *exp2*.

In each of the above expressions, if *file* is of the form **/dev/fd/***n*, where *n* is an integer, then the test is applied to the open file whose descriptor number is *n*.

A compound expression can be constructed from these primitives by using any of the following, listed in decreasing order of precedence.

(*expression*)
> True, if *expression* is true. Used to group expressions.

! *expression* True if *expression* is false.

expression1 **&&** *expression2*
> True, if *expression1* and *expression2* are both true.

expression1 || *expression2*
> True, if either *expression1* or *expression2* is true.

Input/Output

Before a command is executed, its input and output may be redirected using a special notation interpreted by the shell. The following may appear anywhere in a simple-command or may precede or follow a *command* and are *not* passed on to the invoked command. Command substitution, parameter expansion, and arithmetic substitution occur before *word* or *digit* is used except as noted below. File name generation occurs only if the shell is interactive and the pattern matches a single file. Field splitting is not performed.

In each of the following redirections, if *file* is of the form **/dev/tcp**/*host*/*port*, or **/dev/udp**/*host*/*port*, where *host* is a hostname or host address, and *port* is an integer port number, then the redirection attempts to make a **tcp** or **udp** connection to the corresponding socket.

<*word*	Use file *word* as standard input (file descriptor 0).
>*word*	Use file *word* as standard output (file descriptor 1). If the file does not exist then it is created. If the file exists, and the **noclobber** option is on, this causes an error; otherwise, it is truncated to zero length.
>|*word*	Same as >, except that it overrides the **noclobber** option.
>>*word*	Use file *word* as standard output. If the file exists then output is appended to it (by first seeking to the end-of-file); otherwise, the file is created.
<>*word*	Open file *word* for reading and writing as standard input.
<<[–]*word*	The Korn shell input is read up to a line that is the same as *word*, or to an end-of-file. No parameter substitution, command substitution or file name generation is performed on *word*. The resulting document, called a *here-document*, becomes the standard input. If any character of *word* is quoted, then no interpretation is placed upon the characters of the document; otherwise, parameter and command substitution occurs, \new-line is ignored, and \ must be used to quote the characters \, $, `, and the first character of word. If – is appended to <<, then all leading tabs are stripped from *word* and from the document.

<&digit	The standard input is duplicated from file descriptor *digit* (see **dup(2)**). Similarly for the standard output using >& *digit*.
<&–	The standard input is closed. Similarly for the standard output using >&–.
<&p	The input from the co-process is moved to standard input.
>&p	The output to the co-process is moved to standard output.

If one of the above is preceded by a *digit*, then the file descriptor number referred to is that specified by the digit (instead of the default **0** or **1**). For example:

> **... 2>&1**

means file descriptor 2 is to be opened for writing as a duplicate of file descriptor 1.

The order in which redirections are specified is significant. The Korn shell evaluates each redirection in terms of the file descriptor/file association at the time of evaluation. For example:

> **... 1 >*fname* 2>&1**

first associates file descriptor 1 with file *fname*. It then associates file descriptor 2 with the file associated with file descriptor 1 (i.e. *fname*). If the order of redirections were reversed, file descriptor 2 would be associated with the terminal (assuming file descriptor 1 had been) and then file descriptor 1 would be associated with file *fname*.

If a command is followed by & and job control is not active, then the default standard input for the command is the empty file **/dev/null**. Otherwise, the environment for the execution of a command contains the file descriptors of the invoking shell as modified by input/output specifications.

Environment

The *environment* (see **environ**(7)) is a list of name-value pairs that is passed to an executed program in the same way as a normal argument list. The names must be *identifiers* and the values are character strings. The shell interacts with the environment in several ways. On invocation, the shell scans the environment and creates a variable for each name found, giving it the corresponding value and attributes and marking it *export*. Executed commands inherit the environment. If the user modifies the values of these variables or creates new ones, using the **export** or **typeset**-x commands, they become part of the environment. The environment seen by any executed command is thus composed of any name-value pairs originally inherited by the shell, whose values may be modified by the current shell, plus any additions which must be noted in **export** or **typeset**-x commands.

The environment for any *simple-command* or function may be augmented by prefixing it with one or more variable assignments. A variable assignment argument is a word of the form *identifier=value*. Thus:

    TERM=450   cmd   args   and
    (export TERM; TERM=450; cmd args)

are equivalent (as far as the above execution of *cmd* is concerned except for special built-in commands listed below - those that are preceded with a dagger).

If the obsolete **-k** option is set, *all* variable assignment arguments are placed in the environment, even if they occur after the command name. The following first prints **a=b c** and then **c**:

```
echo  a=b  c
set  -k
echo  a=b  c
```

This feature is intended for use with scripts written for early versions of the shell and its use in new scripts is strongly discouraged. It is likely to disappear someday.

Functions

For historical reasons, there are two ways to define functions, the *name*( ) syntax and the **function** *name* syntax, described in the **Commands** later in this appendix. Shell functions are read in and stored internally. Alias names are resolved when the function is read. Functions are executed like commands with the arguments passed as positional parameters. (See**Execution** later in this appendix.)

Functions defined by the **function** *name* syntax and called by name execute in the same process as the caller and share all files and present working directory with the caller. Traps caught by the caller are reset to their default action inside the function. A trap condition that is not caught or ignored by the function causes the function to terminate and the condition to be passed on to the caller. A trap on **EXIT** set inside a function is executed in the environment of the caller after the function completes. Ordinarily, variables are shared between the calling program and the function. However, the **typeset** special built-in command used within a function defines local variables whose scope includes the current function and all functions it calls. Errors within functions return control to the caller.

Functions defined with the   *name*( ) syntax and functions defined with the**function** *name* syntax that are invoked with the . special built-in command are executed in the caller's environment and share all variables and traps with the caller. Errors within these function executions cause the script that contains them to abort.

The special built-in command **return** is used to return from function calls.

Function names can be listed with the **-f** or **+f** option of the **typeset** special built-in command. The text of functions, when available, will also be listed with-**f**. Functions can be undefined with the **-f** option of the **unset** special built-in command.

Ordinarily, functions are unset when the shell executes a shell script. Functions that need to be defined across separate invocations of the shell should be placed in a directory and the **FPATH** variable should contain the name of this directory. They may also be specified in the **ENV** file.

Discipline Functions

Each variable can have zero or more discipline functions associated with it. The shell initially understands the discipline names **get**, **set**, and **unset** but on most systems others can be added at run time via the C programming interface extension provided by the **builtin** built-in utility. If the **get** discipline is defined for a variable, it is invoked whenever the given variable is referenced. If the variable.**sh.value** is assigned a value inside the discipline function, the referenced variable will evaluate to this value instead. If the **set** discipline is defined for a variable, it is invoked whenever the given variable is assigned a value. The variable .**sh.value** is given the value of the variable before invoking the discipline, and the variable will be assigned the value of.**sh.value** after the discipline completes. If.**sh.value** is unset inside the discipline, then that value is unchanged. If the **unset** discipline is defined for a variable, it is invoked whenever the given variable is unset. The variable will not be unset unless it is unset explicitly from within this discipline function.

The variable **.sh.name** contains the name of the variable for which the discipline function is called, **.sh.subscript** is the subscript of the variable, and **.sh.value** will contain the value being assigned inside the **.set** discipline function. For the **set** discipline, changing **.sh.value** will change the value that gets assigned.

Jobs

If the **monitor** option of the **set** command is turned on, an interactive shell associates a job with each pipeline. It keeps a table of current jobs, printed by the **jobs** command, and assigns them small integer numbers. When a job is started asynchronously with &, the shell prints a line which looks like:

[1] 1234

indicating that the job which was started asynchronously was job number 1 and had one (top-level) process, whose process id was 1234.

This paragraph and the next require features that are not in all versions of the Unix operating system and may not apply. If you are running a job and wish to do something else you may hit the key **^Z** (control-Z) which sends a **STOP** signal to the current job. The shell will then normally indicate that the job has been '**Stopped**', and print another prompt. You can then manipulate the state of this job, putting it in the background with the **bg** command, or run some other commands and then eventually bring the job back into the foreground with the foreground command **fg**. A **^Z** takes effect immediately and is like an interrupt in that pending output and unread input are discarded when it is typed.

A job being run in the background will stop if it tries to read from the terminal. Background jobs are normally allowed to produce output, but this can be disabled by giving the command "**stty tostop**". If you set this **tty** option, then background jobs will stop when they try to produce output like they do when they try to read input.

There are several ways to refer to jobs in the shell. A job can be referred to by the process id of any process of the job or by one of the following:

%*number*   The job with the given number.
%*string*   Any job whose command line begins with
             string.
%?*string*   Any job whose command line contains *string*.
%%   Current job.
%+   Equivalent to %%.
%−   Previous job.

The shell learns immediately whenever a process changes state. It normally informs you whenever a job becomes blocked so that no further progress is possible, but only just before it prints a prompt. This is done so that it does not otherwise disturb your work.

When the **monitor** mode is on, each background job that completes triggers any trap set for **CHLD**.

When you try to leave the shell while jobs are running or stopped, you will be warned that **"You have stopped(running) jobs."**. You may use the **jobs** command to see what they are. If you do this or immediately try to exit again, the shell will not warn you a second time, and the stopped jobs will be terminated.

Korn Shell User and Programming Manual

Signals

The **INT** and **QUIT** signals for an invoked command are ignored if the command is followed by & and job **monitor** option is not active. Otherwise, signals have the values inherited by the shell from its parent (but see also the **trap** command earlier in this appendix).

Execution

Each time a command is read, the above substitutions are carried out. If the command name matches one of the **Special Built-in Commands** listed later in this appendix, it is executed within the current shell process. Next, the command name is checked to see if it matches a user defined function. If it does, the positional parameters are saved and then reset to the arguments of the *function* call. A function is also executed in the current shell process. When the *function* completes or issues a **return**, the positional parameter list is restored. For functions defined with the **function** *name* syntax, any trap set on **EXIT** within the function is executed. The exit value of a *function* is the value of the last command executed. If a command name is not a *special built-in command* or a user defined *function*, but it is one of the built-in commands listed later in this section, it is executed in the current shell process.

The shell variable **PATH** defines the search path for the directory containing the command. Alternative directory names are separated by a colon (**:**). The default path is **/bin:/usr/bin:** (specifying **/bin**, **/usr/bin**, and the current directory in that order). The current directory can be specified by two or more adjacent colons, or by a colon at the beginning or end of the path list. If the command name contains a **/**, then the search path is not used. Otherwise, each directory in the path is searched for an executable file that is not a directory. If the shell determines that there is a built-in version of a command corresponding to a given pathname, this built-in is invoked in the current process. A process is created and an attempt is made to execute the command via *exec*(2). If the file has execute permission but is not an **a.out** file, it is assumed to be a file containing shell commands. A separate shell is spawned to read it. All non-exported variables are removed in this case. If the shell command file doesn't have read permission, or if the *setuid* and/or *setgid* bits are set on the file, then the shell executes an agent whose job it is to set up the permissions and execute the shell with the shell command file passed down as an open file. A parenthesized command is executed in a sub-shell without removing non-exported variables.

Command Re-entry

The text of the last **HISTSIZE** (default 128) commands entered from a terminal device is saved in a *history* file. The file **$HOME/.sh_history** is used if the **HISTFILE** variable is not set or if the file it names is not writable. A shell can access the commands of all *interactive* shells which use the same named **HISTFILE**. The built-in command **hist** is used to list or edit a portion of this file. The portion of the file to be edited or listed can be selected by number or by giving the first character or characters of the command. A single command or range of commands can be specified. If you do not specify an editor program as an argument to **hist** then the value of the variable **HISTEDIT** is used. If **HISTEDIT** is unset, the obsolete variable **FCEDIT** is used. If **FCEDIT** is not defined, then **/bin/ed** is used. The edited command(s) is printed and re-executed upon leaving the editor unless you quit without writing. The **-s** option (and in obsolete versions, the editor name **-**) is used to skip the editing phase and to re-execute the command. In this case a substitution parameter of the form *old=new* can be used to modify the command before execution. For example, with the preset alias **r**, which is aliased to '**hist -s**', typing `r bad=good c' will re-execute the most recent command which starts with the letter **c**, replacing the first occurrence of the string **bad** with the string **good**.

In-line Editing Options

Normally, each command line entered from a terminal device is simply typed followed by a **new-line** ('RETURN' or 'LINE FEED'). If either the **emacs**, **gmacs**, or **vi** option is active, the user can edit the command line. To be in either of these edit modes **set** the corresponding option. An editing option is automatically selected each time the **VISUAL** or **EDITOR** variable is assigned a value ending in either of these option names.

The editing features require that the user's terminal accept 'RETURN' as carriage return without line feed and that a space (' ') must overwrite the current character on the screen.

The editing modes implement a concept where the user is looking through a window at the current line. The window width is the value of **COLUMNS** if it is defined, otherwise 80. If the window width is too small to display the prompt and leave at least 8 columns to enter input, the prompt is truncated from the left. If the line is longer than the window width minus two, a mark is displayed at the end of the window to notify the user. As the cursor moves and reaches the window boundaries the window will be centered about the cursor. The mark is a > (<, *) if the line extends on the right (left, both) side(s) of the window.

The search commands in each edit mode provide access to the history file. Only strings are matched, not patterns, although a leading ^ in the string restricts the match to begin at the first character in the line.

Each of the edit modes has an operation to list the files or commands that match a partially entered word. When applied to the first word on the line, or the first word after a **;**, **|**, **&**, or **(**, and the word does not begin with ~ or contain a **/**, the list of aliases, functions, and executable commands defined by the

PATH variable that could match the partial word is displayed. Otherwise, the list of files that match the given word is displayed. If the partially entered word does not contain any file expansion characters, a * is appended before generating these lists. After displaying the generated list, the input line is redrawn. These operations are called command name listing and file name listing, respectively. There are additional operations, referred to as command name completion and file name completion, which compute the list of matching commands or files, but instead of printing the list, replace the current word with a complete or partial match. For file name completion, if the match is unique, a / is appended if the file is a directory and a space is appended if the file is not a directory. Otherwise, the longest common prefix for all the matching files replaces the word. For command name completion, only the portion of the file names after the last / are used to find the longest command prefix. If only a single name matches this prefix, then the word is replaced with the command name followed by a space.

Key Bindings

The **KEYBD** trap can be used to intercept keys as they are typed and change the characters that are actually seen by the shell. This trap is executed after each character (or sequence of characters when the first character is ESC) is entered while reading from a terminal. The variable **.sh.edchar** contains the character or character sequence which generated the trap. Changing the value of **.sh.edchar** in the trap action causes the shell to behave as if the new value were entered from the keyboard rather than the original value.

The variable **.sh.edcol** is set to the input column number of the cursor at the time of the input. The variable **.sh.edmode** is set to ESC when in **vi** insert mode (see later in this section) and is null otherwise. By prepending **${.sh.editmode}** to a value assigned to **.sh.edchar** it will cause the shell to change to control mode if it is not already in this mode.

This trap is not invoked for characters entered as arguments to editing directives, or while reading input for a character search.

Emacs Editing Mode

This mode is entered by enabling either the **emacs** or **gmacs** option. The only difference between these two modes is the way they handle ^**T**. To edit, the user moves the cursor to the point needing correction and then inserts or deletes characters or words as needed. All the editing commands are control characters or escape sequences. The notation for control characters is caret (^) followed by the character. For example, ^**F** is the notation for control **F**. This is entered by depressing 'f' while holding down the 'CTRL' (control) key. The 'SHIFT' key is not depressed. (The notation ^**?** indicates the DEL (delete) key.)

The notation for escape sequences is **M-** followed by a character. For example, **M-f** (pronounced Meta f) is entered by depressing ESC (ascii **033**) followed by 'f'. (**M-F** would be the notation for ESC followed by 'SHIFT' (capital) 'F'.)

All edit commands operate from any place on the line (not just at the beginning). Neither the 'RETURN' nor the 'LINE FEED' key is entered after edit commands except when noted.

^**F**	Move cursor forward (right) one character.
M-f	Move cursor forward one word. (The emacs editor's idea of a word is a string of characters consisting of only letters, digits and underscores.)
^**B**	Move cursor backward (left) one character.
M-b	Move cursor backward one word.
^**A**	Move cursor to start of line.
^**E**	Move cursor to end of line.
b^]*char*	Move cursor forward to character *char* on current line.

M-^]_char_	Move cursor back to character _char_ on current line.
^X^X	Interchange the cursor and mark.
erase	Delete previous character. (User defined erase character as defined by the **stty** command, usually **^H** or #.)
^D	Delete current character.
M-d	Delete current word.
M-^H	(Meta-backspace) Delete previous word.
M-h	Delete previous word.
M-^?	(Meta-Delete) Delete previous word (if your interrupt character is (**Delete**, the default) then this command will not work).
^T	Transpose current character with next character in emacs mode. Transpose two previous characters in gmacs mode.
^C	Capitalize current character.
M-c	Capitalize current word.
M-l	Change the current word to lower case.
^K	Delete from the cursor to the end of the line. If preceded by a numerical parameter whose value is less than the current cursor position, then delete from given position up to the cursor. If preceded by a numerical parameter whose value is greater than the current cursor position, then delete from cursor up to given cursor position.
^W	Kill from the cursor to the mark.
M-p	Push the region from the cursor to the mark on the stack.
kill	(User defined kill character as defined by the **stty** command, usually **^G** or @.) Kill the entire current line. If two kill characters are entered in succession, all kill characters from then on cause a line feed (useful when using paper terminals).

^Y	Restore last item removed from line. (Yank item back to the line.)
^L	Line feed and print current line.
^@	(Null character) Set mark.
M-space	(Meta space) Set mark.
^J	(New line) Execute the current line.
^M	(Return) Execute the current line.
eof	End-of-file character, normally **^D**, is processed as an End-of-file only if the current line is null.
^P	Fetch previous command. Each time **^P** is entered the previous command back in time is accessed. Moves back one line when not on the first line of a multi-line command.
M-<	Fetch the least recent (oldest) history line.
M->	Fetch the most recent (youngest) history line.
^N	Fetch next command line. Each time **^N** is entered the next command line forward in time is accessed.
^Rstring	Reverse search history for a previous command line containing string. If a parameter of zero is given, the search is forward. String is terminated by a **Return** or **Newline**. If string is preceded by a ^, the matched line must begin with string. If string is omitted, then the next command line containing the most recent string is accessed. In this case a parameter of zero reverses the direction of the search.
^O	Operate - Execute the current line and fetch the next line relative to current line from the history file.
M-digits	(**Escape**) Define numeric parameter, the *digits* are taken as a parameter to the next command. The commands that accept a parameter are **^F**, **^B**, *erase*, **^C**, **^D**, **^K**, **^R**, **^P**, **^N**, **M-.**, **M-^]**, **M-_**, **M-b**, **M-c**, **M-d**, **M-f**, **M-h**, **M-l** and **M-^H**.

M- *letter*   Soft-key - Your alias list is searched for an alias by the name *letter* and if an alias of this name is defined, its value will be inserted on the input queue. The letter must not be one of the above meta-functions.

M-] *letter*   Soft-key - Your alias list is searched for an alias by the name letter and if an alias of this name is defined, its value will be inserted on the input queue. The can be used to program functions keys on many terminals.

M-.   The last word of the previous command is inserted on the line. If preceded by a numeric parameter, the value of this parameter determines which word to insert rather than the last word.

M-_   Same as **M-.**.

M-*   Attempt file name generation on the current word. An asterisk is appended if the word doesn't match any file or contain any special pattern characters.

M-Esc   File name completion. Replaces the current word with the longest common prefix of all filenames matching the current word with an asterisk appended. If the match is unique, a / is appended if the file is a directory and a space is appended if the file is not a directory.

M-=   List files matching current word pattern if an asterisk were appended.

^U   Multiply parameter of next command by **4**.

\   Escape next character. Editing characters, the user's *erase*, *kill* and *interrupt* (normally **^?**) characters may be entered in a command line or in a search string if preceded by a \. The \ removes the next character's editing features (if any).

^V   Display version of the Korn shell.

M-#   Insert a # at the beginning of the line and execute it. This causes a comment to be inserted in the history file.

Vi Editing Mode

There are two typing modes. Initially, when you enter a *command* you are in the *input* mode. To edit, the user enters control mode by typing **Escape** (033) and moves the cursor to the point needing correction and then inserts or deletes characters or words as needed. Most control commands accept an optional repeat count prior to the command.

When in **vi** mode on most systems, canonical processing is initially enabled and the command will be echoed again if the speed is 1200 baud or greater and it contains any control characters or less than one second has elapsed since the prompt was printed. The **Escape** character terminates canonical processing for the remainder of the command and the user can then modify the command line. This scheme has the advantages of canonical processing with the type-ahead echoing of raw mode.

If the option **viraw** is also set, the terminal will always have canonical processing disabled. This mode is implicit for systems that do not support two alternate end of line delimiters, and may be helpful for certain terminals.

Input Edit Commands

By default the editor is in *input* mode.

erase   (User defined erase character as defined by the **stty** command, usually ^H or #.) Delete previous character.

^W   Delete the previous blank separated word.

^D   Terminate the shell.

^V   Escape next character. Editing characters, the user's *erase* or *kill* characters may be entered in a command line or in a search string if preceded by a ^V. The ^V removes the next character's editing features (if any).

\qquad \\qquad Escape the next *erase* or *kill* character.

Motion Edit Commands

These commands will move the cursor.

[*count*]l	Cursor forward (right) one character.
[*count*]w	Cursor forward one alpha-numeric word.
[count]W	Cursor to the beginning of the next word that follows a blank.
[*count*]e	Cursor to end of word.
[*count*]E	Cursor to end of the current blank delimited word.
[*count*]h	Cursor backward (left) one character.
[*count*]b	Cursor backward one word.
[*count*]B	Cursor to preceding blank separated word.
[*count*]l	Cursor to column 1 count.
[*count*]f *c*	Find the next character *c* in the current line.
[*count*]F *c*	Find the previous character *c* in the current line.
[*count*]t *c*	Equivalent to **f** followed by **h**.
[*count*]T *c*	Equivalent to **F** followed by **l**.
[*count*];	Repeats count times, the last single character find command, **f**, **F**, **t**, or **T**.
[*count*],	Reverses the last single character find command count times.
0	Cursor to start of line.
^	Cursor to first non-blank character in line.
$	Cursor to end of line.

Search Edit Commands

These commands access your command history.

[*count*] **k**	Fetch previous command. Each time **k** is entered the previous command back in time is accessed.
[*count*]–	Equivalent to **k**.

[*count*]**j**   Fetch next command. Each time **j** is entered the next command forward in time is accessed.

[*count*]+   Equivalent to **j**.

[*count*]**G**   The command number *count* is fetched. The default is the least recent history command.

/string   Search backward through history for a previous command containing *string*. String is terminated by a **Return** or **Newline**. If *string* is preceded by a ^, the matched line must begin with *string*. If *string* is null the previous string will be used.

? *string*   Same as / except that search will be in the forward direction.

n   Search for next match of the last pattern to / or **?** commands.

N   Search for next match of the last pattern to / or **?**, but in reverse direction. Search history for the string entered by the previous / command.

Text Modification Edit Commands

These commands will modify the line.

a   Enter input mode and enter text after the current character.

A   Append text to the end of the line. Equivalent to **$a**.

[*count*]**c***motion*
c[*count*]*motion*

Delete current character through the character that motion would move the cursor to and enter input mode. If *motion* is **c**, the entire line will be deleted and input mode entered.

C   Delete the current character through the end of line and enter input mode **c$**. Equivalent to **c$**.

S   Equivalent to **cc**.

D   Delete the current character through the end of line. Equivalent to **d$**.

[*count*]**d***motion*
d[*count*]*motion*

> Delete current character through the character that motion would move to. If *motion* is **d**, the entire line will be deleted.

i

> Enter input mode and insert text before the current character.

I

> Insert text before the beginning of the line. Equivalent to **i**.

[*count*]**P**

> Place the previous text modification before the cursor.

[*count*]**p**

> Place the previous text modification after the cursor.

R

> Enter input mode and replace characters on the screen with characters you type overlay fashion.

[*count*]**r***c*

> Replace the count character(s) starting at the current cursor position with *c*, and advance the cursor.

[*count*]**x**

> Delete current character.

[*count*]**X**

> Delete preceding character.

[*count*]**.**

> Repeat the previous text modification command.

[*count*]**~**

> Invert the case of the count character(s) starting at the current cursor position and advance the cursor.

[*count*]**_**

> Causes the *count* word of the previous command to be appended and input mode entered. The last word is used if *count* is omitted. Causes an * to be appended to the current word and file name generation attempted. If no match is found, it rings the bell. Otherwise, the word is replaced by the matching pattern and input mode is entered.

| \ | Filename completion. Replaces the current word with the longest common prefix of all filenames matching the current word with an asterisk appended. If the match is unique, a/ is appended if the file is a directory and a space is appended if the file is not a directory. |

Other Edit Commands

Miscellaneous commands.

[*count*]**y***motion*	
y[*count*]*motion*	Yank current character through character that motion would move the cursor to and puts them into the delete buffer. The text and cursor are unchanged.
Y	Yanks from current position to end of line. Equivalent to **y$**.
u	Undo the last text modifying command.
U	Undo all the text modifying commands performed on the line.
[*count*]**v**	Returns the command **fc −e ${VISUAL:− ${EDITOR:−vi}}** *count* in the input buffer. If *count* is omitted, then the current line is used.
^L	Line feed and print current line. Has effect only in control mode.
^J	(New line) Execute the current line, regardless of mode.
^M	(Return) Execute current line, regardless of mode.
#	Sends the line after inserting a # in front of the line. If line already commented, then remove the # character. Useful for causing the current line to be inserted in the history without being executed.
=	List the file names that match the current word if an asterisk were appended it.

@letter   Your alias list is searched for an alias *letter* and if defined, its value is inserted on the input queue.

%   find the matching (), {}

Built-in Commands

The following simple-commands are executed in the shell process. Input/Output redirection is permitted. Unless otherwise indicated, the output is written on file descriptor 1 and the exit status, when there is no syntax error, is zero. Except for **:**, **true**, **false**, **echo**, **command**, **newgrp**, and **login**, all built-in commands accept — to indicate end of options. They also interpret the option **-?** as a help request and print a *usage* message on standard error. Commands that are preceded by one or two § symbols are special built-in commands and are treated specially in the following ways:

1.   Variable assignment lists preceding the command remain in effect when the command completes.
2.   I/O redirections are processed after variable assignments.
3.   Errors cause a script that contains them to abort.
4.   They are not valid function names.
5.   Words following a command preceded by §§ that are in the format of a variable assignment are expanded with the same rules as a variable assignment. This means that tilde substitution is performed after the = sign and field splitting and file name generation are not performed.

§ **:** [*arg* . . .]
    The command only expands parameters.

§ **.** *name* [*arg* . . .]
    If *name* is a function defined with the **function** *name* reserved word syntax, the function is executed in the current environment (as if it had been defined with the

name() syntax.) Otherwise if *name* refers to a file, the file is read in its entirety and the commands are executed in the current shell environment. The search path specified by **PATH** is used to find the directory containing the file. If any arguments *arg* are given, they become the positional parameters while processing the **.** command and the original positional parameters are restored upon completion. Otherwise the positional parameters are unchanged. The exit status is the exit status of the last command executed.

§§ **alias** [**-ptx**] [*name*[=*value*]] . . .

alias with no arguments prints the list of aliases in the form *name=value* on standard output. The **-p** option causes the word **alias** to be inserted before each one. When one or more arguments are given, an *alias* is defined for each *name* whose *value* is given. A trailing space in *value* causes the next word to be checked for alias substitution. The obsolete -t option is used to set and list tracked aliases. The value of a tracked alias is the full pathname corresponding to the given *name*. The value becomes undefined when the value of **PATH** is reset but the alias remains tracked. Without the **-t** option, for each *name* in the argument list for which no *value* is given, the name and value of the alias is printed. The obsolete **-x** option has no effect. The exit status is non-zero if a *name* is given, but no value, and no alias has been defined for the *name*.

bg [*job* . . .]

This command is only on systems that support job control. Puts each specified *job* into the background. The current job is put in the background if *job* is not specified. See *Jobs* for a description of the format of *job*.

§ **break** [*n*]

Exit from the enclosing **for**, **while**, **until**, or **select** loop, if any. If *n* is specified, then break *n* levels.

builtin [-ds] [-f *file* **] [** *name* **. . .]**

> If *name* is not specified, and no **-f** option is specified, the built-ins are printed on standard output. The **-s** option prints only the special built-ins. Otherwise, each *name* represents the pathname whose basename is the name of the built-in. The entry point function name is determined by prepending **b_** to the built-in name. Special built-ins cannot be bound to a pathname or deleted. The **-d** option deletes each of the given built-ins. On systems that support dynamic loading, the **-f** option names a shared library containing the code for built-ins. Once a library is loaded, its symbols become available for subsequent invocations of **builtin**. Multiple libraries can be specified with separate invocations of the **builtin** command. Libraries are searched in the reverse order in which they are specified. When a library is loaded, it looks for a function in the library whose name is **lib_init()** and invokes this function with an argument of **0**.

cd [-LP] [*arg* **]**
cd [-LP] *old new*

> This command can be in either of two forms. In the first form it changes the current directory to *arg*. If *arg* is **-** the directory is changed to the previous directory. The shell variable **HOME** is the default *arg*. The variable **PWD** is set to the current directory. The shell variable **CDPATH** defines the search path for the directory containing *arg*. Alternative directory names are separated by a colon (**:**). The default path is **<null>** (specifying the current directory). Note that the current directory is specified by a null path name, which can appear immediately after the equal sign or between the colon delimiters anywhere else in the path list. If *arg* begins with a **/** then the search path is not used. Otherwise, each directory in path is searched for *arg*.

The second form of **cd** substitutes the string *new* for the string *old* in the current directory name, **PWD**, and tries to change to this new directory.

By default, symbolic link names are treated literally when finding the directory name. This is equivalent to the **-L** option. The **-P** option causes symbolic links to be resolved when determining the directory. The last instance of **-L** or **-P** on the command line determines which method is used. The **cd** command may not be executed by **rsh.**

command [-pvV] *name* [*arg . . .*]

Without the **-v** or **-V** options, **command** executes *name* with the arguments given by *arg*. The **-p** option causes a default path to be searched rather than the one defined by the value of **PATH**. Functions will not be searched for when finding *name*. In addition, if *name* refers to a special built-in, none of the special properties associated with the leading daggers will be honored. (For example, the predefined alias **redirect='command exec'** prevents a script from terminating when an invalid redirection is given.) With the **-v** option, **command** is equivalent to the built-in **whence** command described below. The **-V** option causes **command** to act like **whence -v**.

§ **continue** [*n*]

Resume the next iteration of the enclosing **for while until** or **select** loop. If *n* is specified then resume at the *nth* enclosing loop.

disown [*job . . .*]

Causes the shell not to send a HUP signal to each given *job*, or all active jobs if *job* is omitted, when a login shell terminates.

echo *arg* ...

When the first *arg* does not begin with a -, and none of the arguments contain a \, then **echo** prints each of its arguments separated by a space and terminated by a new-line. Otherwise, the behavior of **echo** is system dependent and **print** or **printf** described below should be used. See *echo*(1) for usage and description.

§ **eval** [*arg* ...]

The arguments are read as input to the shell and the resulting command(s) executed.

§ **exec** [*arg* ...]

If *arg* is given, the command specified by the arguments is executed in place of this shell without creating a new process. The **-c** option causes the environment to be cleared before applying variable assignments associated with the **exec** invocation. The **-a** option causes *name* rather than the first *arg*, to become **argv[0]** for the new process. Input/output arguments may appear and affect the current process. If *arg* is not given, the effect of this command is to modify file descriptors as prescribed by the input/output redirection list. In this case, any file descriptor numbers greater than 2 that are opened with this mechanism are closed when invoking another program.

§ **exit** [*n*]

Causes the shell to exit with the exit status specified by *n*. The value will be the least significant 8 bits of the specified status. If *n* is omitted, then the exit status is that of the last command executed. An end-of-file will also cause the shell to exit except for a shell which has the **ignoreeof** option (see **set** below) turned on.

§§ **export** [**-p**] [*name* [=*value*]] . . .

If *name* is not given, the names and values of each variable with the export attribute are printed with the values quoted in a manner that allows them to be re-input. The **-p** option causes the word **export** to be inserted before each one. Otherwise, the given *name*s are marked for automatic export to the *environment* of subsequently-executed commands.

false   Does nothing, and exits 1. Used with **until** for infinite loops.

fg [*job* ...]

This command is only on systems that support job control. Each *job* specified is brought to the foreground and waited for in the specified order. Otherwise, the current job is brought into the foreground. See *Jobs* for a description of the format of *job*.

getconf [*name* [*pathname*]]

Prints the current value of the configuration parameter given by *name*. The configuration parameters are defined by the IEEE POSIX 1003.1 and IEEE POSIX 1003.2 standards. (See *pathconf*(2) and *sysconf*(2).) The *pathname* argument is required for parameters whose value depends on the location in the file system. If no arguments are given, **getconf** prints the names and values of the current configuration parameters. The pathname / is used for each of the parameters that requires *pathname*.

getopts [-a *name*] *optstring vname* [*arg* ...]

Checks *arg* for legal options. If *arg* is omitted, the positional parameters are used. An option argument begins with a + or a -. An option not beginning with + or - or the argument - - ends the options. *optstring* contains the letters that **getopts** recognizes. If a letter is followed by a :, that option is expected to have an argument. The options can be separated from the argument by blanks. The option -? causes **getopts** to generate a usage message on standard error. The **-a** argument can be used to specify the name to use for the usage message, which defaults to **$0**. **getopts** places the next option letter it finds inside variable *vname* each time it is invoked. The option letter will be prepended with a + when *arg* begins with a +. The index of the next *arg* is stored in **OPTIND**.

The option argument, if any, gets stored in **OPTARG**. A leading **:** in *optstring* causes **getopts** to store the letter of an invalid option in **OPTARG**, and to set *vname* to **?** for an unknown option and to **:** when a required option is missing. Otherwise, **getopts** prints an error message. The exit status is non-zero when there are no more options. There is no way to specify any of the options **:, +, -, ?, [,** and **]**. The option **#** can only be specified as the first option.

hist [**-e** *ename*] [**-nlr**] [*first* [*last*]]

hist -s [*old=new*] [*command*]

In the first form, a range of commands from *first* to *last* is selected from the last **HISTSIZE** commands that were typed at the terminal. The arguments *first* and *last* may be specified as a number or as a string. A string is used to locate the most recent command starting with the given string. A negative number is used as an offset to the current command number. If the **-l** option is selected, the commands are listed on standard output. Otherwise, the editor program *ename* is invoked on a file containing these keyboard commands. If *ename* is not supplied, then the value of the variable **HISTEDIT** is used. If **HISTEDIT** is not set, then **FCEDIT** (default **/bin/ed**) is used as the editor. When editing is complete, the edited command(s) is executed if the changes have been saved. If *last* is not specified, then it will be set to *first*. If *first* is not specified, the default is the previous command for editing and -16 for listing. The option **-r** reverses the order of the commands and the option **-n** suppresses command numbers when listing. In the second form, *command* is interpreted as *first* described above and defaults to the last command executed. The resulting command is executed after the optional substitution *old =new* is performed.

jobs [**-lnp**] [*job* . . .]

Lists information about each given job; or all active jobs if *job* is omitted. The **-l** option lists process ids in addition to the normal information. The **-n** option only displays jobs that have stopped or exited since last notified. The **-p** option causes only the process group to be listed.

kill [**-s** *signame*] *job* . . .
kill [**-n** *signum*] *job* . . .
kill -l [*sig* . . .]

Sends either the TERM (terminate) signal or the specified signal to the specified jobs or processes. Signals are either given by number with the **-n** option or by name with the **-s** option (as given in **<signal.h>**, stripped of the prefix "SIG" with the exception that SIGCLD is named CHLD). For backward compatibility, the **n** and **s** can be omitted and the number or name placed immediately after the -. If the signal being sent is TERM (terminate) or HUP (hangup), then the job or process will be sent a CONT (continue) signal if it is stopped. The argument *job* can be the process id of a process that is not a member of one of the active jobs. See *Jobs* for a description of the format of *job*. In the third form, **kill -l**, if *sig* is not specified, the signal names are listed. Otherwise, for each *sig* that is a name, the corresponding signal number is listed. For each *sig* that is a number, the signal name corresponding to the least significant 8 bits of *sig* is listed.

let *arg* ...

Each *arg* is a separate *arithmetic expression* to be evaluated. See **Arithmetic Evaluation** earlier in this section, for a description of arithmetic expression evaluation. The exit status is 0 if the value of the last expression is non-zero, and 1 otherwise.

§ **newgrp** [*arg* . . .]

> Equivalent to **exec /bin/newgrp** *arg* . . . .

print [**-Rnprs**] [**-u** *unit*] [**-f** *format*] [*arg* . . .]

> With no options or with option - or - -, each *arg* is printed on standard output. The **-f** option causes the arguments to be printed as described by **printf**. In this case, any **n**, **r**, **R** options are ignored. Otherwise, unless the **-R** or **-r**, are specified, the following escape conventions will be applied: \a   The   alert character (ascii **07**).

> \b   The backspace character (ascii **010**).

> \c   Causes **print** to end without processing more arguments and not adding a new-line.

> \f   The formfeed character (ascii **014**).

> \n   The new-line character (ascii **012**).

> \r   The carriage return character (ascii **015**).

> \t   The tab character (ascii **011**).

> \v   The vertical tab character (ascii **013**).

> \E   The escape character (ascii **033**).

> \\   The backslash character \.

> \0*x*   The character defined by the 1, 2, or 3-digit octal string given by *x*.

> The **-R** option will print all subsequent arguments and options other than **-n**. The **-p** option causes the arguments to be written onto the pipe of the process spawned with |**&** instead of standard output. The **-s** option causes the arguments to be written onto the history file instead of standard output. The **-u** option can be used to specify a one digit file descriptor unit number *unit* on which the output will be placed. The default is 1. If the option **-n** is used, no **new-line** is added to the output.

printf *format* [*arg* . . .]

> The arguments *arg* are printed on standard output in accordance with the ANSI-C formatting rules associated with the format string *format*. If the number

of arguments exceeds the number of format specifications, the **format** string is reused to format remaining arguments. The following extensions can also be used:

- A **%b** format can be used instead of **%s** to cause escape sequences in the corresponding *arg* to be expanded as described in **print.**

- A **%P** format can be used instead of **%s** to cause *arg* to be interpreted as an extended regular expression and be printed as a shell pattern.

- A **%q** format can be used instead of **%s** to cause the resulting string to be quoted in a manner than can be reinput to the shell.

- The precision field of the **%d** format can be followed by a **.** and the output base.

pwd [-LP]

Outputs the value of the current working directory. The **-L** option is the default; it prints the logical name of the current directory. If the **-P** option is given, all symbolic links are resolved from the name. The last instance of **-L** or **-P** on the command line determines which method is used.

read [-Aprs] [-d *delim* **] [-t** *timeout* **] [-u** *unit* **] [** *vname?prompt* **] [** *vname . . .* **]**

The shell input mechanism. One line is read and is broken up into fields using the characters in **IFS** as separators. The escape character, \, is used to remove any special meaning for the next character and for line continuation. The **-d** option causes the read to continue to the first character of *delim* rather than new-line. In raw mode, **-r,** the \ character is not treated specially. The first field is assigned to the first *vname*, the second field to the second *vname*, etc., with leftover fields assigned to the last *vname*. The **-A** option causes the variable *vname* to be unset and each field that is read to be stored in successive elements of the indexed array *vname*. The **-p** option causes the input line to be taken from the input pipe of a process spawned by the shell using |**&**. If the **-s** option is present, the input will be saved as a command in the history file. The option **-u** can be used to specify a one digit file descriptor unit *unit* to read from. The file descriptor can be opened with the **exec** special built-in command. The default value of unit *n* is 0. The option **-t** is used to specify a timeout in seconds when reading from a terminal or pipe. If *vname* is omitted, then **REPLY** is used as the default *vname*. An end-of-file with the **-p** option causes cleanup for this process so that another can be spawned. If the first argument contains a **?**, the remainder of this word is used as a *prompt* on standard error when the shell is interactive. The exit status is 0 unless an end-of-file is encountered or **read** has timed out.

§§ **readonly** [**-p**] [*vname*[=*value*]] . . .

If *vname* is not given, the names and values of each variable with the readonly attribute are printed with the values quoted in a manner that allows them to be re-inputted. The **-p** option causes the word **readonly** to be inserted before each one. Otherwise, the given *vname*s are marked readonly and these names cannot be changed by subsequent assignment.

§ **return** [*n*]

Causes a shell *function* or **.** script to return to the invoking script with the exit status specified by *n*. The value will be the least significant 8 bits of the specified status. If *n* is omitted, then the return status is that of the last command executed. If **return** is invoked while not in a *function* or a **.** script, then it behaves the same as **exit**.

§ **set** [±**Cabefhkmnopstuvx**] [±**o** [*option*]] . . . [±**A** *vname*] [*arg* . . .]

The options for this command have meaning as follows:

-A   Array assignment. Unset the variable *vname* and assign values sequentially from the *arg* list. If **+A** is used, the variable *vname* is not unset first.

-C   Prevents redirection > from truncating existing files. Files that are created are opened with the O_EXCL mode. Requires >| to truncate a file when turned on.

-a   All subsequent variables that are defined are automatically exported.

-b   Prints job completion messages as soon as a background job changes state rather than waiting for the next prompt.

-e   If a command has a non-zero exit status, execute the **ERR** trap, if set, and exit. This mode is disabled while reading profiles.

-f   Disables file name generation.

-h   Each command becomes a tracked alias when first encountered.

-k   (Obsolete). All variable assignment arguments are placed in the environment for a command, not just those that precede the command name.

-m   Background jobs will run in a separate process group and a line will print upon completion. The exit status of background jobs is reported in a completion message. On systems with job control, this option is turned on automatically for interactive shells.

-n   Read commands and check them for syntax errors, but do not execute them. Ignored for interactive shells.

-o   The following argument can be one of the following option names:

allexport	Same as **-a**.
errexit	Same as **-e**.
bgnice	All background jobs are run at a lower priority. This is the default mode.

emacs	Puts you in an *emacs* style in-line editor for command entry.
gmacs	Puts you in a *gmacs* style in-line editor for command entry.
ignoreeof	The shell will not exit on end-of-file. The command **exit** must be used.
keyword	Same as **-k**.
markdirs	All directory names resulting from file name generation have a trailing / appended.
monitor	Same as **-m**.
noclobber	Same as **-C**.
noexec	Same as **-n**.
noglob	Same as **-f**.
nolog	Do not save function definitions in the history file.
notify	Same as **-b**.
nounset	Same as **-u**.
privileged	Same as **-p**.
verbose	Same as **-v**.
trackall	Same as **-h**.
vi	Puts you in insert mode of a *vi* style in-line editor until you hit the escape character **033**. This puts you in control mode. A return sends the line.
viraw	Each character is processed as it is typed in *vi* mode.
xtrace	Same as **-x**.

If no option name is supplied, then the current option settings are printed.

-p   Disables processing of the **$HOME/.profile** file and uses the file **/etc/suid_profile** instead of the **ENV** file. This mode is on whenever the effective uid (gid) is not equal to the real uid (gid). Turning this off causes the effective uid and gid to be set to the real uid and gid.

-s   Sort the positional parameters lexicographically.

-t   (Obsolete). Exit after reading and executing one command.

-u   Treat unset parameters as an error when substituting.

-v   Print shell input lines as they are read.

-x   Print commands and their arguments as they are executed.

- -   Do not change any of the options; useful in setting **$1** to a value beginning with -. If no arguments follow this option then the positional parameters are unset.

As an obsolete feature, if the first *arg* is - then the **-x** and **-v** options are turned off and the next *arg* is treated as the first argument. Using + rather than - causes these options to be turned off. These options can also be used upon invocation of the shell. The current set of options may be found in **$-**. Unless **-A** is specified, the remaining arguments are positional parameters and are assigned, in order, to **$1 $2** . . . . If no arguments are given, then the names and values of all variables are printed on the standard output.

§**shift** [*n*]

The positional parameters from **$***n***+1** . . . are renamed **$1** . . . , default *n* is 1. The parameter *n* can be any arithmetic expression that evaluates to a non-negative number less than or equal to **$#**.

sleep *seconds*

Suspends execution for the number of decimal seconds or fractions of a second given by *seconds*.

§ **trap** [**-p**] [*action*] [*sig*] . . .

The **-p** option causes the trap action associated with each trap as specified by the arguments to be printed with appropriate quoting. Otherwise, *action* will be processed as if it were an argument to **eval** when the shell receives signal(s) *sig*. Each *sig* can be given as a number or as the name of the signal. Trap commands are executed in order of signal number. Any attempt to set a trap on a signal that was ignored on entry to the current shell is ineffective. If *action* is omitted and the first *sig* is a number, or if *action* is -, then the trap(s) for each *sig* are reset to their original values. If *action* is the null string then this signal is ignored by the shell and by the commands it invokes. If *sig* is **ERR** then *action* will be executed whenever a command has a non-zero exit status. If *sig* is **DEBUG** then *action* will be executed before each command. If *sig* is **0** or **EXIT** and the **trap** statement is executed inside the body of a function, then the command *action* is executed after the function completes. If *sig* is **0** or **EXIT** for a **trap** set outside any function then the command *action* is executed on exit from the shell. If *sig* is **KEYBD**, then *action* will be executed whenever a key is read while in **emacs**, **gmacs**, or **vi** mode. The **trap** command with no arguments prints a list of commands associated with each signal number.

true   Does nothing, and exits 0. Used with **while** for infinite loops.

§§ **typeset** [±**AHflnprtux**] [±**EFLRZi** [*n*]] [*vname* [=*value*]] . . .

Sets attributes and values for shell variables and functions. When invoked inside a function, a new instance of the variable *vname* is created. The variable's value and type are restored when the function completes. The following list of attributes may be specified:

-A   Declares *vname* to be an associative array. Subscripts are strings rather than arithmetic expressions.

-E   Declares *vname* to be a double precision floating point number. If *n* is non-zero, it defines the number of significant figures that are used when expanding *vname*. Otherwise, ten significant figures will be used.

-F   Declares *vname* to be a double precision floating point number. If *n* is non-zero, it defines the number of places after the decimal point that are used when expanding *vname*. Otherwise ten places after the decimal point will be used.

-H This option provides Unix to host-name file mapping on non-Unix machines.

-L Left justify and remove leading blanks from *value*. If *n* is non-zero, it defines the width of the field, otherwise it is determined by the width of the value of first assignment. When the variable is assigned to, it is filled on the right with blanks or truncated, if necessary, to fit into the field. The **-R** option is turned off.

-R Right justify and fill with leading blanks. If *n* is non-zero, it defines the width of the field, otherwise it is determined by the width of the value of first assignment. The field is left filled with blanks or truncated from the end if the variable is reassigned. The **-L** option is turned off.

-Z Right justify and fill with leading zeros if the first non-blank character is a digit and the **-L** option has not been set. Remove leading zeros if the **-L** option is also set. If *n* is non-zero, it defines the width of the field, otherwise it is determined by the width of the value of first assignment.

-f The names refer to function names rather than variable names. No assignments can be made and the only other valid options are **-t**, **-u** and **-x**. The **-t** option turns on execution tracing for this function. The **-u** option causes this function to be marked undefined. The **FPATH** variable will be searched to find the function definition when the function is referenced.

-i Declares *vname* to be represented internally as integer. The right hand side of an assignment is evaluated as an arithmetic expression when assigning to an integer. If *n* is non-zero, it defines the output arithmetic base, otherwise the output base will be ten.

-l   All upper-case characters are converted to lower-case. The upper-case option, **-u**, is turned off.

-n   Declares *vname* to be a reference to the variable whose name is defined by the value of variable *vname*. This is usually used to reference a variable inside a function whose name has been passed as an argument.

-r   The given *vname*s are marked readonly and these names cannot be changed by subsequent assignment.

-t   Tags the variables. Tags are user definable and have no special meaning to the shell.

-u   All lower-case characters are converted to upper-case. The lower-case option, **-l**, is turned off.

-x   The given *vname*s are marked for automatic export to the *environment* of subsequently-executed commands. Variables whose names contain a **.** cannot be exported.

The **-i** attribute cannot be specified along with **-R**, **-L**, **-Z**, or **-f**.

Using **+** rather than **-** causes these options to be turned off. If no *vname* arguments are given, a list of *vnames* (and optionally the *values*) of the *variables* is printed. (Using **+** rather than **-** keeps the values from being printed.) The **-p** option causes **typeset** followed by the option letters to be printed before each name rather than the names of the options. If any option other than **-p** is given, only those variables which have all of the given options are printed. Otherwise, the *vname*s and *attributes* of all *variables* are printed.

ulimit [-HSacdfmnpstv] [*limit*]

Set or display a resource limit. The available resource limits are listed below. Many systems do not support one or more of these limits. The limit for a specified resource is set when *limit* is specified. The value of *limit* can be a number in the unit specified below with each resource, or the value **unlimited**. The **-H** and **-S** options specify whether the hard limit or the soft limit for the given resource is set. A hard limit cannot be increased once it is set. A soft limit can be increased up to the value of the hard limit. If neither the **H** nor **S** options is specified, the limit applies to both. The current resource limit is printed when *limit* is omitted. In this case, the soft limit is printed unless **H** is specified. When more than one resource is specified, then the limit name and unit is printed before the value.

-a Lists all of the current resource limits.

-c The number of 512-byte blocks on the size of core dumps.

-d The number of K-bytes on the size of the data area.

-f The number of 512-byte blocks on files that can be written by the current process or by child processes (files of any size may be read).

-m The number of K-bytes on the size of physical memory.

-n The number of file descriptors plus 1.

-p The number of 512-byte blocks for pipe buffering.

-s The number of K-bytes on the size of the stack area.

-t The number of CPU seconds to be used by each process.

-v The number of K-bytes for virtual memory.

If no option is given, **-f** is assumed.

umask [-S] [*mask*]

The user file-creation mask is set to *mask* (see *umask*(2)). *mask* can either be an octal number or a symbolic value as described in *chmod*(1). If a symbolic value is given, the new umask value is the complement of the result of applying *mask* to the complement of the previous umask value. If *mask* is omitted, the current value of the mask is printed. The **-S** option causes the mode to be printed as a symbolic value. Otherwise, the mask is printed in octal.

§ **unalias** [**-a**] *name* . . .

> The aliases given by the list of *name*s are removed from the alias list. The **-a** option causes all the aliases to be unset.

§**unset** [**-fnv**] *vname* . . .

> The variables given by the list of *vname*s are unassigned, i.e., their values and attributes are erased. Readonly variables cannot be unset. If the **-f** option is set, then the names refer to *function* names. If the **-v** option is set, then the names refer to *variable* names. The **-f** option overrides **-v**. If **-n** is set and *name* is a name reference, then *name* will be unset rather than the variable that it references. The default is equivalent to **-v**. Unsetting **LINENO**, **MAILCHECK**, **OPTARG**, **OPTIND**, **RANDOM**, **SECONDS**, **TMOUT**, and _ removes their special meaning even if they are subsequently assigned to.

wait [*job* . . .]

> Wait for the specified *job* and report its termination status. If *job* is not given, then all currently active child processes are waited for. The exit status from this command is that of the last process waited for. See *Jobs* for a description of the format of *job*.

whence [**-afpv**] *name* . . .

> For each *name*, indicate how it would be interpreted if used as a command name. The **-v** option produces a more verbose report. The **-f** options skips the search for functions. The **-p** option does a path search for *name* even if name is an alias, a function, or a reserved word. The **-a** option is similar to the **-v** option but causes all interpretations of the given name to be reported.

Invocation

    If the shell is invoked by **exec**(2), and the first character of argument zero (**$0**) is **-**, then the shell is assumed to be a *login* shell and commands are read from **/etc/profile** and then from either **.profile** in the current directory or **$HOME/.profile**, if either file exists. Next, for interactive shells, commands are read from the file named by performing parameter expansion, command substitution, and arithmetic substitution on the value of the environment variable **ENV** if the file exists. If the **-s** option is not present and *arg* is, then a path search is performed on the first *arg* to determine the name of the script to execute. The script *arg* must have read permission and any *setuid* and *setgid* settings will be ignored. If the script is not found on the path, *arg* is processed as if it named a built-in command or function. Commands are then read as described below; the following options are interpreted by the shell when it is invoked:

-c   If the **-c** option is present, then commands are read from the first *arg*. Any remaining arguments become positional parameters starting at **0**.

-s   If the **-s** option is present or if no arguments remain, then commands are read from the standard input. Shell output, except for the output of the special commands listed earlier in this appendix, is written to file descriptor 2.

-i   If the **-i** option is present or if the shell input and output are attached to a terminal (as told by **tcgetattr**(2)), then this shell is *interactive*. In this case TERM is ignored (so that **kill 0** does not kill an interactive shell) and INTR is caught and ignored (so that **wait** is interruptible). In all cases, QUIT is ignored by the shell.

-r   If the **-r** option is present, the shell is a restricted shell.

-D   A list of all double quoted strings that are preceded by a **$** will be printed on standard output and the shell will exit. This set of strings will be subject to language translation when the locale is not C or POSIX. No commands will be executed.

-I *filename*

The **-R** *filename* option is used to generate a cross reference database that can be used by a separate utility to find definitions and references for variables and commands.

The remaining options and arguments are described under the **set** command above. An optional - as the first argument is ignored.

Rsh Only

Rsh is used to set up login names and execution environments whose capabilities are more controlled than those of the standard shell. The actions of **rsh** are identical to those of **sh**, except that the following are disallowed:

- changing directory (see *cd*(1))
- setting or unsetting the value or attributes of **SHELL**, **ENV**, or **PATH**
- specifying path or command names containing /
- redirecting output (>, >|, <>, and >>)
- adding or deleting built-in commands

The restrictions above are enforced after **.profile** and the **ENV** files are interpreted.

When a command to be executed is found to be a shell procedure, **rsh** invokes **sh** to execute it. Thus, it is possible to provide to the end-user shell procedures that have access to the full power of the standard shell, while imposing a limited menu of commands; this scheme assumes that the end-user does not have write and execute permissions in the same directory.

The net effect of these rules is that the writer of the **.profile** has complete control over user actions, by performing guaranteed setup actions and leaving the user in an appropriate directory (probably *not* the login directory).

The system administrator often sets up a directory of commands (for example **/usr/rbin**) that can be safely invoked by **rsh**.

EXIT STATUS

Errors detected by the shell, such as syntax errors, cause the shell to return a non-zero exit status. Otherwise, the shell returns the exit status of the last command executed (see also the **exit** command above). If the shell is being used non-interactively, then execution of the shell file is abandoned. Run time errors detected by the shell are reported by printing the command or function name and the error condition. If the line number that the error occurred on is greater than one, then the line number is also printed in square brackets ([]) after the command or function name.

CAVEATS

If a command is executed, and then a command with the same name is installed in a directory in the search path before the directory where the original command was found, the shell will continue to *exec* the original command. Use the **-t** option of the **alias** command to correct this situation.

Some very old shell scripts contain a^ as a synonym for the pipe character |.

Using the **hist** built-in command within a compound command will cause the whole command to disappear from the history file.

The built-in command . *file* reads the whole file before any commands are executed. Therefore, **alias** and **unalias** commands in the file will not apply to any commands defined in the file.

Traps are not processed while a job is waiting for a foreground process. Thus, a trap on **CHLD** won't be executed until the foreground job terminates.

It is a good idea to leave a space after the comma operator in arithmetic expressions to prevent the comma from being interpreted as the decimal point character in certain locales.

Appendix F: Pdksh

The Public Domain Korn Shell, or pdksh, is a free, public domain version of the Korn shell. It's compatible with most any version of Unix such as SCO, BSD, Solaris, HP-UX, but is mostly used on Linux-based systems. It has most of the features of ksh88, as well as some ksh93 and additional features that are not in either. Here are a few of the features not in pdksh:

- Exported aliases and functions
- Set -t
- Signals/traps not cleared during functions
- Trap DEBUG, local ERR and EXIT traps in functions
- ERRNO parameter
- Float and structure datatypes
- Compound and nameref variables
- Associative arrays
- Discipline functions
- Search, replace, and substring operators

The source distribution contains more details on features not found in pdksh as well as current bugs/anomolies.

Downloading the Source

Pdksh bundled with versions of Linux, including Red Hat's, and the source distribution is available from the following sites:

> **ftp://ftp.cs.mun.ca/pub/pdksh/**

The following sites have been known to mirror the above directory:

> Austria:
> **http://gd.tuwien.ac.at/utils/shells/pdksh/**

> France:
> **ftp://ftp.lip6.fr/pub/unix/shells/pdksh/**

> United Kingdom:
> **ftp://ftp.demon.net/pub/mirrors/pdksh/**

> United States:
> **ftp://ftp.rge.com/pub/shells/pdksh/**

More information is available at this URL**http://www.kornshell.com/resources/.**

Building Pdksh

Once downloaded, it is fairly easy to build a runnable version. The first step is to run the configure script. This is a GNU script that will generate a **Makefile** and **config.h** files. Some of the useful options to configure are:

Table F.1: Pdksh Build Steps

1) configure configure PDKSH and prepare for build.

2) make build binaries and docs.

3) make check verify the build.

4) make install run the installation step.

5) set default shell add pdksh path to **/etc/shells** for default login shell (this step is optional)

prefix=*PATH*
indicates the directory tree under which the binary and man page are installed (*PATH*/**bin/ksh** and *PATH*/**man/man1/ksh.1**). The default prefix is **/usr/local.**

exec-prefix=*PATH*
overrides **-prefix** for machine dependent files

program-prefix=*pd*
install binary and man page as **pdksh** and **pdksh.1**

verbose
show what is being defined as script runs

There is also an option to enable/disable features during the configure step. More information about this can be viewed by running "**configure -help | more**".

For the Red Hat distribution of Linux, make sure that **/dev/tty** has mode **0666** (not mode **0644**). Otherwise, you will get warnings about not being able to do job control.

The next step is to actually build the binary or runnable version and is done by running "**make**". If you get compile/link errors, look at the **Readme** file in the distribution for details. You may need to obtain the GNU public domain C compiler if you don't have one with your system.

Once you've built the binary, you can sanity check it by running "**make check**". If you don't have Perl available, you can also do this by running "**ENV= pdksh misc/Bugs pdksh**", where **pdksh** is the path to pdksh.

If it checks out ok, you can then install it by running "**make install**". If you want to make pdksh your default login shell, then you should add this to the **/etc/shells** file.

Appendix G: Pdksh Quick Reference

Command Execution

The primary prompt (**PS1** - default $ or # for super-users) is displayed whenever the Korn shell is ready to read a command. The secondary prompt (**PS2** - default >) is displayed when the Korn shell needs more input.

Command Execution Format

command1 ; *command2*

        execute *command1* followed by *command2*

command &   execute *command* asynchronously in the background; do not wait for completion

command1 | *command2*

        pass the standard output of *command1* to standard input of *command2*

command1 && *command2*

        execute *command2* if *command1* returns zero (successful) exit status

command1 || *command2*

        execute *command2* if *command1* returns non-zero (unsuccessful) exit status

command |&	execute *command* asynchronously with its standard input and output attached to the parent shell; use **read** −**p**/**print** −**p** to manipulate the standard input/output
command \	continue *command* onto the next line
{ *command* ; }	execute *command* in the current shell
(*command*)	execute *command* in a subshell

Redirecting Input/Output

The Korn shell provides a number of operators that can be used to manipulate command input/output, files, and co-processes.

I/O Redirection Operators

<*file*	redirect standard input from *file*
>*file*	redirect standard output to *file*. Create *file* if non-existent, else overwrite.
>>*file*	append standard output to *file*. Create *file* if non-existent.
>|*file*	redirect standard output to *file*. Create *file* if non-existent, else overwrite even if **noclobber** is set.
<>*file*	open *file* for reading & writing as standard input
<&−	close standard input
>&−	close standard output
<&*n*	redirect standard input from file descriptor *n*
>&*n*	redirect standard output to file descriptor *n*
n<*file*	redirect file descriptor *n* from *file*
n>*file*	redirect file descriptor *n* to *file*
n>>*file*	redirect file descriptor *n* to *file*. Create *file* if non-existent, else overwrite.
n>|*file*	redirect file descriptor *n* to *file*. Create *file* if non-existent, else overwrite even if **noclobber** is set.
n<&*m*	redirect file descriptor *n* from file descriptor *m*

n>&m	redirect file descriptor *n* to file descriptor *m*
n<>file	open *file* for reading & writing as file descriptor *n*
n<<word	redirect to file descriptor *n* until *word* is read
n<<–word	redirect to file descriptor *n* until *word* is read; ignore leading tabs
n<&–	close file descriptor *n* for standard input
n>&–	close file descriptor *n* for standard output
*n<&**p**	redirect input from co-process to file descriptor *n*. If *n* is not specified, use standard input.
*n>&**p**	redirect output of co-process to file descriptor *n*. If *n* is not specified, use standard output.

Filename Substitution

File name substitution is a feature which allows special characters and patterns to substituted with file names in the current directory, or arguments to the **case** and [[...]] commands.

Pattern-Matching Characters/Patterns

?	match any single character
*	match zero or more characters, including null
[abc]	match any characters between the brackets
[x–z]	match any characters in the range **x** to **z**
[a–c e–g]	match any characters in the range **a** to **c**, **e** to **g**
[!abc]	match any characters not between the brackets
[!x–z]	match any characters not in the range **x** to **z**
.	strings starting with '.' must be explicitly matched
?(*pattern-list*)	match zero or one occurrence of any *pattern*
*(*pattern-list*)	match zero or more occurrences of any *pattern*
+(*pattern-list*)	match one or more occurrence of any *pattern*
@(*pattern-list*)	match exactly one occurrence of any *pattern*
!(*pattern-list*)	match anything except any *pattern*
pattern-list	multiple patterns must be separated with a '|' character

Variables

Like in other high-level progamming languages, variables are used by the Korn shell to store values. Variable names can begin with an alphabetic or underscore character, followed by one or more alphanumeric or underscore characters. Other variable names that contain only digits or special characters are reserved for special variables (called *parameters*) set directly by the Korn shell. Data types (called *attributes*) and one-dimensional arrays are also supported by the Korn shell.

Variable/Attribute Assignment Format

variable=   declare *variable* and set it to null
typeset *variable=*

        declare *variable* and set it to null. If used within a function, then a local variable is declared.

variable=value

        assign *value* to *variable*

typeset *variable=value*

        assign *value* to *variable*. If used within a function, then a local variable is declared.

typeset *−attribute variable=value*

        assign *attribute* and *value* to *variable*

typeset *−attribute variable*

        assign *attribute* to *variable*

typeset *+attribute variable*

        remove *attribute* from *variable* (except **readonly**)

Variable/Attribute Listing Format

typeset −*attribute*
> display a list of variable names and their values that
> have attribute set

typeset +*attribute*
> display a list of variable names that have attribute set

Variable Attributes

Variables can have one or more attributes that specify their internal
representation, scope, or the way they are displayed.

Variable Attribute Assignment Format

typeset −**H** *variable*
> Set Unix to host-name file mapping for non-Unix
> systems

typeset −**i** *variable*
> Set *variable* to be integer type

typeset −**i***n variable*
> Set *variable* to be integer type with base *n*

typeset −**l** *variable*
> Set *variable* to lower case

typeset −**L** *variable*
> Left justify *variable*; the field width is specified by the
> first assignment

typeset −**L***n variable*
> Left justify *variable*; set field width to *n*

typeset −**LZ***n variable*
> Left justify *variable*; set field width to *n* and strip
> leading zeros

typeset −r *variable*

> Set *variable* to be readonly (same as **readonly**)

typeset −R *variable*

> Right justify *variable*; the field width is specified by the first assignment

typeset −R*n variable*

> Right justify *variable*; set field width to *n*

typeset −RZ*n variable*

> Right justify *variable*; set field width to *n* and fill with leading zeros

typeset −t *variable*

> Set the user-defined attribute for *variable*. This has no meaning to the Korn shell.

typeset −u *variable*

> Set *variable* to upper case

typeset −x *variable*

> Automatically export variable to the environment (same as **export**)

typeset −Z *variable*

> Same as **typeset −RZ**

Variable Substitution

Variable values can be accessed and manipulated using variable expansion. Basic expansion is done by preceding the variable name with the $ character. Other types of expansion can be used to return portions or the length of variables, use default or alternate values, assign default or alternate values, and more.

Variable Expansion Format

${*variable*}   value of *variable*

${#*variable*}   length of *variable*

${*variable*:−*word*}

> value of *variable* if set and not null, else print *word*. If : is omitted, *variable* is only checked if it is set.

${*variable*:=*word*}

> value of *variable* if set and not null, else variable is set to *word*, then expanded. If : is omitted, *variable* is only checked if it is set.

${*variable*:?} value of *variable* if set and not null, else print **"variable: parameter null or not set"**. If : is omitted, *variable* is only checked if it is set.

${*variable*:?*word*}

> value of *variable* if set and not null, else print value of *word* and exit. If : is omitted, *variable* is only checked if it is set.

${*variable*:+*word*}

> value of *word* if *variable* is set and not null, else nothing is substituted. If : is omitted, *variable* is only checked if it is set.

${*variable*#*pattern*}

> value of *variable* without the smallest beginning portion that matches *pattern*

${*variable*##*pattern*}

> value of *variable* without the largest beginning portion that matches *pattern*

${*variable*%*pattern*}

> value of *variable* without the smallest ending portion that matches *pattern*

${*variable*%%*pattern*}

> value of *variable* without the largest ending portion that matches *pattern*

Special Parameters

Some special parameters are automatically set by the Korn shell, and usually cannot be directly set or modified.

$#	number of positional parameters
$@	all positional parameters ("$1", "$2", ..., "$n")
$*	all positional parameters ("$1 $2 ... $n")
$?	exit status of the last command
$$	process id of the current shell
$–	current options in effect
$!	process id of last background command

Special Variables

There are a number of variables provided by the Korn shell that allow you to customize your working environment. Some are automatically set by the Korn shell, some have a default value if not set, while others have no value unless specifically set.

CDPATH	search path for **cd** when not given a full pathname (no default)
COLUMNS	window width for in-line edit mode and **select** command lists (default **80**)
EDITOR	pathname of the editor for in-line editing (default **/bin/ed**)
ENV	pathname of the environment file (no default)
FCEDIT	default editor for the **fc** command
FPATH	search path for auto-loaded functions
	pathname of the history file
HISTFILE	pathname of the history file (default **$HOME/.sh_history**)
HISTSIZE	number of commands to save in history file (default **128**)

HOME	home directory
IFS	internal field separator (default space, tab, newline)
LINES	specifies column length for **select** lists
MAIL	name of mail file
MAILCHECK	specifies how often to check for mail (default **600** seconds)
MAILPATH	search path for mail files (no default)
OLDPWD	previous working directory
OPTARG	value of the last **getopts** option argument
OPTIND	index of the last **getopts** option argument
PATH	search path for commands (default **/bin:/usr/bin:**)
PPID	process id of the parent shell
PS1	primary prompt string (default $, #)
PS2	secondary prompt string (default >)
PS3	**select** command prompt (default #?)
PS4	debug prompt string (default +)
RANDOM	contains a random number
REPLY	contains input to **read** command when no variables given
SECONDS	contains number of seconds since Korn shell invocation
SHELL	pathname of shell
TERM	specifies your terminal type (no default)
TMOUT	Korn shell timeout variable (default **0**)
VISUAL	pathname of the editor for in-line editing

Array Variables

One-dimensional arrays are supported by the Korn shell. On most systems, arrays can have a maximum of 512 elements. Array subscripts start at 0 and go up to 511. Any variable can become an array by simply referring to it with a subscript.

Array Variable Assignment Format

variable[0]=*value variable*[1]=*value* ... *variable*[*n*]=*value*
set −A *variable value0 value1 ... valuen*
typeset *variable*[0]=*value variable*[1]=*value* ... *variable*[n]=*value*
        assign values to array variable elements
set +A *variable value0 value1 ... valuen*
        reassign values to array variable elements
typeset *−attributes variable*[0]=*value variable*[1]=*value* ...
        variable[*n*]=*value*
        assign *attributes* and values to array variable elements
typeset *−attributes variable*
        assign *attributes* to array variable
typeset *+attributes variable*
        remove *attributes* from array variable (except
        readonly)

Array Variable Evaluation

${*array*}, $*array*
        array element zero
${*array*[*n*]}   array element *n*
${*array*[*]}, ${*array*[@]}
        all elements of an array
${#*array*[*]}, ${#*array*[@]}
        number of array elements
${#*array*[*n*]}   length of array element *n*

Misc Substitution

$(*command*)   replace with the standard output of *command*
$((*arithmetic-expression*)
        replace with the result of *arithmetic-expression*

382

$(<*file*)	replace with the contents of *file*
\`*command*\`	replace with the standard output of *command*
~	replace with **$HOME**
~*user*	replace with the home directory of *user*
~−	replace with **$OLDPWD** (previous directory)
~+	replace with **$PWD** (current directory)

Quoting

Quotes are used when assigning values containing whitespace or special characters, to delimit variables, and to assign command output. They also improve readability by separating arguments from commands.

'...'	remove the special meaning of enclosed characters except '
"..."	remove the special meaning of enclosed characters except $, ', and \
c	remove the special meaning of character *c*
\`*command*\`	replace with the standard output of *command*

In-Line Editors

In-line editing provides the ability to edit the current or previous commands before executing them. There are three in-line editing modes available: **emacs**, **gmacs**, and **vi**. The **emacs** and **gmacs** modes are basically the same, except for the way **Ctl-t** is handled. The in-line editing mode is specified by setting the **EDITOR** or **VISUAL** variables, or with the **set −o** command. The editing window width is specified by the **COLUMNS** variable. For lines longer than the window width, a mark is displayed to notify position. The marks >, <, and * specify that the line extends to the right, left, or both sides of the window.

Vi Input Mode Commands

#, \<Backspace\>

        delete previous character

Ctl-d   terminate the Korn shell

Ctl-v   escape next character

Ctl-w   delete previous word

Ctl-x, @   kill the entire line

\<Return\>   execute current line

\   escape next *erase* or *kill* character

Vi Motion Edit Commands

[*n*]**h**, [*n*]\<Backspace\>

        move left one character

[*n*]**l**, [*n*]\<Space\>

        move forward one character

[*n*]**b**   move backward one word

[*n*]**B**   move backward one word; ignore punctuation

[*n*]**w**   move forward one word

[*n*]**W**   move forward one word; ignore punctuation

[*n*]**e**   move to end of next word

[*n*]**E**   move to end of next word; ignore punctuation

[*n*]**f***c*   move forward to character *c*

[*n*]**F***c*   move backward to character *c*

[*n*]**t***c*   move forward to character before character *c*

[*n*]**T***c*   move backward to character before character *c*

[*n*]**;**   repeat last **f**, **F**, **t**, or **T** command

[*n*]**,**   repeat last **f**, **F**, **t**, or **T** command, but in opposite direction

0   move cursor to start of line

^   move cursor to first non-blank character in line

$ move cursor to end of line

Vi Search/Edit History Commands

[*n*]**G**	get last command (or command *n*)
[*n*]**j**, [*n*]+	get next command from history file
[*n*]**k**, [*n*]−	get previous command from history file
n	repeat last / or ? search
N	repeat last / or ? search, except in opposite direction
/*string*	search backward in history file for command that matches *string*
?*string*	search forward in history file for command that matches *string*

Vi Text Modification Commands

a	add text after current character
A	append text to end of current line
[*n*]**c**X, **c**[*n*]X	change current character up to cursor position defined by X
[*n*]**d**X, **d**[*n*]X	delete current character up to cursor position defined by X
[*n*]**y**X, **y**[*n*]X	copy current character up to cursor position defined by X into buffer
X	used to define ending cursor position for **c**, **d**, or **y** commands

	b	backwards to beginning of word
	e	cursor to end of current word
	w	cursor to beginning of next word
	W B E	same as **w b e**, but ignore punctuation
	0	before cursor to end of current line
	$	cursor to end of current line

C	change current character to end of line
D	delete current character through end of line
i	insert text left of the current character
I	insert text before beginning of line

[n]p	put previously yanked/deleted text after cursor
[n]**P**	put previously yanked/deleted text before cursor
[n]**r**c	replace current character with c
R	replace text from cursor to <ESCAPE>
S	delete entire line and enter input mode
yy	copy current line into buffer
[n]x	delete current character
[n]X	delete previous character
[n].	repeat last text modification command
[n]~	toggle case of current character
[n]_	append last word of previous **ksh** command
\	replace current word with filename that matches word*. For unique matches, append a / to directories and " " (space) for files.

Vi Other Edit Commands

u	undo last text modification command
U	undo text modification commands on current line
[n]**v**	return output of **fc −e** command
Ctl-l	redisplay current line
Ctl-j	execute current line
Ctl-m	execute current line
#	insert a # (comment) at beginning of current line
=	list files that match current word*
*	replace current word with files that match word*
@_c	insert value of alias c

Emacs/Gmacs In-Line Editor Commands

Ctl-b	move left one character
Ctl-f	move right one character
Esc-b	move left one word

Esc-f	move right one word
Ctl-a	move to beginning of line
Ctl-e	move to end of line
Ctl-h	delete preceding character
Ctl-x	delete the entire line
Ctl-k	delete from cursor to end of line
Ctl-d	delete current character
Esc-d	delete current word
Ctl-w	delete from cursor to mark
Ctl-y	undo last delete (w/**Esc-p**)
Ctl-p	get previous command from history file
Ctl-n	get next command from history file
Ctl-o	execute current command line and get next command line
Ctl-r*string*	search backward in history file for command that contains *string*
Ctl-c	change current character to upper case
Esc-c	change current word to upper case
Esc-l	change current character to lower case
Esc-p	save to buffer from cursor to mark
Esc-<SPACE>, **Ctl-@**	
	mark current location
Ctl-l	redisplay current line
Ctl-]*c*	move cursor forward to character *c*
Ctl-xCtl-x	interchange the cursor and mark
erase	delete previous character
Esc-Ctl-h	delete previous word
Esc-h	delete previous word
Ctl-t	transpose current and next character (**emacs**)
Ctl-t	transpose two previous characters (**gmacs**)
Ctl-j	execute current line
Ctl-m	execute current line
Esc-<	get oldest command line
Esc->	get previous command line
Esc-*n*	define numeric parameter *n* for next command (command can be **Ctl-c**, **Ctl-d**, **Ctl-k**, **Ctl-n**, **Ctl-p**,

	Ctl-r, **Esc-.**, **Ctl-]***c*, **Esc-_**, **Esc-b**, **Esc-c**, **Esc-d**, **Esc-f**, **Esc-h**, **Esc-l**, **Esc-Ctl-h**)
Esc-*c*	insert value of alias _*c* (*c* cannot be **b**, **c**, **d**, **f**, **h**, **l**, or **p**)
Esc-., **Esc-_**	insert last word of previous command
Esc-Esc	replace current word with filename that matches *word**. For unique matches, append a / to directories and " " (space) for files
Esc-=	list files that match current *word**
Ctl-u	multiply parameter of next command by 4
\	escape next character
Ctl-v	display version of shell
Esc-#	insert a # (comment) at beginning of current line

Job Control

Job control is a process manipulation feature found in the Korn shell. It allows programs to be stopped and restarted, moved between the foreground and background, their processing status to be displayed, and more. To enable job control, the **monitor** option must be enabled. By default, this is enabled on systems that support the job control feature. When a program is run in the background, a job number and process id are returned.

Job Control Commands

bg	put current stopped job in the background
bg %*n*	put stopped job *n* in the background
fg	move current background job into the foreground
fg %*n*	move background job *n* into the foreground
jobs	display status of all jobs
jobs –l	display status of all jobs along with process ids
jobs –p	display process ids of all jobs

kill −l list all valid signal names

kill [*−signal*] %*n*

send specified signal to job *n* (default 9)

set −m, **set −o monitor**

enable job control

stty [−]**tostop** allow/prevent background jobs from generating output

wait wait for all background jobs to complete

wait %*n* wait for background job *n* to complete

Ctl-z stop the current job

Job Name Format

%*n*	job *n*
%+, %%	current job
%−	previous job
%*string*	job whose name begins with *string*
%?*string*	job that matches part or all of *string*

Arithmetic

Integer arithmetic is performed with the **let** and **((...))** commands. All of the operators from the C programming language (except ++, −−, and ?:) are supported by the Korn shell. The format for arithmetic constants is:

> *number*
> or
> *base#number*

where *base* is a decimal number between **2** and **36** that specifies the arithmetic base. If not specified, the default is base **10**. The arithmetic base can also be set with the **typeset −i** command.

Arithmetic Commands

let "*arithmetic-expression*"
((*arithmetic-expression*))
> evaluate arithmetic expression

integer *variable*
> declare an integer variable

integer *variable=integer-value*
> declare an integer variable and set it to a value

integer *variable="arithmetic-assignment-expression"*
> declare an integer variable and assign it the value of
> the *arithmetic-assignment-expression*

typeset –i*n variable*[=*value*]
> declare a base *n* integer variable, and optionally assign
> it a value

Arithmetic Operators

–	unary minus
!	logical negation
~	bitwise negation
*, /, %	multiplication, division, remainder (modulo)
+, –	addition, subtraction
<<, >>	left shift, right shift
<=, <	less than or equal to, less than
>=, >	greater than or equal to, greater than
==, !=	equal to, not equal to
&	bitwise AND
^	bitwise exclusive OR
|	bitwise OR
&&	logical AND
||	logical OR
=	assignment
*=, /=, %=	multiply assign, divide assign, modulo assign

+=, −=	increment, decrement
<<=, >>=	left shift assign, right shift assign
&=, ^=, |=	bitwise AND assign, bitwise exclusive OR assign, bitwise OR assign
(...)	grouping (used to override precedence rules)

Options

The Korn shell has a number of options that specify your environment and control execution. They can be enabled/disabled with the **set** command or on the **ksh** command line.

Enabling/Disabling Options

ksh [−/+*options*]
> enable/disable specified options

set [−/+*options*]
> enable/disable specified options

List of Options

−a	automatically export variables that are defined
−b	execute all background jobs at a lower priority
−c *cmds*	read and execute *cmds* (w/**ksh** only)
−e	execute **ERR** trap (if set) on non-zero exit status from any commands
−f	disable file name expansion
−h	make commands tracked aliases when first encountered
−i	execute in interactive mode (w/**ksh** only)
−k	put variable assignment arguments in environment

−m	enable job control (system dependent)
−n	read commands without executing them
−o allexport	automatically export variables that are defined
−o bgnice	execute all background jobs at a lower priority
−o emacs	use emacs-style editor for in-line editing
−o errexit	execute **ERR** trap (if set) on non-zero exit status from any commands
−o gmacs	use gmacs-style editor for in-line editing
−o ignoreeof	do not exit on end of file (default **Ctl-d**); use **exit**
−o keyword	put variable assignment arguments in environment
−o markdirs	display trailing / on directory names resulting from file name substitution
−o monitor	enable job control (system dependent)
−o noclobber	prevent I/O redirection from truncating existing files
−o noexec	read commands without executing them
−o noglob	disable file name expansion
−o nolog	do not save function definitions in history file
−o nounset	return error on substitution of unset variables
−o privileged	disable processing of **$HOME/.profile**, and use **/etc/suid_profile** instead of **ENV** file
−o trackall	make commands tracked aliases when first encountered
−o verbose	display input lines as they are read
−o vi	use vi-style editor for in-line editing
−o viraw	process each character as it is typed in vi mode
−o xtrace	display commands and arguments as executed
−p	disable processing of **$HOME/.profile**, and use **/etc/suid_profile** instead of **ENV** file
−r	run a restricted shell (w/**ksh** only)
−s	read commands from standard input
−u	return error on substitution of unset variables
−v	display input lines as they are read
−x	display commands and arguments as executed
−	disable −v and −x flags; don't process remaining flags

Aliases

Aliases are command macros and are used as shorthand for other commands, especially frequently-used ones.

Alias Commands

alias	display a list of aliases and their values
alias *name*	display the value for alias *name*
alias *name='value'*	
	create an alias *name* set to *value*
alias −t	display a list of tracked aliases
alias −t *name='value'*	
	create a tracked alias *name* set to *value*
unalias *name*	remove the alias name

Some Preset Aliases

Alias	Value	Definition
autoload	typeset −fu	define an autoloading function
echo	print −	display arguments
functions	typeset −f	display list of functions
hash	alias −t −	display list of tracked aliases
history	fc −l	list commands from history file
integer	typeset −i	declare integer variable
r	fc −e −	re-execute previous command
stop	kill −STOP	suspend job
type	whence −v	display information about commands

Conditional Expressions

The [[...]] command is used to evaluate conditional expressions with file attributes, strings, and integers. The basic format is:

[[*expression*]]

where *expression* is the condition you are evaluating. There must be whitespace after the opening brackets, and before the closing brackets. Whitespace must also separate the expression arguments and operators. If the expression evaluates to true, then a zero exit status is returned, otherwise the expression evaluates to false and a non-zero exit status is returned.

[[...]] String Operators

−n *string*	true if length of *string* is not zero
−o *option*	true if *option* is set
−z *string*	true if length of *string* is zero
string1 = *string2*	true if *string1* is equal to *string2*
string1 != *string2*	true if *string1* is not equal to *string2*
string = *pattern*	true if *string* matches *pattern*
string != *pattern*	true if *string* does not match *pattern*
string1 < *string2*	true if *string1* is less than *string2*
string1 > *string2*	true if *string1* is greater than *string2*

[[...]] File Operators

−a *file*	true if *file* exists
−b *file*	true if *file* exists and is a block special file
−c *file*	true if *file* exists and is a character special file
−d *file*	true if *file* exists and is a directory
−f *file*	true if *file* exists is a regular file

−**g** *file*	true if *file* exists and its setgid bit is set
−**G** *file*	true if *file* exists and its group id matches the current effective group id
−**k** *file*	true if *file* exists and its sticky bit is set
−**L** *file*	true if *file* exists and is a symbolic link
−**O** *file*	true if *file* exists and is owned by the effective user id
−**p** *file*	true if *file* exists and is a fifo special file or a pipe
−**r** *file*	true if *file* exists and is readable
−**s** *file*	true if *file* exists and its size is greater than zero
−**S** *file*	true if *file* exists and is a socket
−**t** *n*	true if file descriptor *n* is open and associated with a terminal device
−**u** *file*	true if *file* exists and its set user-id bit is set
−**w** *file*	true if *file* exists and is writable
−**x** *file*	true if *file* exists and is executable. If *file* is a directory, then true indicates that the directory is readable.
file1 −**ef** *file2*	true if *file1* and *file2* exist and refer to same file
file1 −**nt** *file2*	true if *file1* exists and is newer than *file2*
file1 −**ot** *file2*	true if *file1* exists and is older than *file2*

[[...]] Integer Operators

exp1 −**eq** *exp2* true if *exp1* is equal to *exp2*

exp1 −**ne** *exp2* true if *exp1* is not equal to *exp2*

exp1 −**le** *exp2* true if *exp1* is less than or equal to *exp2*

exp1 −**lt** *exp2* true if *exp1* is less than *exp2*

exp1 −**ge** *exp2* true if *exp1* is greater than or equal to *exp2*

exp1 −**gt** *exp2* true if *exp1* is greater than *exp2*

Other [[...]] Operators

!*expression*   true if *expression* is false
(*expression*)   true if *expression* is true; used to group expressions
[[*expression1* && *expression2*]]
        true if both *expression1* and *expression2* are true
[[*expression1* || *expression2*]]
        true either *expression1* or *expression2* are true

Control Commands

case *value* **in**
    pattern1)   *commands1* **;;**
    pattern2)   *commands2* **;;**
    . . .
    patternn)   *commandsn* **;;**
esac
Execute *commands* associated with the *pattern* that matches *value*.

for *variable* **in** *word1 word2 . . . wordn*
do
    commands
done
Execute *commands* once for each *word*, setting *variable* to successive *words* each time.

for *variable*
do
    commands
done
Execute *commands* once for each positional parameter, setting *variable* to successive positional parameters each time.

if *command1*
then
    commands
fi
Execute *commands* if *command1* returns a zero exit status.

if *command1*
then
    commands2
else
    commands3
fi
Execute *commands2* if *commands1* returns a zero exit status, otherwise execute *commands3*.

if *command1*
then
    commands
elif *command2*
then
    commands
. . .
elif *commandn*
then
    commands
else
    commands
fi
If *command1* returns a zero exit status, or *command2* returns a zero exit status, or *commandn* returns a zero exit status, then execute the *commands* corresponding to the **if/elif** that returned a zero exit status. Otherwise, if all the **if/elif** commands return a non-zero exit status, execute the commands between **else** and **fi**.

select *variable* **in** *word1 word2 . . . wordn*
do
  commands
done
Display a menu of numbered choices *word1* through *wordn* followed by a prompt (**#?** or **$PS3**). Execute *commands* for each menu selection, setting *variable* to each selection and **REPLY** to the response until a **break**, **exit**, or EOF is encountered.

select *variable*
do
  commands
done
Display a menu of numbered choices for each positional parameter followed by a prompt (**#?** or **$PS3**). Execute *commands* for each menu selection, setting *variable* to each selection and **REPLY** to the response until a **break**, **exit**, or EOF is encountered.

until *command1*
do
  commands
done
Execute *commands* until *command1* returns a zero exit status

while *command1*
do
  commands
done
Execute *commands* while *command1* returns a zero exit status.

Commands

:	null command; returns zero exit status
. *file*	read and execute commands in *file*
break	exit from current enclosing **for**, **select**, **until**, or **while** loop
break *n*	exit from *nth* enclosing **for**, **select**, **until**, or **while** loop
cd *dir*	change directory to *dir*(default **$HOME**)
cd *dir1 dir2*	change to directory where *dir1* in current pathname is substituted with *dir2*
cd −	change directory to previous directory
echo *args*	display arguments
eval *cmds*	read and execute commands
exec *I/O-redirection-command*	
	perform I/O redirection on file descriptors
exec *command*	
	replace current process with *command*
exit	exit from current program with exit status of the last command. If given at command prompt, terminate the login shell.
exit *n*	exit from current program with exit status *n*
export	display list of exported variables
export *var=val*	
	set *var* to *value* and export
export *vars*	export *vars*
false	return non-zero exit status
fc −l[*options*] [*range*]	
	display *range* commands from history file according to *options*. If no *range* argument given, display last 16 commands.Options can be:
	−**n** do not display command numbers
	−**r** reverse order (latest commands first)
	and *range* can be:

        n1 [*n2*]   display list from command *n1* to command *n2*. If *n2* not specified, display all commands from current command back to command *n1*.

        −count   display last *count* commands

        string   display all previous commands back to command that matches *string*

fc [*options*] [*range*]

edit and re-execute range commands from history file according to *options*. If no *range* argument given, edit and re-execute last command. Options can be:

−e *editor*   use specified editor (default **FCEDIT** or /**bin/ed**)

−r   reverse order (latest commands first)

and *range* can be:

n1 n2   edit command *n1* to command *n2*

n   edit command *n*

−n   edit previous *nth* command

string   use all the previous commands back to the command that matches *string*

fc −e − [*old=new*] [*command*]

edit and re-execute *command* where *old=new* specified to replace string *old* with *new* before executing. If no *command* argument is given, use last command. The *command* can be given as:

n   edit and re-execute command number *n*

−n   edit and re-execute last *nth* command

string   edit and re-execute most previous command that matches *string*

getopts *optsring name arguments*

parse *arguments*, using *optstring* as list of valid options; save option letter in *name*

getopts *optsring name*

parse positional parameters, using *optstring* as list of valid options; save option letter in *name*

newgrp   change group-id to default group-id

Appendix G: Pdksh Quick Reference

newgrp *gid*   change group id to *gid*

pwd   display pathname of current directory

readonly   display a list of readonly variables

readonly *var*   set *var* to be readonly

readonly *var=value*

   set *var* to *value* and make it readonly

set   display list of current variables and their values

set −o   display current option settings

set *args*   set positional parameters

set *−args*   set positional parameters that begin with −

set −s   sort positional parameters

set − −   unset positional parameters

shift   shift positional parameters once left

shift *n*   shift positional parameters *n* times left

test *expression*

   evaluate *expression*

time *command*

   display elapsed, user, and system time spent executing *command*

times   display total user and system time for current Korn shell and its child processes

trap *commands signals*

   execute *commands* when *signals* are received

trap "" *signals*

   ignore *signals*

trap *signals*, **trap** *−signals*

   reset traps to their default values

trap *commands* **0**, **trap** *commands* **EXIT**

   execute *commands* on exit

trap   display a list of current traps

trap *commands* **DEBUG**

   execute *commands* after each command is executed

trap *commands* **ERR**

   if **errexit** (−**e**) option enabled, execute *commands* after commands that have a non-zero exit status

true   return a non-zero exit status

typeset   display a list of current variables and their values

ulimit [*options*] *n*

set a resource limit to *n*. If *n* is not given, the specified resource limit is displayed. If no *option* given, file size limit (–**f**) is displayed.

–**a**	displays all current resource limits
–**c** *n*	set core dump size limit to *n* 512-byte blocks
–**d** *n*	set data area size limit to *n* kilobytes
–**f** *n*	set child process file write limit to *n* 512-byte blocks (default)
–**m** *n*	set physical memory size limit to *n* kilobytes
–**s** *n*	set stack area size limit to *n* kilobytes
–**t** *n*	set process time limit to *n* seconds

umask   display current file creation mask value

umask *mask*   set default file creation mask to *mask*

unset *var*   remove definition of *var*

whence *name* display information about *name*

whence –**v** *name*

display more information about *name*

Functions

Functions are a form of commands like aliases, and scripts. They differ from Korn shell scripts, in that they do not have to read in from the disk each time they are referenced, so they execute faster. They also provide a way to organize scripts into routines, like in other high-level programming languages. Since functions can have local variables, recursion is possible. Functions are defined with the following format:

function *name* { *commands* ; }

Local function variables are declared with the **typeset** command within the function.

Function Commands

return	return from a function
return *n*	return from a function; pass back return value of *n*
typeset −f	display a list of functions and their definitions
typeset +f	display a list of function names only
typeset −fu	display a list of autoloading functions
typeset −fu *name*	

           make function name autoloading

typeset −ft *name*

           display function commands and arguments as they are executed

unset −f *name* remove function *name*

THE print *COMMAND*

print [*options*] *arguments*

           display *arguments* according to *options*

print **Options**

−	treat everything following − as an argument, even if it begins with −
−n	do not add a ending newline to output
−p	redirect the given arguments to a co-process
−r	ignore \ escape conventions
−R	ignore \ escape conventions; do not interpret − arguments as options (except **−n**)
−s	redirect given arguments to history file
−u*n*	redirect arguments to file descriptor *n*. If file descriptor is greater than **2**, it must first be opened with **exec**. If *n* is not specified, default file descriptor is **1** (standard output).

print **Escape Characters**

\a	Bell character
\b	Backspace
\c	Line without ending newline
\f	Formfeed
\n	Newline
\r	Return
\t	Tab
\v	Vertical tab
\\	Backslash
\0*x*	8-bit character whose ASCII code is the 1-, 2-, or 3-digit octal number x

THE read *COMMAND*

read [*options*] *variables*

        read input into *variables* according to *options*

read *name?prompt*

        display *prompt* and read the response into *name*

read **Options**

−p	read input line from a co-process
−r	do not treat \ as line continuation character
−s	save a copy of input line in command history file
−u*n*	read input line from file descriptor *n*. If file descriptor is greater than **2**, it must first be opened with **exec**. If *n* is not specified, default file descriptor is 0.

Miscellaneous

#	anything following a # to the end of the current line is treated as a comment and ignored
#!*interpreter*	if the first line of a script starts with this, then the script is run by the specified interpreter
rsh	running under the restricted shell is equivalent to **ksh**, except that the following is not allowed: • changing directories • setting value of **ENV**, **PATH**, or **SHELL** • specifying path or command names containing / • redirecting command output command with >, >|, <>, or >>

Debugging Korn Shell Scripts

The Korn shell provides a number of options that are useful in debugging scripts: **noexec** (**–n**), **verbose** (**–v**), and **xtrace** (**–x**). The **noexec** (**–n**) option causes commands to be read without being executed and is used to check for syntax errors. The **verbose** (**–v**) option causes the input to displayed as it is read. The **xtrace** (**–x**) option causes commands in Korn shell scripts to be displayed as they are executed. This is the most useful, general debugging option. For example, **tscript** could be run in trace mode if invoked "ksh **–x** tscript".

Files

$HOME/.profile
> contains local environment settings, such as the search path, execution options, local variables, aliases, and more. At login time, it is read in and executed after the **/etc/profile** file.

$HOME/.sh_history
> contains previously executed commands

$ENV contains the name of the file that has aliases, function, options, variables, and other environment settings that are to be available to subshells

Example Commands

```
# Execute multiple commands on one line

      $ pwd ; ls tmp ; print "Hello world"
# Run the find command in the background

      $ find . —name tmp.out —print &
# Connect the output of who to grep

      $ who | grep fred
# Talk to fred if he is logged on

      $ { who | grep fred ; } && talk fred
# Send ls output to ls.out, even if noclobber is set

      $ ls >| ls.out
# Append output of ls to ls.out

      $ ls >> ls.out
# Send invite.txt to  dick, jane, and spot

      $ mail dick jane spot < invite.txt
# List file names that begin with z

      $ ls z*
# List two, three, and four character file names

      $ ls ?? ??? ????
```

\# List file names that begin with **a**, **b**, or **c**

```
$ ls [a-c]*
```
\# List file names that do not end with **.c**

```
$ ls *[!.c]
```
\# List file names that contain any number of consecutive **x**'s

```
$ ls *(x)
```
\# List file names that contain only numbers

```
$ ls +([0-9])
```
\# List file names tha do not end in **.c**, **.Z**, or **.o**

```
$ ls !(*.c|*.Z|*.o)
```
\# Set **NU** to the number of users that are logged on

```
$ NU=$(who | wc -l)
```
\# Set **HOSTS** to the contents of the **/etc/hosts** file

```
$ HOSTS=$(</etc/hosts)
```
\# Set **TOTAL** to the sum of **4 + 3**

```
$ TOTAL=$((4+3))
```
\# Change directory to **jane**'s home directory

```
$ cd ~jane
```
\# Set the right-justify attribute on variable **SUM** and set it to **70**

```
$ typeset -R SUM=70
```
\# Set and export the variable **LBIN**

```
$ typeset -x LBIN=/usr/lbin
```
\# Set the field width of **SUM** to **5**

```
$ typeset -R5 SUM
```
\# Remove the lowercase attribute from **MSYS**

```
$ typeset +l MSYS
```
\# Unset variable **LBIN**

```
$ unset LBIN
```
\# Display the length of variable **FNAME**

```
$ print ${#FNAME}
```
\# Set **SYS** to the hostname if not set, then display its value

```
$ print ${SYS:=$(hostname)}
```

Display an error message if **XBIN** is not set

```
$ : ${XBIN:?}
```
Display the base directory in **LBIN**

```
$ print ${LBIN##*/}
```
Set array variable **MONTHS** to the first four month names

```
$ set —A MONTHS jan feb mar apr
```
Display element 3 of the **XBUF** array variable

```
$ print ${XBUF[3]}
```
Display the length of the **TMP** array element 2

```
$ print ${#TMP[2]}
```
Display **$HOME set to /home/anatole**

```
$ print '$HOME set to' $HOME
```
Display the value of **$ENV**

```
$ print $ENV
```
Display the last five commands from the history file

```
$ history —5
```
Retrieve last **print** command in vi edit mode

```
$ set —o vi; <ESCAPE>/^print<RETURN>
```
Bring background job 3 into the foreground

```
$ fg %3
```
Display all information about current jobs

```
$ jobs —l
```
Terminate job 5

```
$ kill %5
```
Increment variable **X**

```
$ integer X; ((X+=1))
```
Set variable **X** to **5** in base **2**

```
$ typeset —i2 X=5
```
Set variable **X** to **20** modulo **5**

```
$ ((X=20%5))
```
Set **Y** to **5*4** if **X** equals **3**

```
$ ((X==3 && (Y=5*4)))
```

Terminate the Korn shell if no input given in 30 minutes

```
$ TMOUT=1800
```
Automatically export variables when defined

```
$ set -o allexport
```
Set diagnostic mode

```
$ set -x
```
Create an alias for the **ls** command

```
$ alias l='ls -FAc | ${PAGER:-/bin/pg}'
```
Create a tracked alias for the **cp -r** command

```
$ alias -t "cp -r"
```
Put the command number and current directory in the prompt

```
$ typeset -x PS1="!:$PWD> "
```
Check if variable **X** is set to a number

```
$ [[$X=+([0-9])]] && print "$X is num"
```
Check if **X** is set to null

```
$ [[-z $X]] && print "X set to null"
```
Check if **FILE1** is newer than **FILE2**

```
$ [[ $FILE1 -nt $FILE2 ]]
```
Check if **VAR** is set to **ABC**

```
$ [[ $VAR = ABC ]]
```
Check if the **bgnice** option is set

```
$ [[-o bgnice]] && print "bgnice set"
```
Check if **TMP** is a readable directory

```
$ [[ -d $TMP && -x $TMP ]]
```
Check the number of arguments

```
$(($#==0)) && {print "Need arg"; exit 1;}
```
Display an error message, then beep

```
$ print "Unexpected error!\a"
```
Display a message on standard error

```
$ print -u2 "This is going to stderr"
```

\# Write a message to the command history file

```
$ print -s "su attempted on $(date)"
```
\# Take standard input from **FILE**

```
$ exec 0<FILE
```
\# Open file descriptor **5** for reading and writing

```
$ exec <> 5
```
\# Display a prompt and read the reply into **ANSWER**

```
$ read ANSWER?"Enter response: "
```
\# Create a function **md** that creates a directory and **cd**'s to it

```
$ function md {mkdir $1 && cd $1 ; pwd}
```
\# Set a trap to ignore signals **2** and **3**

```
$ trap "" 2 3
```
\# Run **dbtest** in **noexec** mode

```
$ ksh -n dbtest
```
\# Set a trap to execute **pwd** after each command

```
$ trap "pwd" DEBUG
```
\# Set **X** to **1** and make it readonly

```
$ readonly X=1
```
\# Set **VAR** to **1** and export it

```
$ export VAR=1
```
\# Set the positional parametersto **A B C**

```
$ set A B C
```
\# Set the file size creation limit to 1000 blocks

```
$ ulimit 1000
```
\# Disable core dumps

```
$ ulimit -c 0
```
\# Add group write permission to the file creation mask

```
$ umask 013
```
\# Return information about the **true** command

```
$ whence -v true
```

Appendix H: Pdksh Man Page

ksh - Public domain Korn shell

Synopsis

> **ksh** [+-**abCefhikmnprsuvxX**] [+-**o** *option*] [[-**c** *command-string* [*command-name*] | -**s** | *file*] [*argument* ...]]

Description

> **ksh** is a command interpreter that is intended for both interactive and shell script use. Its command language is a superset of the **sh**(1) shell language.

Shell Startup

> The following options can be specified only on the command line:

> -**c** *command-string*
>> the shell executes the command(s) contained in command-string
>
> -**i**   interactive mode - see below
>
> -**l** *login shell*
>> see below interactive mode
>
> -**s**   the shell reads commands from standard input; all non-option arguments are positional parameters
>
> -**r**   restricted mode - see below

> In addition to the above, the options described in the **set** built-in command can also be used on the command line.

If neither the **-c** nor the **-s** options are specified, the first non-option argument specifies the name of a file the shell reads commands from; if there are no non-option arguments, the shell reads commands from standard input. The name of the shell (i.e., the contents of the $0) parameter is determined as follows: if the **-c** option is used and there is a non-option argument, it is used as the name; if commands are being read from a file, the file is used as the name; otherwise the name the shell was called with (i.e., **argv**[0]) is used.

A shell is interactive if the **-i** option is used or if both standard input and standard error are attached to a tty. An interactive shell has job control enabled (if available), ignores the **INT**, **QUIT** and **TERM** signals, and prints prompts before reading input (see **PS1** and **PS2** parameters). For non-interactive shells, the **trackall** option is on by default (see **set** command below).

A shell is restricted if the **-r** option is used or if either the basename of the name the shell is invoked with or the **SHELL** parameter match the pattern ***r*sh** (e.g., **rsh**, **rksh**, **rpdksh**, etc.). The following restrictions come into effect after the shell processes any profile and $ENV files:

- the **cd** command is disabled
- the **SHELL**, **ENV** and **PATH** parameters can't be changed
- command names can't be specified with absolute or relative paths
- the **-p** option of the command built-in can't be used
- redirections that create files can't be used (i.e., >, >|, >>, <>)

A shell is privileged if the **-p** option is used or if the real user-id or group-id does not match the effective user-id or group-id (see **getuid**(2), **getgid**(2)). A privileged shell does not process **$HOME/.profile** nor the **ENV** parameter (see below), instead the file **/etc/suid_profile** is processed. Clearing the privileged

option causes the shell to set its effective user-id (group-id) to its real user-id
(group-id).

If the basename of the name the shell is called with (i.e., **argv**[0]) starts with - or if the **-l** option is used, the shell is assumed to be a login shell and the shell reads and executes the contents of **/etc/profile** and **$HOME/.profile** if they exist and are readable.

If the **ENV** parameter is set when the shell starts (or, in the case of login shells, after any profiles are processed), its value is subjected to parameter, command, arithmetic and tilde substitution and the resulting file (if any) is read and executed. If **ENV** parameter is not set (and not null) and **pdksh** was compiled with the **DEFAULT_ENV** macro defined, the file named in that macro is included (after the above mentioned substitutions have been performed).

The exit status of the shell is 127 if the command file specified on the command line could not be opened, or non-zero if a fatal syntax error occurred during the execution of a script. In the absence of fatal errors, the exit status is that of the last command executed, or zero, if no command is executed.

Command Syntax

The shell begins parsing its input by breaking it into words. Words, which are sequences of characters, are delimited by unquoted white-space characters (space, tab and newline) or meta-characters (<, >, |, ;, &, (and)). Aside from delimiting words, spaces and tabs are ignored, while newlines usually delimit commands. The metacharacters are used in building the following tokens: <, <&, <<, >, >&, >>, etc. are used to specify redirections (see **Input/Output Redirection** below); |
is used to create pipelines; |& is used to create co-processes (see **Co-Processes** later in this appendix); ; is used to separate

commands; & is used to create asynchronous pipelines; &&
and || are used to specify conditional execution; ;; is used in case
statements; ((..)) are used in arithmetic expressions; and lastly,
(..) are used to create subshells.

Whitespace and metacharacters can be quoted individually
using backslash (\), or in groups using double (") or single (')
quotes. Note that the following characters are also treated
specially by the shell and must be quoted if they are to represent
themselves: \, ", ', #, $, `, ~, {, }, *, ? and [. The first three of
these are the above mentioned quoting characters (see **Quoting**
later in this appendix); #, if used at the beginning of a word,
introduces a comment - everything after the # up to the nearest
newline is ignored; $ is used to introduce parameter, command
and arithmetic substitutions (see **Substitution** later in this
appendix); ' introduces an old-style command substitution (see
Substitution below); ~ begins a directory expansion (see **Tilde
Expansion** later in this appendix); { and } delimit **csh**(1) style
alternations (see **Brace Expansion** later in this appendix); and,
finally, *, ? and [are used in file name generation (see **File
Name Patterns** later in this appendix).

As words and tokens are parsed, the shell builds commands, of
which there are two basic types: simple-commands, typically
programs that are executed, and compound-commands, such as
for and **if** statements, grouping constructs and function
definitions.

A simple-command consists of some combination of parameter
assignments (see **Parameters** later in this appendix), input/
output redirections (see **Input/Output Redirections** later in
this appendix), and command words; the only restriction is that
parameter assignments come before any command words. The
command words, if any, define the command that is to be
executed and its arguments. The command may be a shell built-
in command, a function or an external command, i.e., a separate

executable file that is located using the **PATH** parameter (see **Command Execution** later in this appendix). Note that all command constructs have an exit status: for external commands, this is related to the status returned by **wait**(2) (if the command could not be found, the exit status is 127, if it could not be executed, the exit status is 126); the exit status of other command constructs (built-in commands, functions, compound-commands, pipelines, lists, etc.) are all well defined and are described where the construct is described. The exit status of a command consisting only of parameter assignments is that of the last command substitution performed during the parameter assignment or zero if there were no command substitutions.

Commands can be chained together using the | token to form pipelines, in which the standard output of each command but the last is piped to the standard input of the following command. The exit status of a pipeline is that of its last command. A pipeline may be prefixed by the ! reserved word which causes the exit status of the pipeline to be logically complemented: if the original status was 0 the complemented status will be 1, and if the original status was not 0, then the complemented status will be 0.

Lists of commands can be created by separating pipelines by any of the following tokens: &&, ||, &, |& and ;. The first two are for conditional execution: *cmd1* && *cmd2* executes cmd2 only if the exit status of *cmd1* is zero; || is the opposite - *cmd2* is executed only if the exit status of *cmd1* is non-zero. && and || have equal precedence which is higher than that of &, |& and ;, which also have equal precedence. The & token causes the preceding command to be executed asynchronously, that is, the shell starts the command, but does not wait for it to complete (the shell does keep track of the status of asynchronous commands - see **Job Control** later in this appendix). When an asynchronous command is started when job control is disabled (i.e., in most scripts), the command is started with signals **INT** and **QUIT** ignored and with input redirected from **/dev/null** (however, redirections specified in the asynchronous command have precedence). The |& operator starts a co-process which is special kind of asynchronous process (see **Co-Processes** later in this appendix). Note that a command must follow the && and || operators, while a command need not follow &, |& and ;. The exit status of a list is that of the last command executed, with the exception of asynchronous lists, for which the exit status is 0.

Compound commands are created using the following reserved words - these words are only recognized if they are unquoted and if they are used as the first word of a command (i.e., they can't be preceded by parameter assignments or redirections):

> **case else function then ! do esac if time [[done fi in until { elif for select while }**

Note: Some shells (but not this one) execute control structure commands in a subshell when one or more of their file descriptors are redirected, so any environment changes inside them may fail. To be portable, the **exec** statement should be used instead to redirect file descriptors before the control structure.

In the following compound command descriptions, command lists (denoted as list) that are followed by reserved words must end with a semi-colon, a newline or a (syntactically correct) reserved word. For example,

> **{ echo foo; echo bar; }**
> **{ echo foo; echo bar}**
> **{ { echo foo; echo bar; } }**

are all valid, but

> **{ echo foo; echo bar }**

is not.

(*list*) Execute list in a subshell. There is no implicit way to pass environment changes from a subshell back to its parent.

{ *list* } Compound construct; list is executed, but not in a subshell. Note that { and } are reserved words, not meta-characters.

case *word* **in [[(|** *pattern* **[|** *pattern***] ...)** *list* **;;] ... esac**

The **case** statement attempts to match *word* against the specified patterns; the *list* associated with the first successfully matched pattern is executed. Patterns used in **case** statements are the same as those used for file name patterns except that the restrictions regarding . and / are dropped. Note that any unquoted space before and after a pattern is stripped; any space with a pattern must be quoted. Both the word and the patterns are subject to parameter, command, and arithmetic substitution as well as tilde substitution. For historical reasons, open and close braces may be used instead of in and esac (e.g., **case $foo { *) echo bar; }**). The exit status of a **case** statement is that of the executed list; if no list is executed, the exit status is zero.

for *name* **[in** *word* **...** *term* **] do** *list* **done**

where *term* is either a newline or a ;. For each word in the specified word *list*, the parameter *name* is set to the *word* and *list* is executed. If **in** is not used to specify a word list, the positional parameters ("$1", "$2", etc.) are used instead. For historical reasons, open and close braces may be used instead of **do** and **done** (e.g., **for i; { echo $i; }**). The exit status of a **for** statement is the last exit status of *list*; if *list* is never executed, the exit status is zero.

if *list* **then** *list* **[elif** *list* **then** *list***] ... [else** *list***] fi**

If the exit status of the first list is zero, the second list is executed; otherwise the list following the **elif**, if any, is executed with similar consequences. If all the lists

417

following the **if** and **elifs** fail (i.e., exit with non-zero status), the list following the **else** is executed. The exit status of an **if** statement is that of non-conditional list that is executed; if no non-conditional list is executed, the exit status is zero.

select *name* **[in** *word* **...** *term* **] do** *list* **done**

where *term* is either a newline or a ;. The **select** statement provides an automatic method of presenting the user with a menu and selecting from it. An enumerated list of the specified words is printed on standard error, followed by a prompt (**PS3**, normally '#? '). A number corresponding to one of the enumerated words is then read from standard input, *name* is set to the selected *word* (or is unset if the selection is not valid), **REPLY** is set to what was read (leading/trailing space is stripped), and *list* is executed. If a blank line (i.e., zero or more **IFS** characters) is entered, the menu is re-printed without executing list. When *list* completes, the enumerated list is printed if **REPLY** is null, the prompt is printed and so on. This process is continues until an end-of-file is read, an interrupt is received or a break statement is executed inside the loop. If **in** *word* ... is omitted, the positional parameters are used (i.e., "$1", "$2", etc.). For historical reasons, open and close braces may be used instead of do and done (e.g., **select i; { echo $i; }**). The exit status of a **select** statement is zero if a break statement is used to exit the loop, non-zero otherwise.

until *list* **do** *list* **done**

This works like **while**, except that the body is executed only while the exit status of the first list is non-zero.

while *list* **do** *list* **done**

A while is a prechecked loop. Its body is executed as often as the exit status of the first list is zero. The exit status of a **while** statement is the last exit status of the list in the body of the loop; if the body is not executed, the exit status is zero.

function *name* { *list* }

Defines the function *name*. See **Functions** later in this appendix. Note that redirections specified after a function definition are performed whenever the function is executed, not when the function definition is executed.

name () *command*

Mostly the same as **function**. See **Functions** later in this appendix.

time [**-p**] [*pipeline*]

The **time** reserved word is described in the **Command Execution** section.

((*expression*))

The arithmetic expression expression is evaluated; equivalent to **let** *"expression"*. See **Arithmetic Expressions** and the **let** command later in this appendix.

[[*expression*]]

Similar to the **test** and [...] commands (described later), with the following exceptions: Field splitting and file name generation are not performed on arguments. The **-a** (and) and **-o** (or) operators are replaced with && and ||, respectively. Operators (e.g., -f, =, !, etc.) must be unquoted. The second operand of != and = expressions are patterns (e.g., the comparison in **[[foobar = f*r]]** succeeds). There are two additional binary operators: < and > which return true if their first string operand is less than, or greater than, their second string operand, respectively. The single argument form of **test**, which tests if the argument has non-zero length, is not valid - explicit operators must be always be used, e.g., instead of [*str*] use [[**-n** *str*]]

Parameter, command and arithmetic substitutions are performed as expressions are evaluated and lazy expression evaluation is used for the && and || operators. This means that in the statement **[[-r foo && $(< foo) = b*r]]** the **$(< foo)** is evaluated if and only if the file **foo** exists and is readable.

Quoting

Quoting is used to prevent the shell from treating characters or words specially. There are three methods of quoting: First, \ quotes the following character, unless it is at the end of a line, in which case both the \ and the newline are stripped. Second, a single quote (') quotes everything up to the next single quote (this may span lines). Third, a double quote (") quotes all characters, except $, ' and \, up to the next unquoted double quote. $ and ' inside double quotes have their usual meaning (i.e., parameter, command or arithmetic substitution) except no field splitting is carried out on the results of double-quoted substitutions. If a \ inside a double-quoted string is followed by \, $, ' or ", it is replaced by the second character; if it is followed by a newline, both the \ and the newline are stripped; otherwise, both the \ and the character following are unchanged. Note: see POSIX Mode below for a special rule regarding sequences of the form "...`...\"...`..".

Aliases

There are two types of aliases: normal command aliases and tracked aliases. Command aliases are normally used as a short hand for a long or often used command. The shell expands command aliases (i.e., substitutes the alias name for its value) when it reads the first word of a command. An expanded alias is re-processed to check for more aliases. If a command alias ends in a space or tab, the following word is also checked for alias expansion. The alias expansion process stops when a word that is not an alias is found, when a quoted word is found or when an alias word that is currently being expanded is found.

The following command aliases are defined automatically by the shell:

> **autoload='typeset -fu'**
> **functions='typeset -f'**
> **hash='alias -t'**
> **history='fc -l'**
> **integer='typeset -i'**
> **local='typeset'**
> **login='exec login'**
> **newgrp='exec newgrp'**
> **nohup='nohup '**
> **r='fc -e -'**
> **stop='kill -STOP'**
> **suspend='kill -STOP $$'**
> **type='whence -v'**

Tracked aliases allow the shell to remember where it found a particular command. The first time the shell does a path search for a command that is marked as a tracked alias, it saves the full path of the command. The next time the command is executed, the shell checks the saved path to see that it is still valid, and if so, avoids repeating the path search. Tracked aliases can be listed and created using **alias -t**. Note that changing the **PATH** parameter clears the saved paths for all tracked aliases. If the trackall option is set (i.e., **set -o trackall** or **set -h**), the shell tracks all commands. This option is set automatically for non-interactive shells. For interactive shells, only the following commands are automatically tracked: **cat**, **cc**, **chmod**, **cp**, **date**, **ed**, **emacs**, **grep**, **ls**, **mail**, **make**, **mv**, **pr**, **rm**, **sed**, **sh**, **vi** and **who**.

Substitution

The first step the shell takes in executing a simple-command is to perform substitutions on the words of the command. There are three kinds of substitution: parameter, command and arithmetic. Parameter substitutions, which are described in detail in the next section, take the form $name or ${...}; command substitutions take the form $(*command*) or '*command*'; and arithmetic substitutions take the form $((*expression*)). If a substitution appears outside of double quotes, the results of the substitution are generally subject to word or field splitting according to the current value of the **IFS** parameter. The **IFS** parameter specifies a list of characters which are used to break a string up into several words; any characters from the set space, tab and newline that appear in the **IFS** characters are called **IFS** white space. Sequences of one or more **IFS** white space characters, in combination with zero or one non-**IFS** white space characters delimit a field. As a special case, leading and trailing **IFS** white space is stripped (i.e., no leading or trailing empty field is created by it); leading or trailing non-**IFS** white space does create an empty field. Example: if **IFS** is set to ':', the sequence of characters '**A:B::D**' contains four fields: 'A', 'B', '' and 'D'. Note that if the **IFS** parameter is set to the null string, no field splitting is done; if the parameter is unset, the default value of space, tab and newline is used.

The results of substitution are, unless otherwise specified, also subject to brace expansion and file name expansion.

A command substitution is replaced by the output generated by the specified command, which is run in a subshell. For $(*command*) substitutions, normal quoting rules are used when command is parsed, however, for the '*command*' form, a \ followed by any of $, ' or \ is stripped (a \ followed by any other character is unchanged). As a special case in command substitutions, a command of the form < *file* is interpreted to mean substitute the contents of file(**$(< foo)** has the same effect as **$(cat foo)**, but it is carried out more efficiently because no process is started). **NOTE**: $(*command*) expressions are currently parsed by finding the matching parenthesis, regardless of quoting. This will hopefully be fixed soon.

Arithmetic substitutions are replaced by the value of the specified expression. For example, the command echo **$((2+3*4))** prints 14. See **Arithmetic Expressions** for a description of an expression.

Parameters

Parameters are shell variables; they can be assigned values and their values can be accessed using a parameter substitution. A parameter name is either one of the special single punctuation or digit characterparameters described later in this appendix, or a letter followed by zero or more letters or digits ('_' counts as a letter). The latter form can be treated as arrays by appending an array index of the form: [*expr*] where *expr* is an arithmetic expression. Array indices are currently limited to the range 0 through 1023, inclusive. Parameter substitutions take the form $*name*, ${*name*} or ${*name*[*expr*]}, where *name* is a parameter name. If substitution is performed on a parameter (or an array parameter element) that is not set, a null string is substituted unless the nounset option (**set -o nounset** or **set -u**) is set, in which case an error occurs. Parameters can be assigned values in a number of ways. First, the shell implicitly sets some parameters like #, **PWD**, etc.; this is the only way the special single character parameters are set. Second, parameters are imported from the shell's environment at startup. Third, parameters can be assigned values on the command line, for example, '**FOO=bar**' sets the parameter **FOO** to **bar**; multiple parameter assignments can be given on a single command line and they can be followed by a simple-command, in which case the assignments are in effect only for the duration of the command (such assignments are also exported). Note that both the parameter name and the = must be unquoted for the shell to recognize a parameter assignment. The fourth way of setting a parameter is with the **export**, **readonly** and **typeset** commands; see their descriptions in the **Command Execution** section later in this appendix. Fifth, **for** and **select** loops set parameters as well as the **getopts**, **read** and **set -A** commands. Lastly, parameters can be assigned values using assignment operators inside arithmetic expressions (see **Arithmetic Expressions** later in this appendix) or using the ${*name=value*} form of parameter substitution.

Parameters with the export attribute (set using the **export** or **typeset -x** commands, or by parameter assignments followed by simple commands) are put in the environment (see **environ**(5)) of commands run by the shell as *name=value* pairs. The order in which parameters appear in the environment of a command is unspecified. When the shell starts up, it extracts parameters and their values from its environment and automatically sets the export attribute for those parameters.

Modifiers can be applied to the ${*name*} form of parameter substitution:

${*name*:-*word*}
> if *name* is set and not null, it is substituted, otherwise *word* is substituted.

${*name*:+*word*}
> if *name* is set and not null, *word* is substituted, otherwise nothing is substituted.

${*name*:=*word*}
> if *name* is set and not null, it is substituted, otherwise it is assigned *word* and the resulting value of *name* is substituted.

${*name*:?*word*}
> if *name* is set and not null, it is substituted, otherwise *word* is printed on standard error (preceded by *name*:) and an error occurs (normally causing termination of a shell script, function or .-script). If *word* is omitted the string '**parameter null or not set**' is used instead. In the above modifiers, the : can be omitted, in which case the conditions only depend on *name* being set (as opposed to set and not null). If *word* is needed,

parameter, command, arithmetic and tilde substitution are performed on it; if *word* is not needed, it is not evaluated.

The following forms of parameter substitution can also be used:

${#*name*}

> The number of positional parameters if *name* is *, @ or is not specified, or the length of the string value of parameter *name*.

${#*name*[*]}, ${#*name*[@]}

> The number of elements in the array *name*.

${*name*#*pattern*}, ${*name*##*pattern*}

> If *pattern* matches the beginning of the value of parameter *name*, the matched text is deleted from the result of substitution. A single # results in the shortest match, two #'s results in the longest match.

${*name*%*pattern*}, ${*name*%%*pattern*}

> Like ${..#..} substitution, but it deletes from the end of the value.

The following special parameters are implicitly set by the shell and cannot be set directly using assignments:

!   Process id of the last background process started. If no background processes have been started, the parameter is not set.

The number of positional parameters (i.e., **$1**, **$2**, etc.).

$ The process ID of the shell, or the PID of the original shell if it is a subshell.

-       The concatenation of the current single letter options (see **set** command below for list of options).

?   The exit status of the last non-asynchronous command executed. If the last command was killed by a signal, $? is set to 128 plus the signal number.

0   The name the shell was invoked with (i.e., **argv**[0]), or the command-name if it was invoked with the **-c** option and the command-name was supplied, or the file argument, if it was supplied. If the posix option is not set, **$0** is the name of the current function or script.

1 ... 9   The first nine positional parameters that were supplied to the shell, function or .-script. Further positional parameters may be accessed using ${*number*}.

*   All positional parameters (except parameter **0**), i.e., **$1 $2 $3**.... If used outside of double quotes, parameters are separate words (which are subjected to word splitting); if used within double quotes, parameters are separated by the first character of the **IFS** parameter (or the empty string if **IFS** is null).

@   Same as $*, unless it is used inside double quotes, in which case a separate word is generated for each positional parameter - if there are no positional parameters, no word is generated ("$@" can be used to access arguments, verbatim, without loosing null arguments or splitting arguments with spaces).

The following parameters are set and/or used by the shell:

_ (underscore)
    When an external command is executed by the shell, this parameter is set in the environment of the new process to the path of the executed command. In interactive use, this parameter is also set in the parent shell to the last word of the previous command. When **MAILPATH** messages are evaluated, this parameter contains the name of the file that changed (see **MAILPATH** parameter later in this appendix).

CDPATH
    Search path for the **cd** built-in command. Works the same way as **PATH** for those directories not beginning

with / in cd commands. Note that if **CDPATH** is set and does not contain . nor an empty path, the current directory is not searched.

COLUMNS

Set to the number of columns on the terminal or window. Currently set to the **cols** value as reported by **stty**(1) if that value is non-zero. This parameter is used by the interactive line editing modes, and by **select**, **set -o** and **kill -l** commands to format information in columns.

EDITOR

If the **VISUAL** parameter is not set, this parameter controls the command line editing mode for interactive shells. See **VISUAL** parameter later in this appendix for how this works.

ENV If this parameter is found to be set after any profile files are executed, the expanded value is used as a shell start-up file. It typically contains function and alias definitions.

ERRNO

Integer value of the shell's errno variable - indicates the reason the last system call failed. **Not implemented yet.**

EXECSHELL

If set, this parameter is assumed to contain the shell that is to be used to execute commands that **execve**(2) fails to execute and which do not start with a '#! *shell*' sequence.

FCEDIT

The editor used by the **fc** command.

FPATH

Like **PATH**, but used when an undefined function is executed to locate the file defining the function. It is also searched when a command can't be found using **PATH**. See **Functions** later in this appendix for more information.

HISTFILE

The name of the file used to store history. When assigned to, history is loaded from the specified file. Also, several invocations of the shell running on the same machine will share history if their **HISTFILE** parameters all point at the same file. **NOTE**: if **HISTFILE** isn't set, no history file is used. This is different from the original Korn shell, which uses **$HOME/.sh_history**; in future, **pdksh** may also use a default history file.

Index

—